This study of narrative technique in Victorian novels introduces the concept of "narrative annexes" whereby unexpected characters, impermissible subjects, and plot-changing events are introduced within fictional worlds which otherwise exclude them. They are marked by the crossing of borders into previously unrepresented places and new genres or modes, challenging Victorian cultural and literary norms. Suzanne Keen's original readings of novels by Charlotte Brontë, Dickens, Disraeli, Hardy, Kingsley, Trollope, and Wells show these writers negotiating the boundaries of representation to reveal in narrative annexes the subjects (notably sexuality and social class) which contemporary critics sought to exclude from the realm of the novel. Fears of disease, of working men, of Popery, of dark-skinned others, of the poor who toil and starve in close proximity to the rectories, homes, clubs, and walled gardens of Victorian polite society draw readers down narrow alleys, through hedges, across desolate heaths, into narrative annexes.

CAMBRIDGE STUDIES IN NINETEENTH-CENTURY
LITERATURE AND CULTURE 15

VICTORIAN RENOVATIONS
OF THE NOVEL

CAMBRIDGE STUDIES IN NINETEENTH-CENTURY
LITERATURE AND CULTURE 15

General editors
Gillian Beer, *University of Cambridge*
Catherine Gallagher, *University of California, Berkeley*

Editorial board
Isobel Armstrong, *Birkbeck College, London*
Terry Eagleton, *University of Oxford*
Leonore Davidoff, *University of Essex*
D. A. Miller, *Columbia University*
J. Hillis Miller, *University of California, Irvine*
Mary Poovey, *The Johns Hopkins University*
Elaine Showalter, *Princeton University*

Nineteenth-century British literature and culture have been rich fields for interdisciplinary studies. Since the turn of the twentieth century, scholars and critics have tracked the intersections and tensions between Victorian literature and the visual arts, politics, social organization, economic life, technical innovations, scientific thought – in short, culture in its broadest sense. In recent years, theoretical challenges and historiographical shifts have unsettled the assumptions of previous scholarly syntheses and called into question the terms of older debates. Whereas the tendency in much past literary critical interpretation was to use the metaphor of culture as "background," feminist, Foucauldian, and other analyses have employed more dynamic models that raise questions of power and of circulation. Such developments have re-animated the field.

This series aims to accommodate and promote the most interesting work being undertaken on the frontiers of the field of nineteenth-century literary studies: work which intersects fruitfully with other fields of study such as history, or literary theory, or the history of science. Comparative as well as interdisciplinary approaches are welcomed.

A complete list of titles published will be found at the end of the book.

VICTORIAN RENOVATIONS
OF THE NOVEL

Narrative Annexes and the Boundaries of Representation

SUZANNE KEEN

Department of English
Washington and Lee University
Lexington, Virginia

Dear Kathy,

From the start, your responses to this project have been woven into my thinking. I hope it pleases you in the end! I can't wait to see your book.

Much love,

Suzanne

CAMBRIDGE
UNIVERSITY PRESS

PUBLISHED BY THE PRESS SYNDICATE OF THE UNIVERSITY OF CAMBRIDGE
The Pitt Building, Trumpington Street, Cambridge CB2 1RP, United Kingdom

CAMBRIDGE UNIVERSITY PRESS
The Edinburgh Building, Cambridge CB2 2RU, United Kingdom
40 West 20th Street, New York, NY 10011-4211, USA
10 Stamford Road, Oakleigh, Melbourne 3166, Australia

First published 1998

Printed in the United Kingdom at the University Press, Cambridge

Typeset in Baskerville 11/12½ pt   [VN]

A catalogue record for this book is available from the British Library

Library of Congress cataloguing in publication data
Keen, Suzanne.
Victorian renovations of the novel: narrative annexes and the
boundaries of representation / Suzanne Keen.
p.   cm – (Cambridge studies in nineteenth-century literature
and culture; 15)
Includes bibliographical references and index.
ISBN 0 521 58344-6 (hardback)
1. English fiction – 19th century – History and criticism.
2. Literature and society – Great Britain – History – 19th century.
3. Mimesis in literature.   4. Narration (rhetoric)   1 Title.
II. Series.
PR871.K44   1998
823'.809355 – dc21
97-23903 CIP

ISBN 0 521 58344 6 hardback

For Beth Tamar Schulman

Contents

Acknowledgments

To enumerate adequately the debts of gratitude I owe, I must begin with my parents, Bill and Sally Keen, who fostered my life-long habit of novel-reading. Among my many wonderful teachers, Michael S. Harper, Susanne Woods, George P. Landow, Roland Greene, and Barbara Lewalski stand out. Philip Fisher's courses showed me the way from Renaissance literature to the Victorian novel; I am fortunate indeed to have benefited from this advisor's exacting criticism and always-stimulating suggestions. Marjorie Garber, Roland Greene, Dorrit Cohn, Deborah Nord, Helen Vendler, Patricia Yaeger, Joseph Allen Boone, George P. Landow, John Norman, Douglas Bruster, Joseph Lease, Katherine Rowe, Elizabeth Spiller, and the participants in the Feminist Colloquium at Harvard made invaluable suggestions in the early stages of the project. The generous responses of Susan Stanford Friedman and Janice Carlisle to my preliminary thinking both encouraged and challenged me. The members of the Works in Progress group at Yale University – including Mark Wollaeger, William Jewett, Lynn Enterline, Heather James, Katherine Rowe, Elizabeth Heckendorn Cook, and Elizabeth Fowler – helped me along the way with always-acute criticism. I am indebted to Catherine Gallagher, Ian Duncan, Linda Peterson, Thomas Whitaker, John Hollander, Peter J. Rabinowitz, and two anonymous readers for detailed comments on the entire manuscript at various stages, and to Elizabeth Heckendorn Cook, Roland Greene, Carla Kaplan, and Rosemarie Morgan for responses to individual chapters. Among my beloved colleagues at the Berkeley College Fellows lunch table, I must thank, for their encouragement and always-interesting conversation, Larry Manley, Claude Rawson, Vasily Rudich and Karl Turekian. Josie Dixon has been an attentive editor and I am also grateful to Linda Bree and Leigh Mueller at Cambridge University Press. Without the support of a Morse Junior Faculty Fellowship, generously granted to me by Yale University for 1993–4, I could not have completed work on this book, begun as a dissertation supported by a Rudmose Fellowship from the Harvard Graduate School of Arts and Sciences. Final preparation of the manuscript has been completed with the aid of a Glenn Grant from Washington and Lee University. I received immeasurable help from librarians at Sterling Memorial Library, Yale University; Widener Library, Harvard University; Beinecke Library, Yale University; the John Hay Library, Brown University; and Leyburn Library, Washington and Lee University. Child Library at Harvard, cheerfully staffed by a phalanx of graduate students, is always a home away from home. Countless novel-reading friends and acquaintances have pointed out examples of narrative annexes to me; though I could not write about them all, I am grateful for each suggestion. No one reader has more patiently read and reread my work than my husband, Fran MacDonnell. Naturally, any errors that remain in this book are solely my responsibility.

A NOTE ON EDITIONS OF NOVELS

Whenever possible I have used Penguin or Oxford paperback editions of the novels discussed in detail in the chapters that follow. When one of these readily available teaching editions does not exist, I have chosen a standard or easily accessible edition likely to remain in print. In the remainder of cases, I have resorted to the first edition of the novel in question.

CHAPTER 1

Narrative annexes: altered spaces, altered modes

INTRODUCTION

This study of the Victorian novel identifies a technique employed across its various kinds – in social fictions, fictional autobiographies, *Bildungsromanen*, Condition of England novels, romances, and realistic novels – to renovate the nineteenth-century house of fiction. *Narrative annexes*, as I name them, allow unexpected characters, impermissible subjects, and plot-altering events to appear, in a bounded way, within fictional worlds that might be expected to exclude them. Like other Victorian renovations, narrative annexes may appear to disfigure the structure they alter, but they at the same time reveal Victorian novelists' creative responses to the capacities and limitations of their form. Annexes are initiated by a combined shift in genre and setting that changes the fictional world of the novel, and they work by interrupting the norms of a story's world, temporarily replacing those norms, and carrying the reader, the perceiving and reporting characters, and the plot-line across a boundary and through an altered, particular, and briefly realized zone of difference. In small spaces and few pages, narrative annexes challenge both cultural and literary norms to form imaginative worlds more variously, in sometimes distracting or dissonant interludes. Yet annexes never stop the plot, but serve the story by modifying the story-world. As alternatives to the techniques of fantasy or multiplied plot lines, Victorian annexes simultaneously anticipate the fragmentation associated with modern fiction, and resemble the flexible worldmaking of prose fiction before the novel. Extending and qualifying the boundaries of representation, narrative annexes draw attention and contribute to the generic diversity of the Victorian novel, complicating the traditional opposition of realism and romance. Narrative annexes are sites of Victorian novelists' negotiation with the conventional, and as such they reveal not only the effort to employ alternative representational strategies, but also the subjects that instigate that effort.

All narrative annexes possess a shift to a previously unrepresented place and a simultaneous alteration in narrative language that sends signals of adjusted genre. All narrative annexes make a change within the primary level of a fictional world without departing it entirely, as an embedded text or an interpolated story does. The connection of the setting and the consistency of the narrative situation permit the perceiving (and, in the case of the first person, narrating) character to journey through the annex, by crossing a boundary line or border region, marked with signs of generic and spatial difference.

A constitutive feature of annexes, these boundaries or border regions indicate the commitment of Victorian novelists to the representation of spatially coherent fictional worlds, and at the same time allude to the contemporary critical discourse on the proper "realm" of the novel. When, at the end of the century in "The Death of the Lion" (1894), Henry James' characters refer to the new practice of representing in fiction all-too-recently forbidden subjects as "the permissibility of the larger latitude,"[1] the journalists and literary lion self-consciously retail a cliché of the book reviewers. If by the 1890s the "larger latitude" had been opened up for exploration by naturalist novelists who took readers into regions previously unrepresented, and by sensationalist writers who dared, if not actual frankness, forays into the risqué, the new permissibility suggested an older set of prohibitions, copiously attested to in sixty years of book reviews. The "larger latitude" replaces a "narrower sphere." Metaphors of place, zone, realm, and boundary-line proved indispensable to the Victorian reviewers who attempted to define and redefine the role of the novel. The novelists responsible for both continuing and challenging the traditions of representation in fiction shared with the critics a moral vocabulary that expressed possibilities and impossibilities in geographical terms ("latitude"; "over the line"), but they also had close at hand a rich array of literary models for the radical alteration of fictional worlds. For from Shakespeare's drama, *The Faerie Queene*, *Don Quixote*, and romantic poetry, among other sources, Victorian novelists inherited an image of boundary-crossing – into the green world, into the houses of Pride or Holiness, into the cave of Montesinos, into the underworld, through spots of time. Critics' protests against the episodic and the improbable notwithstanding, the place- and genre-shifting strategy I describe in this book as "narrative annexing" belonged in the tool-box of techniques Victorian novelists inherited from earlier narrative artists. Since boundaries, borders, and lines of demarcation evoke not only the long tradition of traversing an ever-altering imaginary terrain, but also the censorious language of the Victorian cultural watchdog, or the formal purist (often but not always the same person), they become a vital element of novelists' manipulation of spatial difference and dramatic generic admixture to challenge representational norms.

For instance, Thomas Hardy simultaneously alters the generic signals and the location of *The Mayor of Casterbridge* (1886) when he conveys Michael Henchard through a border-region that becomes a forbidding barrier around the abode of the weather prophet: "The turnpike became a lane, the lane a cart-track, the cart-track a bridle-path, the bridle-path a foot-way, the foot-way overgrown. The solitary walker slipped here and there, and stumbled over the natural springes formed by the brambles, till at length he reached the house, which, with its garden, was surrounded with a high, dense hedge."[2] This hedge marks the boundary between the ordinary world of Casterbridge and the weather-prophet's house, but the incantatory language and the difficult journey have already combined to suggest an annex, an alternative realm outside Casterbridge where magical forecasts rather than up-to-date technology and practical knowledge might work. Passing through the door in the hedge, Henchard pays for bad advice from Mr. Fall. This action, insulated from the main setting of the novel, makes an essential contribution to the plot, as it precipitates Henchard's financial ruin. The bounded realm of the annex serves the downward turning of Henchard's plot-line, contains the unprecedented action of Henchard's reliance on another's guesswork, and results in Jopp's alienation from his employer, which in turn leads to the work of the novel's later narrative annex (discussed in chapter 4).

This brief example points to a fourth feature present, with changed genre, altered setting, and a crossed boundary, in all annexes (the four markers do vary in prominence). The events contained in narrative annexes, while insulated from the primary fictional world by the passage through the annexes' boundary, are always consequential for the plot. Here Seymour Chatman's distinction between "kernel" and "satellite" plot events helps us to see the tricky narrative work an annex performs. Unlike a satellite event, which can be omitted from a plot summary without misrepresentation of the story, a kernel event contributes in an indispensable way to the story's development and outcome.[3] The combination in narrative annexes of an appearance of digressiveness, differ-

ence, even marginality, and essential kernel plot events with real consequences for the temporarily departed primary fictional world results in
odd deformations of mainly verisimilar Victorian fictional worlds. It is
therefore not surprising to discover that the very episodes I call annexes
were often singled out by critics and contemporary readers as especially
unlikely or peculiar. While for practical reasons this last phenomenon
cannot be used as an infallible test of an annex, I trace in the chapters
that follow the critical reaction to narrative annexes in order to recapture this part of the conversation about representational and formal
norms among Victorian novelists, critics, and readers.

Though the career of Thomas Hardy provides perhaps the most
well-known example of the consequences of contesting social norms for
representation, I do not attempt in this book to retell a story of causes
and effects. Instead, my focus on the Victorian strategy of annexing, and
my attention to the prescriptive theory of the novel emerging in the
same period, recovers to view one of the fundamental techniques
novelists used to negotiate the "latitude" of the novel. That they did so
to a chorus of "Unlikely!" "Improbable!" and graver cries of disapproval from contemporaries means not that critical strictures ultimately
confined them, but that their attempt to broaden the representational
range and generic flexibility of narrative fiction attracted notice. The
spatial metaphors for social norms so often employed by Victorian
critics can be observed at work both literally and figuratively in the
novels, calling attention to the shared vocabulary of this decades-long
negotiation. The "permissibility" of the 1890s and subsequent years,
and some of the most significant formal innovations of early twentieth-
century fiction, in fact build upon the testing of limitations observable in
annexes of the earlier Victorian decades.

My goal in this study is not to contest the importance of French,
Russian, and American narrative technique for the development of
modern form, but to focus on an aspect of the English novelistic
tradition that shows us Victorians thinking through, and sometimes
working their way past, the representational barriers associated with
nineteenth-century fiction. Hedges or hedgerows, for instance, often
appear in annexes as particularly English figures for the boundary
between the likely and the unlikely, the possible and the improbable.
The character who traverses the changing terrain of the annex may
doubt the powers of the alternative realm (Henchard says that he does
not "altogether believe in forecasts" [260]), or she may desire the
impossible thing that lies in the other place. In the annex in George

Eliot's *Adam Bede* (1859), Hetty Sorrel seeks a hidden pool in which to drown herself, to "get among the flat green fields with the high hedges round them, where nobody could see her or know her; and there, perhaps, when there was nothing else she could do, she should get courage to drown herself in some pond."[4] Eliot's rendering of Hetty's fear sets the social world of the novel against a private, hidden place where she considers but does not accomplish suicide. When Hetty realizes that her out-of-wedlock pregnancy will result in the public humiliation of going to the parish, or in the necessity of seeking help from strangers, her fantasy of self-sufficiency creates an imaginary realm into which she will escape the "far-off hideous region of intolerable shame that [she] had all her life thought it impossible she could ever come near" (424–5). The generic register of the novel swerves away from domestic realism and the familiar stopping place of picaresque (the inn), into sensation and melodrama as it follows Hetty's path off the road. Eliot allows Hetty to enter her annex on the other side of the "bushy tree-studded hedgerows" (429), but exposes the insufficiency of the solitary zone and hidden pool in preventing Hetty from finding herself in the nearer-than-imagined "hideous region of intolerable shame." As her later confession to Dinah reiterates, Hetty cannot drown herself, no more than she can fathom that a rescuer might ignore her exposed baby's cries. The privacy of the annex not only fails Hetty's purpose, but also allows her capital crime, infanticide.

In contrast, the radical isolation and privation of the annex in Charles Dickens' *Martin Chuzzlewit* (1843–4) makes possible Martin's awareness of his selfishness. To reach an appropriate landscape for killing self-love, Dickens conveys his American travellers in chapter 23 to the fatal locale of "New Eden." This American dead-end owes as much to the imaginary terrain of English Renaissance romance and Coleridgean horror as it does to Dickens' actual travels. The Spenserian features of the landscape animate generic as well as physical alterations in the novel's fictional world:

As they proceeded further on their track, and came more and more towards their journey's end, the monotonous desolation of the scene increased to the degree, that for any redeeming feature it presented to their eyes, they might have entered, in the body, on the grim domains of the Giant Despair. A flat morass, bestrewn with fallen timber; a marsh on which the good growth of the earth seemed to have been wrecked and cast away, that from its decomposing ashes vile and ugly things might rise; where the very trees took the aspect of huge weeds, begotten of the slime from which they sprung, by the hot sun that burnt them up; where fatal maladies, seeking whom they might infect, came forth at night in misty shapes, and creeping out upon the water, hunted them like spectres until day; where even the blessed sun, shining down on festering elements of corruption and disease, became a horror; this was the realm of Hope through which they moved.[5]

In an elaborate mutation, the corrupting water of *The Rime of the Ancient Mariner* and the threatening domains of the Giant Despair turn America into an isolating, abandoned, and fantastically lethal swamp, from an over-crowded zone of social comedy. Martin and Mark Tapley may have reached their dead-end physically, but the increased figurative power of the narrative annex's language and location drives a psychological transformation that comes straight out of Book 1 of *The Faerie Queene*.

Changes in setting alone, unaccompanied by a shift in generic register and a vividly realized boundary-crossing, cannot be considered narrative annexes, for the term would then dissolve into more mundane or merely pragmatic place-changes, of which there are copious examples in Victorian fiction. The "New Eden" annex of *Martin Chuzzlewit* provides a helpful contrast between the unsettling and complicated alterations of fictional worlds in narrative annexes and simple shifts in setting. The journey to America, for instance, certainly alters the scene of one of *Martin Chuzzlewit*'s plot strands, but, except for the striking "New Eden" annex, the American episodes maintain a consistent generic backdrop for scenes of social satire. By way of contrast with Dickens' "New Eden," in William Thackeray's *Vanity Fair* (1847–8) virtually the entire cast of the novel removes to the Low Countries without disrupting the prevailing modes of social comedy and satire. Thackeray's narrator underlines the continuity of the world of home and the world of tourists accompanying the Duke of Wellington's army: "In the meanwhile the business of life and living, and the pursuits of pleasure, especially, went on as if no end were to be expected to them, and no enemy in front."[6] Thackeray represents the war itself, when it arrives, in the most general terms, deferring to his contemporary readers' knowledge of the events; the single paragraph reporting the battle of Waterloo contains the corpse of the one character whose perspective might have lent an alternative view to the novel. Instead of sharing George Osbourne's experience, we carry away the indelible impression of Jos Sedley's life-endangering *faux* uniform. Though Thackeray changes the setting, and the war literally challenges real boundaries, an annex has not been deployed here, for the genre has remained ironically consistent.

When a change in place in a novel is accompanied by a shift in time, most often the device employed by the novelist is not an annex, but a flashback (or analepsis). Anachrony, or the disordering of story events in their presentation, may be a complicating factor in an annex, but a flashback rarely exhibits all of the traits of an annex. When George Eliot's narrator relates the background of Dr. Lydgate, she moves the reader of *Middlemarch* (1871–2) to the Continent and back in time. The additional shift in genre to the melodrama of Lydgate's infatuation with the actress Laure makes it tempting to consider this episode a narrative annex, but most annexes, like most Victorian novels, unfold without disrupting the consecutive time of the narration. In this instance, the representation of a boundary-crossing is missing, and the narrative content, though it illuminates Lydgate's character, does not make up a kernel plot event. To take an even more extreme example of a flashback that shares some but not all of the traits of a narrative annex, when Sir Arthur Conan Doyle abruptly transports his readers from Sherlock Holmes' London to the Great Alkali Plain in *A Study in Scarlet* (1887), the place and time both change drastically, and kernel events are related, but the narrative of murder, detection, and revenge possesses strong generic continuities with the London episodes. The analepsis provides not an alternative world, but a prior world in which the original crime sought by Holmes occurs. Similarly, the gap-filling depositions of the multiple narrators in Wilkie Collins' *The Moonstone* (1868) make up the very fabric of the fictional world.

While detective fiction relies for its resolution on the reconstruction (by confession, discovered document, or investigator's brainwork) of the criminal scene in the past, other sub-genres of the novel depend upon changes in location to instigate their whole action. This, too, differs from the briefer, shorter, and norm-challenging narrative annex. In Bram Stoker's *Dracula* (1897), for instance, gothic conventions demand a departure from the normal, rational world, and Jonathan Harker's journal immediately notes "I read that every known superstition in the world is gathered into the horseshoe of the Carpathians, as if it were the centre of some sort of imaginative whirlpool."[7] That whirlpool becomes the fictional world of the entire novel, not a narrative annex with its short-lived variances from predominant fictional norms.

Many novels achieve an effect of temporary difference by means of interpolation or embedding, in which a frame contains multiple, contrasting voices (*The Moonstone*); or a secondary narrator tells a tale; or a document makes available information presented in contrasting discourse. These alterations in narrative level[8] work differently than narrative annexes. Embedded tales such as the stories in Charles Dickens' *The Pickwick Papers* (1836–7) create a subsidiary level of narrative distinct from the primary world of episodic narration. Elizabeth Gaskell's *Mary Barton* (1848) is enriched by significant interpolations, such as Margaret Legh's song, "The Oldham Weaver"; and the same character's anecdote of the reanimation of the dormant scorpion (like John Barton, the insect appears harmless, but turns dangerous when he gets heated up); and the narrator's allusions to Dives and Lazarus. Because they add subsidiary layers (stories within the story) to the primary fictional world, however, these interpolations do not constitute narrative annexes. Nor do the "criminal nightworld"[9] of Manchester, the crime scene, and the squalid basements of the most wretched inhabitants of the city make annexes just because one rarely finds such places in earlier fiction. These settings together make up the primary world of *Mary Barton*.[10]

If there is a narrative annex in *Mary Barton*, it occurs when the title character leaves Manchester and dry land in a race to exonerate her falsely accused beloved. Place could not be more strikingly altered, for here is Mary, hazarding Liverpool, the docks, and the sailors in a "new world of sight and sound" (342), pursuing the witness who can clear Jem's name, "rocking and tossing in a boat for the first time in her life, alone with two rough, hard-looking men" (345). Genre changes, too, as Mary and her rough guides leave the shore. Though Gaskell admonishes her readers that we cannot "read the lot of those who daily pass [us] by in the street," nor "know the wild romances of their lives" (70), here she breaks from *Mary Barton*'s predominant mode of anxiety-producing delay, of dread, anticipation of the worst, of misunderstanding, missing information, and waiting, to produce an anomalous episode of pure romance chase starring an action heroine. The stressful, strange world of the Liverpool annex brings Mary Barton to an almost catatonic state, but not before she accomplishes the task that brings her out on the water, and not before she learns to use her voice ("a loud, harsh whisper") in the service of an "errand of life and death" (348).

One of the most important tasks of a narrative annex, as in Mary Barton's race, is to provide a space for the accomplishment of an action or event that otherwise could not occur in the novel. George Meredith's *The Ordeal of Richard Feverel* (1859) suggests that Victorian novelists sometimes see the construction of an alternative world within a world in terms of an opposition between romance and novel that can free characters not for marvellous experiences, but for perfectly ordinary actions forbidden by social prescriptions.[11] In *The Ordeal of Richard Feverel*, Meredith introduces annexes to carve out a place where the eponymous hero can conduct the love affair that cannot happen anywhere within reach of his father's rigid educational "System."[12] Meredith advertises the shift from the primary fictional world to the annexes, and emphasizes their incompatibility, by parodically renaming the river bank after Prospero's island, and by allowing "Ferdinand" and "Miranda" to act out their love story in terms governed by an outmoded, but still potent, genre: Shakespearian romance (117–27). Narrative annexes thus employ the resources of changed genre and place to serve both plot and the representation of "out of place" behavior.

This brief catalog of examples of narrative annexes, and of techniques that resemble but differ from annexes, suggests that the Victorian novel is replete with peculiar episodes. To sort out all the narrative annexes from all the flashbacks, or interpolations, or from all of the odd places represented in Victorian fiction is not the task of this book, though I have found that every time I describe narrative annexes to a fellow novel-reader, I come away with more examples of the technique in use. Studying these examples has convinced me that while I cannot account for each narrative annex in a book of reasonable length, I can suggest why Victorian novelists broke with the norms of their carefully wrought fictional worlds to employ narrative annexes. The heart of this study lies in the explanation of how Victorian novelists use narrative annexes both to solve problems of plotting and characterization, and to address cultural anxieties, particularly those preoccupations kept out of the novel by the limits of generic conventions, by the prohibitions of contemporary critics, or by shared ideas about the boundaries of representation. In demarking zones in which Victorian novelists struggle to represent improbable, awkward, unsuitable, embarrassing, or downright threatening ideas, characters, actions, and social problems, narrative annexes reveal a great variety of cultural preoccupations. Annexes occur in the novels of great writers, and in the work of contributors to the fascinating "minor" canon of Victorian fiction. Novelists male and female create them, and use them for diverse purposes in novels of various kinds. Because this study can no more hope to encompass all the topics suggested by the contents of annexes than it can interpret every Victorian novel possessing one, I train my attention on the prominent themes of gender, sexuality, and social class (intertwined as they are with religion, politics, and race), to take up the central contestation of the limits of representation made by narrative annexes.

TERMS AND ORGANIZATION

Both product and mirror of the periods from 1832 through the early years of the twentieth century, the Victorian novel has often been described as being bound by conventions that transfer the restrictions and assumptions of the social to representational norms. To take an influential example, George Levine writes, "In a world whose reality is defined . . . according to inherited traditions of social order, no 'inhuman' landscape can occupy much space. Victorian realism's attempt to exclude extremes extends not only to heroism, psychic intensity, or violent behavior, but to geography as well."[13] (Levine is of course interested in the exceptions to the norm he describes.) I demonstrate in the following chapters that, in tandem with narrative annexes' exceptional depictions of place, the generic alternatives proffered by annexes complicate the fictional worlds of the Victorian novel in a way that challenges orderly representation. The attempt to exclude extremes, while standard, is matched by narrative annexes' exceptional inclusions, which controvert both literary and social norms. The strategy of annexing represents one way Victorian novelists struggle with the "inherited traditions of social order," a way as Victorian as the articulation of limits and the drawing of boundaries. My intention is not to discover, again, the presence of romance in the closet of the realistic house of fiction, nor to contest the relationship of social and fictional norms. Instead, in this study I describe a technique of worldmaking employed, at one time or another, by almost every Victorian novelist to construct a space for alternatives. In order to demonstrate the flexibility and diverse uses of this hitherto unrecognized technique, my inquiry extends beyond realism to treat narrative annexes discovered in the kinds (a term I use throughout in the technical sense of a subgenre differing from other kinds in both *how* and *what* it represents[14]) of Victorian fiction. The terms and norms of representation established in the novelistic kinds in which narrative annexes occur vary widely, so I deliberately examine an apparently eclectic group of novels, written over more than half a century by major and minor writers. What *Alton Locke* (1850), *Castle Richmond* (1860), *Coningsby* (1844), *The Mayor of Casterbridge* (1886), and *Villette* (1853) – to name only some of the novels I discuss – have in common is the use of narrative annexes to carry on narration in alternative zones within their primary fictional worlds.

I use the term "fictional world" to denote the assemblage, perceived by the reader, of imagined materials deployed by the author in the

course of novelistic narration. Narrators and their fictional auditors or
implied readers; characters and their actions, speeches, and thoughts;
the duration and order of represented time; the dimensions and details
of settings; and all the items or accessories – material, metonymic, and
metaphorical – denoted or implied by the words of the novel come
together in the reader's mind to form an imagined world. Each fictional
world both opens up and limits the possibilities for representation, for no
fictional world can refer to more than an infinitesimal fraction of the
actual world. Realistic novels asserting their reflection of the actual
world in a way that renders their fictionality transparent may appear to
allude to a real world rather than a fictional one, but they, too, rely on
the reader's capacity to generate a sense of wholeness and actuality out
of a finite number of references. They are as separate from the everyday
world of an actual reader as the most flagrant make-believe. Despite this
separation, readers of fictions realistic and fantastic readily become
familiar with these imaginary worlds, and they can without hesitation
describe the differences between Charles Dickens' fictional worlds and
those of George Eliot, or between the worlds of individual novels by the
same author. (Some Victorian novelists, such as Trollope and Oliphant,
build extensive fictional worlds in series of books.) Part of this common-
sense recognition of fictional worlds derives from the reader's sense that
certain themes, actions, characters, or places would be incongruous in
Eliot, though not in Dickens; or would never appear in *Adam Bede*,
though *Daniel Deronda* would not be the same without them. Faced with a
multiplot novel, the reader accepts not just one setting, but two or more
for separate plot actions, making a geographically and temporally
complex fictional world. Turning the pages of a gothic romance, the
reader engages in the imagining of an entirely different world than that
of everyday life, as readers of a naturalist novel may also do, if they have
not personally frequented the streets and cellars of the East End, or the
industrial cities of the north. A novel's reader simultaneously assembles
its fictional world and learns the norms implicit in its inclusions and
omissions.

Though in a later section of this introduction I relate this idea of
"fictional worlds" and "fictional worldmaking" to what structuralist and
poststructuralist narrative theorists, phenomenological critics, and phil-
osophers of fictional worlds have written, for now I ask my reader to
consider the fictional world of a novel as one of the primary effects of
novel-reading, and one of the virtual requirements of novel-writing.[15]
This study is rooted in the conviction that Victorian fiction makes of

novels imaginary spaces, into which readers can enter and even, temporarily, disappear. Lost in a book, we may find concealment, comfort, consolation, excitement, instruction, and warnings in imaginary situations that shore up and endanger our complacencies. Because readers cannot really get there from here, we can safely indulge in this replacement of actuality with fiction. Thomas Hardy writes, only in part facetiously, that "to get pleasure out of a book is a beneficial and profitable thing, if the pleasure be of a kind, which, while doing no moral injury, affords relaxation and relief when the mind is overstrained or sick of itself." He associates this effect with the habit of entering an imaginary world: "A sudden shifting of the mental perspective into a fictitious world, combined with rest, is well known to be as efficacious for renovation as a corporeal journey afar."[16] Victorian novels carry readers on these renovating trips by imagining the corporeal journeys of characters through space. Further, I hope that my readers can call to mind occasions in reading Victorian fiction when novels are temporarily converted or re-formed by the crossing over into altered places within (but strangely different from) the fictional worlds with which they have grown comfortable. The next step is to recapture the rather more remote nineteenth-century reader's experience. While Victorian readers enjoyed their surrender to fiction, they sometimes encountered startling events, characters, and incongruous views in the novels they read. They repeatedly considered these questions: What belongs in the novel and what should not be found there? What effect ought a novel to have on a reader? Victorian novelists, readers, and critics reinvented boundaries for fictional representation, which they delighted in patrolling, testing, and sometimes violating.

Because "fictional world" is a spatial metaphor, and because Victorians themselves adopted spatial terms for discussing representation in fiction, I describe these bounded, temporary, alternate miniature worlds within worlds with another spatial term: narrative annexes. The architectural meaning of the noun "annex" arises in the nineteenth century from the modern French term for the additional parts of an exhibition building – according to the *Oxford English Dictionary (OED)*, "a supplementary building designed to supply extra accommodation for some special purpose, a wing." If a book were a house, the annex might then be, in this French sense, an appendix. In Victorian novels, however, narrative annexes are entered not at the end of one's reading journey through the house of fiction, but somewhere in the middle. In this study I embrace the pervasive Victorian spatial metaphors that invite readers to imagine narrative fictions as houses or worlds – plural, heterogeneous, but made recognizable by the conventions of novelistic representation. Within the many works that make up "the Victorian novel," diverse conventions govern characters, events, entanglements, and outcomes differently. Despite the heterogeneity of these houses of fiction, each sets its walls and windows and corridors in such a way as to rule out other floor plans. Yet makers can add annexes, as well as windows, to the fictional houses they build.

Entering English in the late Middle Ages from French legal vocabulary, the term "annex" derives its dominant sense from its Latin root, *annexum*, the past participle of *annectere* or *adnectere*, to tie to, or bind. The *OED* shows eight types of attachment described by the verb "annex," only the first of which, "to join, unite," omits a state of subordination. Otherwise, to annex is to add as an accessory; to affix, append; to join as an attribute, qualification, condition, or consequence of some larger region, property, book, or object.[17] Its most familiar use in the twentieth century is barely anticipated by the patriotic definitions of the *OED*; the annexation of modern states by emergent superpowers or neighboring rivals must be imagined in its place after Wellington's use of the word in a quotation chosen by the *OED*'s editors to represent nineteenth-century usage: "The whole country is permanently annexed to the British Empire." I use the term "annexing" to differentiate this technique of narrative fiction from military or colonial "annexation," but I do not mean to whitewash the term. When Victorian fiction includes by representing objects and subjects, such as the starving Irish woman in the annex to Trollope's *Castle Richmond* (discussed in the next chapter), the analogy with empire suggests a complicity that may go hand in hand with critique. Yet no one ideology governs the small territories of annexes, or the more extensive realms of Victorian novels. Instead, annexing reveals the co-presence of multiple, competing modes, linked to alternative spaces within the Victorian novel, and permitting the representation of a variety of troubling figures, topics, and themes. In arguing this, I attempt to augment the influential work of George Levine, Leo Bersani, and Edwin M. Eigner.[18] Attention to annexes reveals a technique of narrative that can be employed to each (or any) of the ends elucidated by Levine (representation of the monstrous), Bersani (containment of desire), and Eigner (the turn towards redemptive mysticism), but annexing is not limited to these themes, and indeed sometimes combines them in unexpected ways.

By discussing narrative annexes in terms of what they *include*, I

concentrate on a variety of the contemporary topics, issues, and problems present in Victorian novels in pressurized forms. To observe the
development of one of the significant innovations in Victorian novelistic
form in response to social and cultural limits on representation inevitably points towards the entangled themes of gender, sexuality, and
anxieties about class and religion. The temporarily altered locus and
mode of the annex calls attention to novelists' exploration not only of
each of these topics individually, but also of the relationships among
sexual behavior, social mobility, violence, and faith. The intertwining of
this cluster of themes reveals many a strange conversion. Michael
Ragussis convincingly argues that in English history, the "trope of
conversion becomes a crucial figure . . . to construct, regulate, maintain,
and erase different racial and national identities."[19] Though Ragussis is
particularly concerned with the nineteenth-century British interest in
the conversion of the Jews, we can see in the annexes to Victorian novels
a wider array of conversions, threats of change, and eruptions of
conscience. Rather than revealing a political unconscious, annexes
provide a record of something like a conscience within the Victorian
novel, a conscience insisting that differences, exceptions, and alternatives appear on the page.

Yet it is equally important to see that when novelists stage challenges
to gender roles in narrative annexes, or represent confrontations with
figures so alien that they demand the redrawing of the boundaries of
fictional worlds, they do not necessarily employ annexes to liberating or
progressive ends. While attention to annexes thus reveals unexpected
aspects of the Victorian novel, it also points out some of the oversimplifi-
cations and omissions of recent theories and criticism. Though the social
and domestic may organize and dominate many Victorian fictional
worlds, annexes disturb the limits of representation and challenge the
recent recasting of the political history of the novel as perpetrating a
single binary opposition along gender lines. In *Desire and Domestic Fiction*,
Nancy Armstrong argues that the source of the eighteenth-century
novel lies in its production of a simpler binary opposition, based on
gender, out of more diverse representations of identity, and that the
nineteenth-century novel further schematizes this male versus female
opposition.[20] Reading the politics of representation in the Victorian
novel leads me to more untidy conclusions, as narrative annexes provide
counter-evidence to this influential thesis by preserving for the novel the
complex and competing means of representation that Armstrong's
argument homogenizes out of existence.

If gender difference is not the only, or primary, ordering principle produced by the Victorian novel, what other matters complicate the picture? Events, controversies, and social problems from the 1840s until the end of the Victorian period affect novelists' concerns and stimulate their desires to represent alternatives. Without attempting to provide an overarching account of social change in the period, I refer in this and subsequent chapters to the Irish Famine; Chartism; enfranchisement; the Corn Law Repeal effort; the Woman Question; Darwinism; and the Condition of England. The relationship of the Victorian novel to reform efforts in social, economic, and political realms; the representation of the moral and religious controversies stimulated by slavery, Methodism, the Oxford Movement, and Darwinism; and the use of fiction to correct abuses (in the Poor Law orphanages; in Yorkshire schools; in marriages and family life) are the subjects of other kinds of books.[21] Using the Victorian epithets "improbable" and "impossible" as touchstones, I treat in this study topics that Victorian novelists, defying incredulity and outright censure, raise in narrative annexes. To identify the limitations that exert pressure on and in Victorian novels, I rely first on the evidence provided by the shape and contents of fictional worlds themselves. Contemporary reactions, in the form of published reviews and private correspondence, augment the internal formal evidence and suggest the extent to which Victorian criticism of the novel participates in the creation of a code for acceptable representation and encourages the use of narrative annexes to make the novel more flexible.

A traditional way of accounting for continuities and innovations in narrative form attends to the sources, analogues, and influences of individual novelists. Very often a bizarre episode or startling turn in a plot bespeaks no pressure to conform, nor burning desire to represent the forbidden, but rather the ineradicable trace of the writer's love for Walter Scott. I assume in this study that the generic variety of narrative annexes shows that Victorian novelists learned their craft not only from one another and from Scott's romances, Thomas Carlyle's histories, and the eighteenth-century novelists, but from Cervantes, Spenser, Shakespeare, Milton, and the Romantic poets. No single study could account for so diverse a set of influences on the Victorian novel and I do not attempt to do so here.[22] Instead, the readings of narrative annexes I undertake show that, for instance, a dream vision and an episode that takes the character (and reader) off the path into unfamiliar territory have in common an impulse to include which appears to defy the consistency, unity, and closed borders of Victorian fiction. Between early modern narratives and modernist fiction lies the novel, whose rise into realism can divert attention from the generic diversity it contains. Not a study or catalog of dreams, digressions, interpolated tales, embedded texts, descriptions, or *exempla* in Victorian fiction, this study inquires instead into an alternative technique for packaging, delivering, and unwrapping the resources of kind within the Victorian novel.[23] Despite the differences among the novels treated in the subsequent pages, their annexes reveal similar strategies of incorporation. I have chosen to discuss, within chapters dealing with various kinds and themes of the Victorian novel, a sufficiently broad array of representative narrative annexes to suggest their contrasting uses, as well as their commonalities of form.

In this introductory chapter, I briefly survey theories of fictional worlds (particularly those of Thomas Pavel, Nelson Goodman, D. A. Miller, and Alexander Gelley), and critical methods for examining place and genre in fiction (with an emphasis on M. M. Bakhtin). Taking Raymond Williams' work on a parallel track to the recent work of Mary Poovey, I suggest that his categories of "dominant," "residual," and "emergent" forms provide the best dynamic model to account for the presence and function of narrative annexes in Victorian novels.[24] While critics, commercial and cultural forces, and novelists collaborated in the production of an idea about appropriate representational realms (as Poovey's description of a process of homogenization into a single culture emphasizes), that idea was always subject to the pressure of the altering form of the novel. Williams' terminology helps to show how novelists used narrative annexes to make both residual and emergent worlds within the dominant worlds of Victorian fiction. Yet as it must be acknowledged that many Victorian novels have *no* annexes, I also consider what their absence tells us about narrative techniques and representational options in subgenres of the novel, such as fantastic fiction which depends upon a shift from primary to secondary worlds.

In the second chapter, "Victorian critics, narrative annexes, and prescriptions for the novel," I focus on a single case, Anthony Trollope's *Castle Richmond*, in order to explore the prescriptive theories of a mainstream realist and his critics. Anthony Trollope's sole narrative annex wrenches *Castle Richmond* off its foundations by staging a confrontation with a starving Irish woman and compelling his readers to consider the condition of Ireland from an uncomfortably close vantage point. Since most Victorian novelists use annexes, it is unusual to find a writer who almost entirely eschews the technique, and whose practical novel theory bans it, employing a narrative annex like the one in *Castle*

Richmond. I suggest here that Trollope increasingly writes multiplot novels (which juxtapose places, contrast modes, and allow for expansions in fictional worlds in a way that renders annexing unnecessary) in order to avoid future uses of narrative annexes. Trollope's internalized fictional literary critic, "Rhadamanthus," makes his first appearance in *Castle Richmond*, in narratorial disquisitions framing the narrative annex. Near the end of his career, Trollope amplifies the prescriptions of Rhadamanthus in his own work of practical novel theory, *An Autobiography* (1883). Real reviewers' reactions to the narrative annex provide a fascinating record of the response to generic mixture and the depiction of subjects that lie in an "interdicted realm," to use Walter Bagehot's phrase.

Contemporary reactions to novels reveal the anxiety caused both by unconventional subjects of representation, and by challenges to normative novelistic techniques. In the third chapter, "Norms and narrow spaces: the gendering of limits on representation," I use Walter Bagehot's criticism to illustrate Victorian critical ideas about norms in novelistic representation and to underline the significance of gender in the formulation of prohibitions. I then focus more closely on reading the unusual materials represented in narrative annexes, drawn from a particularly rich source, for while most Victorian novelists use narrative annexes occasionally, Charlotte Brontë employs annexes in each of her three major novels. I examine the annexes in Brontë's *Jane Eyre* (1847), *Shirley* (1849), and *Villette* (1853), each of which contests convention differently. Brontë's depiction of respectable female characters, such as Lucy Snowe, whose situations test their educations, aspirations, and resourcefulness, makes her novels appropriate sites for the investigation of challenges to norm-generating fictional worlds. In all three novels Brontë uses the image of an aperture through which her questing protagonist peers or passes. This image emphasizes the gendered nature of Brontë's challenges to convention in her border-violating annexes. On a pragmatic as well as a symbolic level, the gender of her protagonists contributes to the need for narrative annexes, which Brontë uses to declare her control over the lines of separation that critics would draw.

Turning in the next two chapters to a selection of novels by five different authors (Charles Dickens, Benjamin Disraeli, Thomas Hardy, Charles Kingsley, and H. G. Wells), I show that narrative annexes work in a variety of contexts simultaneously to diversify representational options and to express qualms about the extension of representation.[25] While the kinds of novels treated in this sequence include

Bildungsromanen, social problem novels, and political fiction, their narrative annexes reveal a shared interest in, and anxiety about, the political, social, and personal agency of the disenfranchised. Gender remains an important imaginative and social category in these works, as in Brontë's, but even more striking is the link between sexuality and conscience, conversion, and political engagement. The temporary realization of lower-class desires, and the presence of alien figures in narrative annexes by no means guarantee the novelists' approval, or a celebratory conclusion. Indeed, Victorian novelists often resort to narrative annexes in order to justify retrograde or punitive plot actions and to qualify seemingly progressive themes with reactionary eruptions of conscience and class-consciousness.

For example, novels by a high Victorian and a late Victorian in favor of political and social reform (and sympathetic to laborers and the poor) contain narrative annexes undermining their prevailingly progressive analyses. In the fourth chapter, "Narrative annexes, social mobility, and class anxiety," I examine Charles Kingsley's *Alton Locke* (1850) and Thomas Hardy's *The Mayor of Casterbridge* (1886), showing how residual and emergent forms within a dominant kind of the Victorian novel, social fiction, work in narrative annexes to figure the difficulties of imagining spaces governed by the desires and judgments of working men and common people. In a mid-century social problem novel and a late Victorian realistic fiction, narrative annexes represent Kingsley's and Hardy's struggles to reconcile representation of members of the lower orders with their potentially threatening enfranchisement. Close readings of the two annexes reveal that the signs of generic difference clustering around the borders demarcating them point towards passageways out of primary social worlds that constrain plot, but that the turns of story made possible by the alternative genres and places of narrative annexes contain punitive responses to the sexual behavior that stands for the hazards of social mobility.

When codes of respectable behavior conflict with the trajectories of plot requiring movement through a variety of locations and genres, narrative annexes can serve liminal and liberating functions, as they do in *Jane Eyre* and *Villette*. Yet the narrative annexes in the three Condition of England novels I treat in chapter 5, "Older, deeper, further: narrative annexes and the extent of the Condition of England," emphasize the existence of others *beyond* political novels' representational range. The placement of the Jew, the expiring worker, and the black murder-victim in annexes suggests the prick of conscience, but a conscience insulated and restrained from having its full effect on the surrounding fictional world. In representing those figures who do not fit in the Condition of England novel, annexes reveal the ambivalence of these novelists towards the necessary but expendable others they depict. I explore in this chapter the role that annexes play in the vexing relationship of conversion narratives to political novels. In *Coningsby* (1844), Disraeli uses conversion *by* a Jew to invert the traditional figure of futurity, in a manifesto for political action that conjures up an idealized feudal past. The problem of overlapping narratives of victimization and spiritual profit, unresolved by Kingsley's Christian Socialism, is reactivated in the annex to Dickens' *Hard Times* (1854), a novel which plays on conventional piety to justify its outrageous human sacrifice in the killing of Stephen Blackpool. At the end of the "long nineteenth-century," H. G. Wells' examination of the corruption at the heart of England's prosperity in *Tono-Bungay* (1908) employs an annex to convert the protagonist into a guilty man, whose self-narrated *Bildungsroman* contains a jarring confession of murder. The critical response to Wells' novel shows that the discontinuity and strangeness of the narrative annex is assimilated to modernity and to the modern novel, even though *Tono-Bungay* closely resembles the big Victorian novels Wells sought to imitate.

The disagreement among critics of *Tono-Bungay* (regarding its modernity) leads directly to a sixth and concluding chapter on the way in which annexes illuminate the continuities among modern, Victorian, and early fiction. The discussion that runs through the study of novelists' and critics' theories of the novel culminates here in an account of the misleading picture of the Victorian novel presented by early criticism of the modern novel. Much of what is putatively modern about the twentieth-century novel can be seen at work two, four, even seven decades earlier in the narrative annexes of Victorian fiction. Yet I do not argue here that annexes are simply modern before their time. I attempt instead to account for continuities in narrative technique from the sixteenth to the twentieth century. Related to the "second worlds" or "green worlds"[26] of early modern literary kinds, narrative annexes preserve in the Victorian novel fiction's ability to shift place and mode for the sake of what can be represented in a specially circumscribed zone. Spenserian romance; dream-vision; Shakespeare's gardens, forests, and islands; and More's Utopia; as well as the play-within-the-play and the interpolated tales of Cervantes – all contribute to the prehistory of narrative annexes. Across the kinds of Victorian fiction, narrative annexes remind us of the diverse heritage of the novel.

Although governed by sequential and spatially consistent actions on the whole, the Victorian novel's peripety does carry characters into worlds *within* the fictional worlds they traverse. When peripety is accompanied by a sudden shift in genre and place, the effect of abandoning the reader's actual world is simultaneously doubled and undone. Entering the altered space and perceiving the difference in mode, the character mimics the reader's world-abandonment and threatens to expose it as an impossible action. This differs markedly from the effects of related narrative techniques mentioned earlier, such as interpolation of secondary narrators' tales, embedding of fictional documents, and metaleptic breaks in narrative level (as when the narrator addresses the reader[27]), which call attention more urgently to the wrought nature of a fictional world. Unlike interpolated stories, narrative annexes can be entered by a character and apprehended by a reader without disrupting the illusion of a continuous fictional world. Bound to orderly, chronological narration which relies on the reporting consciousness of a central character, a Victorian novel may import an alternative place and mode in a narrative annex instead of framing these in an embedded account from a second narrating voice (such as Magwitch's narration of his past in chapter 42 of *Great Expectations* [1860–1]). Annexes maintain the norm of character, although the experiences of the character in the annex often alter her characterization and introduce her to figures who have not been represented in the primary realm of the fiction.

Because annexes deploy alternate modes of story-telling within surrounding fictions, they jar the reader. Yet the annex permits stories, information, places, characters, and points of view that would not be plausible in the primary fictional world to perform work in the novel. Annexes call attention to their difference, jolting the reader out of a smooth journey through a fictional world. The mental map of the fictional world in the reader's mind must be revised. How then does a reader recognize a narrative annex? As striking and individual as the worlds within which they occur, annexes include indoor and outdoor places, bounded by literal and metaphorical barriers. As the spaces represented by narrative annexes differ from one another, so their modes include dream, delirium, travelogue, confession, melodrama, and eyewitness reportage. The employment of the technique described here, a response to limits on representation, does not result in the appearance of the same few alternative spaces, or handful of generic exceptions in an easily cataloged set of instances. A reader discovers a narrative annex by noticing a simultaneous shift in place and genre, a boundary crossed that, without a move to the nested structure of the tale-within-the-tale, suggests a world within the fictional world.

FICTIONAL WORLDS AND THEIR THEORISTS

In order to perceive an anomalous space "within" a fictional world, readers of novels must first apprehend the lineaments of fictional worlds themselves. Earlier in this introduction I assert that readers simultaneously assemble these fictional worlds, learn the norms implied by the author's choices to include and exclude, and recognize surprises or violations of the terms that apparently govern the worldmaking. As will be apparent from the terms in which I describe fictional worlds, I am indebted in my thinking to narratology, to the phenomenological work of Wolfgang Iser, and to the philosophy of worldmaking, particularly that of Thomas Pavel and Nelson Goodman.[28]

D. A. Miller's nuanced description in *Narrative and its Discontents* represents a lucid synthesis of narratological theories of fictional worlds, characterized here as "the field of the narratable."

The anchors of traditional narrative are basically a system of restraints imposed upon the field of the narratable. A story is centered through the establishment of a well-policed periphery, where narratable potentialities are either nullified, reined in, or denied importance. Order and orientation are thus secured by clear distinctions of relevance: between round characters, full of intriguing possibilities, and flat ones, reduced to a prescribed function or gesture that they aren't allowed to overstep; between the primary notation that constitutes an important sequence and the subsidiary notation that is felt merely to fill it in; between motifs that are bound in a pattern of inescapable coherence and motifs that are free to be deleted or not without substantially altering the story.[29]

Bringing together the traditional Anglo-American novel theory of E. M. Forster (on flat and round characters); the French structuralist and poststructuralist contributions of theorists such as Roland Barthes (on the sequences of codes that comprise narrative); and the Russian formalist Boris Tomashevsky's description of bound and free motifs in plot, Miller enumerates some of the elements that contribute to the anchoring restraints on the imagined domain ("field") of the narratable.[30]

Though many narrative theorists would extend Miller's description beyond the traditional narrative upon which he focuses in his study of the dynamics of closure, his discussion of the "narratable" in the novel is particularly useful because it emphasizes both potential and limitation in fictional worldmaking. The "narratable" Miller defines as "the instances of disequilibrium, suspense, and general insufficiency from which a given narrative appears to arise." Covering both "incitements to narrative" and the "dynamic ensuing from such incitements," the narratable "is thus opposed to the 'nonnarratable' state of quiescence assumed by a novel before the beginning and supposedly recovered by it at the end" (*Discontents* ix). However, the opposition of the narratable to what is not narrated before the beginning and (more questionably) after the end only acknowledges one way in which limitation contributes to the shape of fictional worlds. Miller also places the narratable within a "well-policed periphery" which the story also creates. His focus on the nineteenth-century novel, chosen because "it is a text of abundant restrictions and regulations," turns to the symptoms of uneasiness visible in problems of closure, symptoms which he attributes to the novel text's "need for controls" (xiv). It is not necessary to accept a psychologized, needy nineteenth-century novel, nor a Foucauldian disciplinary text policing its own borders, in order to appreciate Miller's reasoning: "for the regulations would be unnecessary if nothing resisted them, and the restrictions come into force for a reason" (xiv). As finite creations made of an exhaustible sequence of words, all fictional worlds, even those that playfully subvert the idea of limitations, set narratable potentialities against the nonnarratable. Miller's choice of the traditional novel, "restricted for a reason," underlines the cultural context(s) in which nineteenth-century fictional worlds were created. Though an earlier generation of structuralist theorists of narrative aimed to create taxonomies that included all narrative forms, from the folk tale to the multiplot novel, poststructuralist narrative theory more often allows for a period focus and admits literary historical evidence as it acknowledges the interplay between narrative form and cultural contexts. (Roland Barthes' designation of a referential or cultural code [REF] in his influential work *S/Z* provides only the most prominent example of such an admixture.) As Alexander Gelley argues in *Narrative Crossings: Theory and Pragmatics of Prose Fiction*, a fictional world "projects the level of agents and actions onto its appropriate backdrop of cultural norms. It accounts for the imbrication of personal choice and contextual determinants that is basic to our representational tradition" (*Narrative Crossings* 8–9).

The relation of the narratable, the nonnarratable, and cultural norms (including generic and social conventions), then, is a fundamental dynamic of fictional worldmaking. Though critics and readers may disagree about the relative importance of context to text, one of the more controversial elements of theories of fictional worlds has proven to be

the adoption of a spatial metaphor for the effect of reading experienced
in time, as the linear text is written and consumed. To paraphrase the
most exacting position, the only real space, in distinction from represented settings, or perceived possibilities and limits on representation, is the
physical space of the page, on which words appear one after another.
Certainly space has been abstracted from its basic meaning by many
theorists, perhaps most strikingly by Joseph Frank, whose 1945 notion of
"spatial form" in modern literature has been reiterated as recently as
1991.[31] Frank's terminology refers to the breaking up of the "time-flow"
in modern narrative, in response to modern poetry's imperative to
suspend orderly, logical reading of word-groups. In their close scrutiny
of forms of narrative disorder (anachrony and achrony), narrative theorists following the Russian formalists (most influentially, Gerard Genette)
have employed the distinction between story-time and discourse-time to
replace an abstract "spatial", with a more precise consideration of
temporal effects in fiction.[32] Yet theorists deploying metaphors for
narrative, for disciplinary practices, and for historical events transpiring
in time persistently invoke space, as Michel de Certeau does when he
writes in *The Practice of Everyday Life* that "every story is a travel story – a
spatial practice."[33] Alexander Gelley's searching critique of spatial
metaphors such as these identifies literary criticism's "incapacity . . . to
mediate between its tropological and its referential language" (*Narrative
Crossings* 37) and pointedly inquires "what allows the notion of space to
be used as a constituent both of the physical world and of linguistic
structures? What is the relation between space as the condition of
phenomenal reality and space as a formal category? Is this relation only
a loose analogy or is it a true homology which, if better understood,
could illuminate both dimensions?" (38). Yet if the metaphorical excesses of theoretical model-makers are especially vulnerable to this sort of
questioning, it is also the case, as Gelley acknowledges, that a significant
constitutive feature of prose fiction, particularly in the nineteenth-
century novel, lies in its projection of a "world model" (28) through
representation of an "ocular" fictional world that can be envisioned (23).
So long as novels proffer imaginable settings, backdrops, or fields of the
narratable, purists will struggle in vain to rid literary criticism of the
spatial metaphors intrinsic to this representational tradition. As I have
already asserted in this introduction, Victorian assumptions about the
novel's role, representational range, and aesthetic achievement are
embodied in a geographical language of "world," "realm," "region,"
"border," "boundary," "house," and "land." The symbolic connection

of cultural norms and limitations on fictional worlds can be observed not only throughout three centuries of novelistic practice, but in the language of critics writing long before recent promulgators of spatial metaphors. Not merely a theoretical vogue or blind spot, spatial descriptions of fictional worlds belong to an accurate literary history of the novel and its theories.

This does not mean that novelists always create or critics always demand purely verisimilar fictional worlds, nor that the establishment of representational boundaries always arises at the prompting of champions of the real, or guardians of the proper. Indeed, readers demonstrably possess appetites for fictional worlds differing from their own, and fictional worlds create the desire that they also satisfy. As Wolfgang Iser puts it in "Toward a Literary Anthropology," the consciousness of a gap or difference between actual and fictional worlds is instigated by the existence of the imaginary:

if we regard the world of the text as being bracketed off from the world it represents, it follows that that which is within the bracket is separated from the reality in which it is usually embedded. Consequently there will be a continual oscillation between the bracketed world and that from which it has been separated. The former therefore becomes a medium for revealing what has remained concealed in the empirical world, and whatever may be the relation between the two, it is the "As if world" that brings about the interplay between them. (*Prospecting* 272)

In the philosophy of possible worlds, the "As if world" referred to by Iser need not be a world of narrative fiction or of artistic construction, but may be scientific, philosophical, etc., so long as it has been constructed through a process of worldmaking entailing composition and decomposition, weighting, ordering, deletion and supplementation, and deformation.[34] The philosopher Nelson Goodman's particular concern in *Ways of Worldmaking* is to bring together the seemingly antithetical worlds of science and art, lest artistic worlds be neglected. They, too, permit "modes of discovery, creation, and enlargement of knowledge in the broad sense of advancement of the understanding" (102). Abstract or purely imaginary worlds may function just as powerfully as denotative worlds in Goodman's view. Yet for Goodman as well as for Iser, the representational worlds of fiction occupy a special position because they can reveal "what has remained concealed in the empirical world" (Iser, *Prospecting* 272), allowing recognition of the familiar in the recasting of the imaginary:

Fiction . . . applies truly neither to nothing nor to diaphanous possible worlds but, albeit metaphorically, to actual worlds . . . the so-called possible worlds of fiction lie within actual worlds. Fiction operates in actual worlds in much the same way as nonfiction. Cervantes and Bosch and Goya, no less than Boswell and Newton and Darwin, take and unmake and remake and retake familiar worlds, recasting them in remarkable and sometimes recondite but eventually recognizable – that is *re-cognizable* – ways. (Goodman, *Ways of Worldmaking* 104–5)

Though Goodman acknowledges the historical and cultural contexts which render particular kinds of representation "recognizable" to a reader, we find a more thorough investigation of a referential theory of fictional worlds in the work of Thomas Pavel.

For Pavel, the movement away from a strictly textualist criticism enables the exploration of a "theory of fiction [that] can respond again to the world-creating powers of imagination and account for the properties of fictional existence and worlds, their complexity, incompleteness, remoteness, and integration within the general economy of culture."[35] The plurality and diversity of fictional worlds for Pavel depends on an admirably flexible view of how this "integration within the general economy of culture" will function in different historical periods. Since no fictional world can ever be made complete, Pavel argues, different cultures will maximize or minimize incompleteness through extensive or intensive strategies. The most extreme form of extensive world assumes first "the completeness of the universe," and second, "the existence of a divine book that describes it in full" (*Fictional Worlds* 108). Nineteenth-century realism, offering a more common sort of extensive fictional world, corresponds to a culture self-defined as occupying "an unbound universe, well-determined and knowable in all its details" (108). Finally, towards the intensive side, "periods of transition and conflict tend to maximize the incompleteness of fictional worlds," a phenomenon Pavel associates with modernist narrative technique (109). Though it will become evident that I differ from Pavel in my characterization of the nineteenth century and its fictional worlds, I rely upon his contention that "the compositional severity of well-focused narration is periodically contradicted by dispersion, faulty arrangement, and incoherence," and not only by modernist and postmodernist fictions (147). I concur with Pavel that "our commitment to coherence is less warranted than it appears" when we privilege nineteenth-century realist fiction (50), but more importantly I find ample evidence within the nineteenth-century novel of the "variety of fictional practice" he discerns in a broader literary history.

Like Goodman and Iser, Pavel sees these various fictional worlds as related to, but separate from the actual world of readers. His description of diverse, but bounded, fictional worlds responds not only to their historical and cultural contexts, but to literary contexts, including the histories and conventions of genres:

> The frontiers of fiction separate it on one side from myth, on another from actuality. To these borders we should add the line that isolates the represented space of fiction from the spectators or readers. Accordingly, fiction is surrounded by sacred borders, by actuality borders, and by representational borders . . . Within these fuzzy, multiple borders, fictional territories grow in accordance with various patterns. (81)

Unabashedly embracing the spatial metaphors that disconcert some theorists, Pavel reminds us that the "various patterns" of generic difference have often been conceptualized in geographical terms. The following section explores the relationship of place and genre in criticism of the ostensibly opposed modes, novel and romance.

PLACE AND GENRE; NOVEL AND ROMANCE

That Victorian novels often contain or imitate the plots, tropes, characters, actions, or themes of a variety of genres and kinds is an assumption, not the subject, of this study. The terms so frequently used by the novelists themselves to distinguish between fictional genres, "novel" and "romance," contribute to a simplifying literary history which forces a great variety of fiction into two vast territories, divided by a fence on which we find perched Scott and Dickens. "Romance" denotes as diverse a group of fictions as does "novel," and romances furnish the novel with a great variety of plot structures, narrative situations, character types, *topoi*, and degrees of distance from the actual world. So many novels contain some aspects of romance that it may seem difficult to distinguish a fiction that is not, in one way or another, indebted to the earlier forms. Yet in some cases, such as gothic and boys' adventure fiction,[36] a dedication to one or several qualities of romance is so basic to the fictional subgenre that the romance inheritance seems absolutely clear, though the cousins may scarcely resemble one another. The precept that "the novel" occupies itself with everyday life, as opposed to the marvellous events of "romance," is of course a common-sense distinction, but in reading Victorian novels we often find the two modes blended. In contemporary novel criticism we find not only the opposition of "novel" and "romance," but also the use of these terms as if they were interchangeable, and the more interesting attempt to specify sub-genres or kinds within fiction. Aside from the French import, realism, a novel that seemed closer to reality might belong to the "literature of social reference," "revolutionary" literature, or "ubiquitous" fiction. If it had a love story in it, a "novel" with the most ordinary protagonists might find itself named "romance." Needless to say, the use of the term "romance" can denote anything from a love plot, to gothic, picaresque, allegorical fiction, or Cervantine anti-romance. Additionally, as Gillian Beer has observed, when read at the distance of a generation or a century's remove, realistic fictions regain many of the qualities of romance.[37]

Why, then, does the opposition between novel and romance appear to be so plain? On the one hand, we look back at the Victorian novel through the 1880s and 1890s, when writers such as Robert Louis Stevenson, Hall Caine, and H. Rider Haggard presented their romances as an escapist alternative to realism. The contrast at the end of the century, when debates about the nature and art of fiction were also so charged, may make it harder to see the intermingling of earlier decades. On the other hand, the difference between nineteenth-century American fiction and the English Victorian novel has been misleadingly schematized in terms of a paradigmatic opposition of realism and romance (or novel and romance), a division that depends on a fantastically homogeneous, realistic English novel, in order that American fiction can occupy the territory of romance.[38]

Mikhail Bakhtin's alternative account of the concoction of the novel out of diverse kinds and voices makes polyphony and heteroglossia more recent commonplaces of novel criticism; however, Bakhtin characterizes the novel as the only mixed form, uniquely containing multiple, contrasting discourses. Readers of romance and epic know differently, for the mixed forms of Renaissance literature obviously antedate and influence the novel, as Bakhtin would acknowledge only in certain quite specific cases.[39] Here an even more drastic opposition between novel and all other narrative kinds (characterized variously as "poetic," "monological," or simply "all other genres") confuses the literary history of the novel and misrepresents the generic complexity of earlier kinds, including romances, epics, other prose narratives, emblem books, and lyric sequences. (Bakhtin admits the presence of dialogical energy only in cases of parody or travesty. On the other hand, his "chronotope" acknowledges that genre, time, and place come together to produce a set of norms characteristic of a particular genre, such as chivalric romance or picaresque. However, Bakhtin sees each of these pre-novelistic kinds as adhering strictly to a single norm, which is clearly not the case. We must look elsewhere for adequate accounts of the history of generic mixture.) Bakhtin's description of novelistic discourse, however, has proven invaluable, and it is as relevant to the small worlds of narrative annexes as to the novel in general. Narrative annexes undoubtedly contribute to the novel's dialogic quality and they are often zones of heightened heteroglossia, where characters from antithetical generic realms speak to one another. However, his genealogy of the novel's qualities depends upon a faulty and oversimplified description of all other narrative genres and of genre history.

Not all or even most criticism of the English novel has been afflicted by such schematizing generic distinctions, and excellent work on authors such as Charles Dickens, Charlotte Brontë, and Elizabeth Gaskell, among others, contributes to an account of Victorian fiction neither shackled in the chains of realism, nor imprisoned in the close space of representational decorum.[40] We are no longer startled to be startled by a Victorian novel. However, certain aspects of fictional narrative have seemed to *belong* to either novel or romance, and the dichotomy effects the analysis of form. Richard Brodhead writes, "Like Cervantes and Fielding, and unlike their English and European contemporaries, Hawthorne and Melville characteristically include within their novels minor narrative forms set off as discrete units of fiction."[41] Here, interpolation belongs to American romance and not to English fiction, despite the embedded narratives in novels by Dickens, Eliot, Gaskell, Reade, Kingsley, Trollope, and Charlotte and Emily Brontë, among others. Because genre entails conventions and because realistic fiction depends upon anti-conventional and anti-literary gestures, "genre" is often associated, by default, with romance.

Victorian novelists, conscious of the norms of the dominant form in which they work (including mixtures of novel and romance), use narrative annexes to alter temporarily the generic and spatial configurations of their fictional worlds. Charles Dickens remarks in a letter on "an idea, which I thought a new one, of making the introduced story so fit into surroundings impossible of separation from the main story, as to make the blood of the book circulate through both."[42] If we imagine interpolated tales as importing their substance through the words of a secondary narrator into the fiction that surrounds them, we might conceive, as Dickens does, that an alternative technique forces the substance of the

novel through the transforming region, "impossible of separation" from
the primary world. The most important distinction between narrative
annexes and interpolated stories is the reliance, in interpolation or
embedding, on a secondary narrator, whose narration may freely roam
away from the place, time, and norms of the surrounding fiction.
Narrative annexes employ peripety instead of an embedded level of
narrative (although annexes often include embedded narratives by
creating circumstances in which new tellers can be introduced). In
maintaining the illusion of connected locations, by means of the characters and narrators who cross the borders between primary texts and
narrative annexes, the technique of annexing emphasizes the centrality
– and flexibility – of *place* in Victorian fiction.[43]

Spaces, or "place" – interiors, institutions, landscapes, towns, cities,
roads, railways, and other architectural objects or geographical areas –
have been examined in a variety of different ways informing criticism of
the novel.[44] A brief survey of the alternatives reveals that only in some of
these contexts does attention to genre or mode accompany the analysis
of spaces and places.[45] As I will discuss shortly, Mikhail Bakhtin's
theories of the "carnivalesque" and "chronotopes" do employ both
space and genre, but I begin with the most obvious candidate, the
analysis of *setting* in literary criticism and narrative theory.

Surprisingly few studies focus on setting in the English novel.[46]
George Levine's suggestive chapter in *The Realistic Imagination*, "The
Landscape of Reality," treats extreme locations outside England, particularly the Alps and the sea, which permit novels to represent "primal
realities beyond the reach of social constraint" (206). Although my work
here does not focus exclusively on realistic fiction, I share Levine's
conviction that "novels need to find appropriate space for realities
unassimilable to the conventions of realism" (205). In Levine's analysis,
the exoticized city, the turbulent sea, and Alpine heights allow "monstrous energies" to be channeled through the ordinary world of the
Victorian novel. He writes that "Truthfulness required not only the
diminution of great expectations, but the admission of violence and
mystery beyond realistic explanation. Thus Victorian novels tend to
establish geographical pockets of excess, 'natural' or 'foreign' places in
which community is no longer implicit" (205–6). These excessive geographical pockets can often be identified as narrative annexes; however,
annexes are not limited to natural settings, foreign places, or extreme
heights for their potential alternative places. In combination with shifted
genres and a dividing line crossed by a character, narrative annexes can

make the most homely and ordinary setting – a humble cottage, or a pool in the woods – into a zone of difference. A character need not journey so far as the Alps to break out of the constraints of a represented world and its community.

Crossing periods and genres, some literary criticism examines the meaning of space in fiction through the analysis of particular elements of setting, such as the house, the road, the garden, the city, the underworld, or the frontier. This sort of criticism may be organized to treat the chosen setting(s) across kinds, as in Raymond Williams' *The Country and the City*, or may be confined to the examples that define a subgenre.[47] A related method, overlapping in many instances with the analysis of a specific kind of fictional space, takes up the characteristic "places" of a particular novelist. Often the subjects of this sort of analysis work from a recognizable (actual) geography, so it is not surprising that the Brontës and Thomas Hardy have been examined in this light.[48] Critics working on individual writers have recognized the close tie between alternative settings and genres, although it is also in this kind of criticism that writers are most often rebuked by critics for representing places that diverge from an ostensibly fixed "sense of place." (We need only think of Anthony Trollope's frustration with readers and critics who expected him to work always in his imaginary Barset or familiar Parliamentary worlds.) On the other hand, interdisciplinary critics such as Rhoda Flaxman, Robert Harbison, and Philippa Tristram have focused on particular settings in work that relates art, architecture, and cultural history to the representation and uses of place in literature.[49]

In the frankly formalist discipline of narratology or narrative poetics, the conventionally opposed categories of "narration" and "description" govern the discussion of place and setting.[50] In works such as Seymour Chatman's *Story and Discourse*, setting and character are both "existents," fictional entities depicted in "discourse," and contributing to the "story." The conventional division in narratology of "story" and "discourse" often results in awkward straddling over categories, as when character belongs to the realm of "story," but characterization and the representation of fictional consciousness belong to the "discourse" level. Setting falls into the same situation.[51] Yet in narrative theory, as in literary criticism, setting is the poor relation of character, receiving little attention even in theories devoted to the analysis of story spaces.[52] Some narrative theory and most criticism of the novel attends to the conventional relationships between certain settings and the generic expectations they generate. Thus a novel set upon a highway, or in a half-decayed castle, alerts a reader to the possibility that picaresque or gothic is in the offing.[53] Obviously, these expectations can be raised by a setting only to be dashed by a debunking, parodic, or otherwise convention-bending plot, as Edwin Eigner has demonstrated in *The Metaphysical Novel* (210–27). In a way that closely resembles the use of scenes in dramas, setting can also be used to differentiate plot strands from one another in multiplot novels. This use of setting should be distinguished from the strategy of employing a frame narrative, for instance, or a play within a play. In drama and narrative fiction, nested levels are created by frames, secondary narrators' stories and interpolated stories, plays within plays, and other instances of embedding and *mise en abyme*. These techniques have been exhaustively cataloged and analyzed by narrative theorists and critics of the novel,[54] while narrative annexes have gone unnoticed because they do not create a nested level of story within the story (though they often contain a secondary narrator and his quoted tale). Although individual instances of "annexing" have been described in criticism of the novel as interruptions, detours, embedded forms, marginal pockets,[55] failures in artistry, or merely puzzling episodes, neither narrative theory nor novel criticism has suggested what these instances have in common, nor what their strange work contributes to the novel.

Cultural poetics and materialist criticism have come closer by scrutinizing a diverse array of textual and historical cases in which the social construction of a space or place either permits or, more commonly, inhibits change. These modes of analysis pick up some of the ways of thinking about spaces and places found in the social science disciplines of anthropology and human geography.[56] Although geography's contribution to literary theory is negligible, considerable traffic runs between anthropology and literary study.[57] Anthropology provides an influential account of the relationship between real and symbolic spaces, and human uses of these zones in "social dramas," as theorized by Victor Turner.[58] Turner's description of the results of social drama's staging emphasizes the dynamic patterning that permits change to occur in social relations. Yet the containing function of the space or occasion corresponding to the "arena" may well uphold hegemonic institutional powers. Then a social drama effectively *prevents* social change.

Mikhail Bakhtin's influential theory of the carnivalesque[59] has been interpreted by cultural materialists in precisely this way. For instance, Terry Eagleton describes carnival as a licensed affair, "a permissible rupture of hegemony, a contained popular blow-off as disturbing and relatively ineffectual as a revolutionary work of art."[60] Bakhtin's own interpretation of the carnivalesque appears, upon closer examination, somewhat less pessimistic. In *Rabelais and his World*, Bakhtin argues that outbreaks of folk carnival humor (ritual spectacles, comic verbal compositions, and various genres of billingsgate) offered medieval people "a completely different nonofficial, extraecclesiastical and extrapolitical aspect of the world, of man, and of human relations; they built a second world and a second life outside officialdom" (5–6). The feudal political structure and framework of class contain this second world in its carnivals and marketplace festivals; Bakhtin sees the festive space as a temporary "utopian realm of community, freedom, equality, and abundance" (9).[61] In this scheme, utopian possibilities are released in a second world where inversions may be tolerated and enjoyed. Though utopian, carnival need not be useless. Genre plays an important role, as the carnivalesque is associated with humor, satire, and the grotesque, modes that flourish in a zone where hierarchies, privileges of rank, norms, and prohibitions have been suspended. Further, Bakhtin sees the development of grotesque as an important step in the history of realism.[62] In Bakhtin's carnivalesque, then, we find a suggestive treatment of fictional and social spaces that draws explicitly on the resources of genre and kind, even rewriting a segment of the history of realism.

The analogy of carnivalesque with narrative annexes, then, appears compelling. Indeed, some annexes permit festive laughter, parody, and ritual inversions to unleash a comic, grotesque point of view or voice within a more strictly governed primary world. Yet it would be precipitous to assume that all annexes serve this function, when some annexes clearly introduce traditional values of culture, rank, and privilege, as in Charlotte Brontë's *Villette*, or Benjamin Disraeli's *Coningsby*. More importantly, it is obvious that a comic or grotesque fictional world with all the trappings of carnivalesque need not be contained within a more orderly framing fiction. When a narrative annex draws on a contrasting genre associated with folk (carnival) humor, it may or *may not* participate in the creation of a utopian realm, for much depends on the perceiving character's perspective. One character's party is another's ordeal. Ultimately, Bakhtin's carnivalesque makes too strict an association of the alternative zone with a particular set of modes to be applicable to all narrative annexes. In a later redaction of the carnivalesque, Stallybrass and White's "trangressive" presents the same problem, for in cases of transgression, "the primary site of contradiction, the site of conflicting desires and mutually incompatible representation is undoubtedly the 'low.'"[63]

The stories of cultural transformation and the development of the Victorian novel take far more complicated forms than a "low" or "transgressive" in contest with a totalizing and dominant realm of officialdom. Officialdom itself, made up of political, economic, educational, literary, and legal hierarchies and systems (among others), underwent rapid and pervasive changes during the Victorian period. If, as Mary Poovey argues in *Making a Social Body*, the dynamics of nineteenth-century cultural formation describe a process, rather than a "unified, homogeneous whole" achieved in a fully formed and fixed British national identity, the sites of difference, contradiction, and contestation will also be revealed in the historical record and in literary texts as diverse and complicated.[64] Using a term that Victorians themselves would have recognized, Poovey describes these epistemological fields as domains, traces their "uneven process of disaggregation," and not only moves towards a recognition of the "imperfect" totality of modern forms of power, but also attends to the irrationality and contradictions inherent in the transformations of domains (14–15). Poovey's model, employed in her work in a broad cultural and historical context, usefully evokes the sorts of generic changes that can alert readers of novels to cultural transformations. Drawing on the same terms as those of Raymond Williams discussed below shortly, Poovey writes: "Because emergent domains develop out of and retain a constitutive relationship to preexistent, or residual, domains, the rationalities and forms of calculation that are institutionalized in new domains tend to carry with them traces of the rationality specific to the domain in which they arise" (14). Just because a trace of this sort has a genealogy or a prehistory (often lending it the dignity and legitimacy of the traditional) does not mean that it will fit neatly or seamlessly in its new context, where "the specific rationality of the residual domain may seem distinctly irrational" (14). Thus we may find the old-fashioned and customary occupying the position of the transgressive or the carnivalesque. My specific focus on the narrative annexes to Victorian novels supports Poovey's view that assumptions about gender, race, nationality, and status are particularly susceptible to transfer from residual to emergent forms, and can be detected in interesting confusions, mixtures, and incoherences in novels with narrative annexes. Rather than clearly moving towards homogeneity, the employment of categories of difference (I would augment Poovey's catalog with religious difference) in narrative annexes bespeaks the capacity of the dominant form, the novel, to diversify its fictional worlds as needed.

RESIDUAL AND EMERGENT FORMS IN VICTORIAN FICTION

Readers of Victorian novels have often regarded the fictional worlds represented in these fictions as mimetic, as does Jerome Buckley in his preface to *The Worlds of Victorian Fiction*: "Since realism was the dominant mode of nineteenth-century fiction, the little world of a given novel usually has a close relationship to the real world, the surfaces of which it can usually reproduce with a photographic accuracy."[65] Describing nineteenth-century fiction, Buckley concedes that fictional worldmaking goes beyond photographic reproduction, especially when alternative genres complicate representation: "A 'world' of fiction may of course be more specialized and exclusive than its real counterpart... Several types or genres [are] each guided by [their] own limiting conventions and assumptions. Each kind establishes its own ambiance, the conditions we must accept if we would explore a strange country of the imagination, a new world with its particular expectations" (vi). Realism in this account is less limited, less conventional, and closer in its fictional worldmaking to the real world than alternative kinds associated with romance. Narratives of the rise of the novel often fix on realism as the highest point of development of the Victorian novel. However, some of the newest "inventions" of the late nineteenth-century novel were reinventions of very old kinds of narrative.

For instance, in the latter part of the Victorian age, when Robert Louis Stevenson, Rider Haggard, and Conan Doyle (among others) reinvigorated romance in adventure fiction, an alternative variant of romance took over some of the territory of gothic in a new mode, Victorian fantastic fiction. The inheritance of romance is particularly noticeable in the representation of the marvellous and the implied contrast of real and fantastic worlds, but it can also be discerned in the fantastic's quest narratives, its embedded tales, and its transitions between primary and secondary worlds. Fantastic fiction in the Victorian period encompasses a diverse group of texts including fairy tales such as Ruskin's *The King of the Golden River* (1851); utopian or dystopian novels of the future such as Richard Jefferies' *After London* (1885); H. G. Wells' scientific romances; and fantastic verse such as Christina Rossetti's *Goblin Market* (1859). Although Rossetti's poem was not intended for children, a great deal of fantastic fiction was written for the new juvenile market.[66] From the 1850s through the end of the century, fantastic fiction and fairy tales augmented rather than contested the fictional worlds of realistic fiction.[67] Fantasy represents an alternative mode that coexists with realistic fiction; for our purposes, its elaborate transitions from world to world highlight the briefer, more abrupt, and more disconcerting shifts of narrative annexes within mainstream fiction.

Fantasy positions itself in relation to the actual world and mimetic fictions by depicting the transition from a realistic world to an often supernatural or marvellous fictional world where the rules and norms differ. (Fairy tales generally begin and end in the marvellous other world.[68]) Theories of the fantastic vary in their breadth, but even at their narrowest they emphasize the effect of the transition between worlds.[69] Accomplished by the passing of the character through what C. S. Lewis' Narnia books call a chink or chasm – a rabbit hole, a mirror, a hidden door, or a picture frame – the passage between worlds may be activated by a talisman: something belonging in that other world, a magical device, or a machine. The "arresting strangeness" of the other world, in Tolkien's term, is established in Victorian fantasy in relation to a first world, often a normal, everyday, realistic world.[70] Yet the secondary world must inspire "secondary belief," must achieve the fullest possible internal consistency, and must not be disabled by a disbelieving frame story (*Tolkien Reader* 49). George MacDonald, a prolific Victorian author of fantastic fiction, lays out the relation between primary and secondary worlds in his essay, "The Fantastic Imagination." He suggests the purpose of sustaining a fantastic world within a world:

The natural world has its laws, and no man must interfere with them in the way of presentment any more than in the way of use; but they themselves may suggest laws of other kinds, and man may, if he pleases, invent a little world of his own, with its own laws; for there is that in him which delights in calling up new forms – which is the nearest, perhaps, he can come to creation.[71]

The fantasist in MacDonald's theory resembles Sidney's poet, who "goeth hand in hand with nature, not enclosed within the narrow warrant of her gifts, but freely ranging only within the zodiac of his own wit," to create a golden world that outdoes the brazen world of everyday existence.[72] MacDonald employs the language of laws which flows so easily from the pen of the Victorian critic of fiction:

His world once invented, the highest law that comes next into play is, that there shall be harmony between the laws by which the new world has begun to exist; and in the process of his creation, the inventor must hold by those laws. The moment he forgets one of them, he makes the story, by its own postulates, incredible. To be able to live a moment in an imagined world, we must see its laws of existence obeyed. Those broken we fall out of it. (*Fantasists* 15)

The "laws" of the interior, secondary world must differ from those that govern the exterior world. MacDonald makes here not the critic's common charge to maintain consistency and probability, but an exacting variation on the theme: the fantasist's invention must meet its own internal standards. The norms of realism (the dominant form) provide necessary counterstructures to the alternative claims of fantasy.[73]

The emphasis in MacDonald's theoretical essay falls on the success of the internal world, but in his fiction his fascination with the problem of conveying his protagonists from one realm to another calls attention to the significance of the transition between worlds and the creation of the necessary sense of difference. In his novel *Phantastes* (1858), the border-crossing between primary and secondary worlds is effected by transforming a domestic interior.[74] *Phantastes* begins by alluding briefly to a world of family and to the coming-of-age of Anodos, the narrator. The speaker places himself in a social world where inheritance functions normally, but an old desk filled with private papers reveals the limitations of realistic genres and ordinary legal transactions. The narrator springs the lock on a hidden chamber, where he discovers a diminutive woman, instead of the papers he expects to find. Leaping onto the floor, she becomes life-sized, reveals herself as his great-grandmother, and promises to introduce him into Fairy Land.

The subsequent transformation wrought on Anodos' bedroom suggests the limitations of ordinary spaces, the absurdities of conventional representation of the natural world, and an exaggerated mutability in which the powers of enchantment erupt into the everyday world. As he lies in bed Anodos hears water running. He sees:

that a large green marble basin, in which I was wont to wash, and which stood on a low pedestal of the same material in a corner of my room, was overflowing like a spring; and that a stream of clear water was running over the carpet, all the length of the room, finding its outlet I know not where. And, stranger still, where this carpet, which I had designed myself to imitate a field of grass and daisies, bordered the course of the little stream, the grass-blades and daisies seemed to wave in a tiny breeze that followed the water's flow. (19)

Rather than exposing the illusion that suggests that a "person" inhabits a "room" with "furniture," the move into the fantastic world dodges, deepening the illusion by transforming commonplace man-made objects into other commonplace natural objects. Inanimate objects come to life and works of art turn into the things that they imitate. Anodos looks at his dressing-table in time to see the carved leaves twining around the drawer handles. He barely completes his toilet before all trace of his room disappears. Following the path and the stream into the dense wood, Anodos does not enter Fairy Land so much as recognize it all around him. In one short scene, the location of the narrative has been turned inside out, in the characteristic transition of fantastic fiction. Any subsequent scene shift or layer of embedding, or encounter with a magical device or personage of the secondary world is governed by the magical precept of metamorphosis.[75]

When houses and furniture become the vehicles of the marvellous, as they are in Spenser's Faerie Land, the relationship of character to setting is susceptible to the abrupt changes of romance. Yet Anodos is the same young man who comes of age in the more reliable and recognizable outer world. A shifted scene in fantasy, as in adventure fiction, signals the opening of possibilities for action and experience that would be forbidden by the ordinary domestic world of home. Even the artificial home and all-male family of university can serve as a point of contrast to the realm of fantastic adventure:

How different is the scene that I have now to tell from that which has just been told! Gone are the quiet college rooms, gone the wind-swayed English elms and cawing rooks, and the familiar volumes on the shelves, and in their place there rise a vision of the great calm ocean gleaming in shaded silver lights beneath the beams of the full African moon.[76]

With beginnings such as Victorian fantasy possesses, their middles break into hitherto unrepresented regions expressly to satisfy the reader's expectation of difference.

When more ordinary novels employ narrative annexes, they draw attention to the limits of fictional worlds. This does not mean that the annex exists outside cultural norms, nor that its work can be done in a chamber free of expectations or conventions, but that the changed backdrop draws attention to the idea of the normative and the appropriate that has hung unremarked in the primary fictional world. Annexes change the rules in a way that draws attention to the presence of rules; they draw and cross borders, emphasizing the incompleteness of fictional worlds; they change the subject without relinquishing the subject. One of the most influential ways of thinking about what we learn from attending both to the normative and to challenges to convention comes not from criticism of individual kinds such as Victorian fantasy, but from the political criticism of Raymond Williams. As we will see, Williams' theory of dominant, residual, and emergent forms fruitfully combines the literary and social meanings of the conventional.

Raymond Williams' paradigm most helpfully frames the ways in which novelists create fictional worlds including spaces for alternatives to and transformations of the normative, in which temporary generic and local differences allow for altered content, events, characterization, and discursive strategies. Williams' terms designate the cultural and artistic forms that exist in a given social moment – the old, the new, and the everyday overlapping. Williams optimistically emphasizes the emergent forms in which new structures of feeling are realized and naturalized: "The effective formations of most actual art relate to already manifest social formations, dominant or residual, and it is primarily to emergent formations (though often in the form of modification or disturbance in older forms) that the structure of feeling, as solution, relates" (*Marxism and Literature* 134). Narrative annexes create these "disturbances," modifying the dominant form of the novel in which they occur, and recording the "structures of feeling" leading to "solutions" of both plot and representational problems. Williams suggests that whatever the dominant form of the day may be, "a new structure of feeling will usually already have begun to form, in the social present" (132). This emergent form can be discerned despite the familiarity of the dominant and residual forms. Williams' terms make it feasible to identify the structure of feeling implicit in the generic mixing that occurs in narrative annexes, as they reach back to recuperate a residual form, shape a new (emergent) vessel, or combine the two impulses within the dominant form. The potent combinations of residual forms with emergent material, and emergent genres with residual impulses further complicate the analysis of the significance of narrative annexes.

Checklists of conventions and the conventional can be the most pedestrian element of genre criticism, but Williams' conviction that conventions represent "the whole body of practices and expectations, over the whole of living: our senses and assignment of energy, our shaping perceptions. . . [our] lived system of meanings and values – constitutive and constituting – which as they are experienced as practices appear as reciprocally confirming" (110) reminds us that examination of conventions reveals "the real grounds of inclusions and exclusions, the styles and ways of seeing that the conventions embody and ratify" (173). The presence of residual and emergent formations in a given social moment or literary text emphasizes the pattern of small alterations that accompanies and participates in change: "there are clear social and historical relations between particular literary forms and the societies and periods in which they were originated and practiced; ... [yet] there are undoubted continuities of literary form through and beyond the societies and periods to which they have such relations. In genre theory, everything depends on the character and process of such continuities" (183). Narrative annexes call attention to the complicated relationships among generic mixture, formal continuity, and change.

Despite the shared qualities that make all of the texts treated in this book recognizable as Victorian novels, the differences embedded in their narrative annexes do not simply repeat the same story. Unlike other Marxist theories working in the service of a millennial teleology, Williams' model leaves heterogeneous possibilities open. A theory of narrative annexes heeds Williams' call for a new generic theory, acknowledging the impact of social and material processes on literary form and vice versa. Heightening the effect of the spatiality of the Victorian novelistic imagination; of the vicissitudes of orderly, chronological narration; and of the struggle to traverse limits for the sake of an expanded range of representation, annexes reveal a lively internal reaction to the formal constraints of fictional worldmaking. In the process, they function as containers of culturally charged subjects, whose presence within fiction is – according to contemporary reactions – peculiar, improbable, and even reprehensible. A signal advantage of Williams' model derives from its focus on what *is* expressed and represented, rather than what is left out. This attention to the narratable, in D. A. Miller's term, allows the reading of the productive tension between what is not, and what might be, represented (*Discontents* ix).

Narrative annexes permit incorporation instead of banishment and proceed by means of presence within both story and discourse rather than through hints of conspicuous or carefully concealed absences.[77] Unlike the fictional world that contains it, the annex is surrounded by fiction. It is always smaller, briefer, and less replete than the narrative in which it occurs; though it may seem awkwardly *added on*, it is always, in essence, *within*. I have suggested that annexes differ from interpolations of, for example, sermons, newspaper accounts, letters, secondary narrations, or authorial mini-essays, in that annexes represent alternative spaces through which the figures of the fiction journey. More closely related to *exemplum*[78] than to ellipsis,[79] annexes commit to discourse materials that a unifying or censoring imagination might omit. In content, however, they are exceptional rather than exemplary. Not to be confused with *mise en abyme,* or "the mirror in the text," an annex acts more like Alice's mirror in *Through the Looking Glass,* drawing the reader into and through an alternative fictional world. Briefer in duration than the secondary worlds of fantastic fiction, annexes disturb the boundaries of fictional worlds, but they quickly dissolve back into those worlds, yielding to the dominant form.

Like episodes, narrative annexes are resources of the *middles* of novels; they cannot alter the normative fictional world until a reader has acquired a sense of being in the middle. If endings and beginnings are the most clearly posted boundaries of fictional worlds, middles make up the ground through which the reader journeys for most of the reading experience. The middle cannot be defined, or sensed by a reader, without the experience of a beginning and the promise of an end. Gerald Prince's *Dictionary of Narratology,* for instance, follows Aristotle in describing the middle as "The set of incidents in a plot or action between the beginning and the end." Yet it is more difficult to say where exactly the middle is, except that it "follows and is followed by other incidents."[80] As resources of the middle, annexes are doubly oriented. They unleash the reader's nostalgia for the previously undisrupted primary fictional world. They make the reader ask, "When will I get back?" Yet they propel the reader forward towards more of the middle, and ultimately towards the fulfilling end. The constancy of a reporting, experiencing consciousness, usually the protagonist, gives the narrative annex its power to extend and deform the middle, because the character's ties to a previously established and coded fictional "existence" are so strong. The familiar figure heightens the effect of the difference of the annex.[81]

When a narrative crux arises in a fictional world, in response to (and despite) the conventions, capacities, and possibilities of that dominant textual realm, a narrative annex may be employed to import a residual or emergent form. When a problem cannot be worked on in the textual world from which it springs, there are several possibilities. It could be banished outright, as inappropriate; it could be ignored and then forgotten; it could become a loose end, left to dangle until a reader gives it a tug. Alternatively, the annex provides a textual space sufficiently different for the problem to be worked on. The annex occupies space, in pages, and provides a workspace. The result of that work – sometimes a solution, always a readjustment of, or challenge to, the trajectory of the narrative – is reimported to the primary world that has generated the problem in the first place. The annex then closes down and the plot moves forward. The annex may be the single aberrant episode in an otherwise orderly text (a text that is obedient to its own assumed boundaries and conventions), or it may be one of a sequence scattered through a novel, marking the fiction's strategic formal readjustments to the challenges of its subjects. Although annexes belong to the realm of "story," by virtue of their characters and actions, they call attention to "discourse," as their generic shift entails alterations in the language of narration.

This book explores the ways that narrative annexes in Victorian novels represent interactions and actions that defy the expectations of the surrounding text; contain confrontations with figures of otherwise unrepresented types; permit narration that figures and defies gender-bound restrictions; and declare the constraints on novelistic representation as a serious topic for the nineteenth-century – not only the late Victorian – novel. Although I do not attempt to make an overarching historical account of the materials that appear in annexes in Victorian novels, I allude to historical details as they illuminate the tensions among dominant, residual, and emergent cultural forms in specific instances. I suggest that a range of materials and topics specific to the period combine with the formal strategy of annexing to produce a fascinating set of instances for the study of the Victorian narrative imagination. In annexes Victorians' fears jostle with Victorians' ambitions and best hopes. While countless Victorian novels carry out their plots in the familiar territories of drawing room, pew, ballroom, and park, I attend to the exceptions. Fears of disease, of working men, of Popery, of dark-skinned others, of the poor who toil and starve in close proximity to the rectories, homes, clubs, and walled gardens of the Victorian self-image draw us down narrow alleys, through thorny hedges, across desolate heaths into narrative annexes.

CHAPTER 2

Victorian critics, narrative annexes, and prescriptions for the novel

Throughout this study I emphasize the prescriptions and warnings of Victorian critics, and I chart their reactions to narrative annexes in order to illuminate Victorians' assumptions about the proper roles, shapes, and subjects of fiction. I introduce in this chapter the vocabulary of realm, domain, and boundary shared by Victorian critics and writers of fiction, and I begin to show how the small alternative zones of narrative annexes fit in a theory of the Victorian novel, even as they test the Victorians' ordinances regarding the shapes and contents of fiction. A related aim of this chapter is to show how recognition of narrative annexing contributes to a broader account of the limitations and capacities of Victorian fiction. For many Victorian novels, not even counting the reams of formula fiction written for the circulating libraries, do *not* employ narrative annexes. Just as most Victorian novels present their events without flashbacks, most first-person narratives do without access to the consciousnesses of other characters, and many novels set in the country do not require an excursion to the city, many Victorian novels accomplish their narrative work without annexes. While keeping in mind the heterogeneity of the Victorian novel in its many genres, its diverse modes of publication, its various (overlapping and sometimes antithetical) aims – to entertain, instruct, titillate, support the author's family, record abuses, instigate reform, indoctrinate, and express visions of community and versions of character – the presence *or absence* of narrative annexes contributes to our understanding of the novel as a product of a particular time and culture. Novels without annexes – suggesting the overall fit among generic conventions, the possibilities of worldmaking, and social norms – bear witness to the capacities of available kinds of Victorian fiction. The less numerous but quite common cases of novels that do use narrative annexes justify our attention by revealing Victorians' responses to the challenges created by their own prescriptive models for representation. More important than an individual novel's freedom from annexes are the modes of Victorian fiction that appear not to require the resources of narrative annexes (such as fantastic and multiplot fiction), for they suggest alternative means for getting beyond the bounded realm of the ideal, appropriate Victorian fictional world. I begin with the rarer phenomenon of an author who eschews narrative annexes.

THE NARROW DOMAIN OF THE NOVEL

In many cases, the best record we possess of the response to the difference of narrative annexes appears in contemporary reviews of fiction. The first critics of Victorian novels were on the whole no more perspicacious or imperceptive about new work than the critics who were to come, and in many cases illuminating criticism appears in the very first notices of novels. In the process of evaluating Victorian fiction, contemporaries writing in periodicals help to create a consensus on the shape and content of the dominant form. Their reactions point towards instances when the residual and emergent forms of narrative annexes contest that consensus. Contemporary reviewers also respond to sensation fiction, to novels-with-a-purpose, and to works of Continental realism with exclamations of puzzlement, startled appreciation, and condemnation. The often-anonymous critics (including in a number of significant cases practicing novelists) are prone to laying down the law in their reviews. This phenomenon does not escape the notice of the critics themselves. In 1860, a review of Anthony Trollope's *Framley Parsonage* (then appearing as a serial in the new *Cornhill Magazine*) notes with exasperation that

It is as yet by no means decided what a novel should be. There is a growing inclination to restrict the domain of the novel within narrower and narrower bounds. Novels with a direct moral purpose, or a historic purpose, or a scientific purpose, are sure to be carped at by the critics . . . Then, tragical subjects are said to be unfit for novels. To choose a tragical subject is instantly pronounced to be a mark of ill-taste. An intricate plot is decried as impossible in real life. Carefully elaborated characters are held up as burlesques of human nature . . . To say that the novel shall represent, without overstepping the modesty of nature, real human life, is no longer a sufficient definition. We are beginning to restrict it within very much narrower bounds.[1]

This lament suggests that constraints on fiction have increased from an appropriate limit, set by "the modesty of nature," to enclose a narrowed sphere that excludes a range of methods, modes, and subjects of fiction.

Not only are social fiction ("novels with a direct moral purpose"), historical fiction, and naturalism ("scientific" fiction) singled out as threatened species, but Aristotle's main ingredients – plot, character, and tragedy – suffer too from the condemnations of the guardians of taste. To this critic, "J. A.," "real human life" runs the risk of exclusion from the genre that is ostensibly dedicated to representing it, and the novel, hemmed in by the admonitions of anxious guardians, becomes like the virgin who is to be protected from the facts of life. The metaphorical language of geography ("domain" and "bounds") suggests that the effort to represent "real human life," or to prevent its appearance in a novel, has political and social significance. The particular aspects of "life" to be excluded cluster around politics, morality, and human tragedy, as well as sexuality. I approach this topic by focusing on Anthony Trollope, in a case study of the response of a mainstream realist novelist and his critics (real and internalized) to the narrowing bounds of Victorian fiction.

It may seem perverse to think of Trollope – the "novel-machine"[2] – as constrained in any way, and yet he was highly conscious of his novels' reception, not only of their earnings, and he read the reviews that excoriated, as well as those that praised, him. Dedicated to an art of sympathetic character, Trollope bridled at objections to love stories, and at prohibitions on sensational plots, for his realism always included substantial doses of romance. Under Jamesian fire for his authorial intrusions (those "little slaps to our credulity")[3] for his voluminous, meandering plots, and not least for his overproduction, Anthony Trollope was none the less regarded as one of the premier realists of his day,[4] and if he was perceived to have broken the clauses of the fictional contract, they were not the statutes of probability[5] and decency. He more subtly depicted female desire than any of his male contemporaries, yet he agreed wholeheartedly with his culture's prohibitions on "overstepping the modesty of nature." In *An Autobiography*, he ponders the temptations facing novelists who hope to delight as well as teach: "The regions of absolute vice are foul and odious. The savour of them, till custom has hardened the palate and the nose, is disgusting. In these [the novelist] will hardly tread. But there are outskirts on these regions, on which sweet-smelling flowers seem to grow, and grass to be green. It is in these border-lands that the danger lies."[6] Here the spatial metaphor maps regions of appropriate and inappropriate representation in terms of vice. When, in *Castle Richmond* (1860), Anthony Trollope treads the grounds of the border-lands that initiate a narrative annex, he enters a place equally disgusting to the palates and noses of his contemporaries. Yet the nature of its contents is political, not sexual. Trollope's experiences and observations in Ireland during the potato famine over a decade earlier compel him to represent his protagonist's close encounter with a starving Irish family, in a journalistic interlude with strong generic links to the first-person "eyewitness to history" account. We can observe in *Castle Richmond* Trollope's struggle to reconcile his representation of direct experience with what he perceives to be the rules of the novelist's craft. Yet even as he creates an annex to avoid restrictions on decorous worldmaking, Trollope begins in *Castle Richmond* to elaborate his condemnation of the "fault of episodes." This becomes a firm principle of his subsequent practice as a novelist and points towards his development of alternative methods of expanding his fictional worlds' horizons. For in the context of this study, Trollope's work is most remarkable for its avoidance of narrative annexes: only one of the forty-seven novels has one. The prohibitions of the imaginary critic "Rhadamanthus," which frame the narrative annex in *Castle Richmond*, transmute into Trollope's own precepts, elaborated in *An Autobiography*. Disappointed with his craftsmanship in *Castle Richmond*, Trollope internalizes the hectoring of Rhadamanthus and develops instead the complex multiply plotted form in which he writes many of his subsequent novels, including his masterworks.

Castle Richmond places a plot of marriage difficulties, blackmail, and changing family fortunes against the backdrop of the Irish potato famine of 1846–7, blending circulating-library fodder (romance and regional novel) with the gentlemanly, journalistic style of the informed insider's letter-to-the-editor about a topic of the day. Unlike the embedded burlesques of letters to the *Jupiter* familiar to readers of *The Warden* (1855), Trollope's technique in *Castle Richmond* dramatizes an encounter, experienced by a character in the fiction, in order to "show the facts" rather than posturing in an identifiably rhetorical style. As I relate above, Trollope himself was uneasy with the strategic alteration of place and genre required to stage this episode of docu-drama, though he manages to get the famine at least onto the backdrop of many of the novel's scenes. Although the main characters, Lady Clara Desmond, Herbert Fitzgerald, Owen Fitzgerald, and the Dowager Countess of Desmond are protected by their station from the direct effects of the famine, both Desmonds and Fitzgeralds work for the relief of the starving peasants. Herbert Fitzgerald organizes and serves in soup kitchens, cooperating on relief committees with priest and parson. The economic effects of the famine (non-payment of rent) reach even the Desmonds and the Fitzgeralds, and a blackmailer takes advantage of the tough economic times to torment the Fitzgeralds with his knowledge of an earlier marriage which renders the current one bigamous. The love plot is sufficiently entangled to add some suspense, as the widow Lady Desmond loves Owen Fitzgerald, who considers himself engaged to her daughter, Clara. Clara succumbs to the family pressure and becomes engaged to Herbert Fitzgerald. The threat of illegitimacy turns fortune's wheel and the less desirable Owen appears to be heir to the family fortunes. Clara refuses to change her mind again. When Herbert is cleared of the taint of illegitimacy, she marries him. In a novel preoccupied with understanding chance occurrences that drastically alter the fortunes of its characters, the famine serves as a terrifying example of the inexplicable nature of God's will. For once, Trollope's capacious fictional world does not seem large enough to take in all the evidence of suffering, and to understand and evaluate the means by which people respond to the famine: "Such discourses of the gods as these," he writes, "are not to be fitly handled in such small measures."[7]

The narrative annex occurs at the nadir of Herbert Fitzgerald's fortune, in "The Last Stage," when the household at Castle Richmond is breaking up after the illegitimacy of the children (by the apparently invalid second marriage) seems to have been established. Before departing, Herbert makes a last trip to Desmond Court, the other household of the novel, where his betrothed lives. Shame drives him to take an alternate route. Herbert's mix of embarrassment, unawareness, and deliberate choice opens the way for the narrative annex, which relates a peculiar eruption of conscience, taking Herbert off the main road of his journey, across a threshold into a zone where he cannot act with authority and effectiveness. It creates a separate and vivid image on the crowded, but otherwise integrated, canvas of Trollope's fictional world, interrupting both the romance plot and the story of coping, and transforming the representation of famine. Early on in *Castle Richmond*, the narrator steps in to emphasize the unforgettable nature of the famine years: "Those who saw its course, and watched its victims, will not readily forget what they saw" (61). Yet the main tasks represented in dealing with the famine are logistical and administrative, and the point of view agrees not only with the station of the main characters, but also with the position of the English government, whose efforts at famine relief Trollope defends.[8]

If Herbert "hardly knew himself whether he had any object in this," Trollope clearly has something he wants to show his readers when he takes Herbert "riding out of the district with which he was most thoroughly acquainted, and passing by cabins and patches of now deserted land which were strange to him. It was a poor, bleak, damp, undrained country, lying beyond the confines of his father's property" (329). On this route a "sudden squall" of rain comes on (330). (As we will see again in Charlotte Brontë's *Villette*, novelists often use unexpected changes in weather to transform the atmosphere of the setting and motivate the boundary-crossings of annexes.) Here the rain provides an excuse for entering the cabin. Trollope explains that in Ireland, travelers customarily shelter themselves and their horses in the cottages of the poor, in the first of a set of overdetermined "factual" assertions that differentiate the outer romance from the docu-drama of the annex. This justifying background information simultaneously reminds readers of the brandishing of credentials of the 1840s social novelists (Elizabeth Gaskell sees inside the homes of the urban poor because she is a minister's wife), and of the attempt to discredit the novelist–witness's report as biased and greatly exaggerated. For instance, it is not uncommon to find a critic such as J. R. Beard condescending to the author, as he does in his review of Gaskell's *Mary Barton* (1848):

We do not mean in the slightest degree to impeach the good faith of the author, so far as the work is based upon the results of actual observation. Still, our impression is, that a somewhat limited experience, and that of an unfortunate kind, has been hastily generalized under the influence of such views as would be the result of reading Lord Ashley's speeches or Mr. Disraeli's Sybil.[9]

Trollope's explanation for Herbert's behavior in entering the cottage insists on its customary nature, and, no less significantly, on its chance occurrence. A sensible gentleman, not an inexperienced, easily misled, or rude intruder, will make his report.

Although, of all the characters in the novel, Herbert has most concerned himself with the fate of the poor, he has never ventured out to their places. The starving have always come to him, which means he has seen only those still capable of walking. The narrator frequently comments on the unforgettable spectacle of the suffering Irish, while insisting that the "yellow meal" has kept death at bay. Though the faces of the poor are sallow from the cornmeal diet, Herbert (and his creator Trollope) believe that people will get enough food to survive, if they will only work. The desolation of the cottage Herbert enters in the

narrative annex shocks him at least temporarily out of these complacent political views, as he observes "the nakedness of the interior"
(*Castle Richmond* 330). No fire, no furniture, and no household objects
can be seen. Herbert descries a person on the earthen floor, under the
dripping roof: "Squatting in the middle of the cabin, seated on her legs
crossed under her, with nothing between her and the wet earth, there
crouched a woman with a child in her arms" (331). The darkness of the
cottage allows for glimpses that enlarge into portraits of suffering, but
they are not to remain silent tableaux. The starving woman's eyes
observe Herbert, initiating the interaction between them: "But as his
eyes became used to the light he saw her eyes gleaming brightly
through the gloom. They were very large and bright as they turned
round upon him while he moved – large and bright, but with a dull,
unwholesome brightness, – a brightness that had in it none of the light
of life" (331). Herbert finds himself here in a liminal zone, where an
unwholesome animation enables the dying woman to present her point
of view.

In a novel that has oriented itself, by means of the class of the
characters and the narrator, into a position above the starving (planning
for them, making policy, dispensing charity to them), this scene of
interlocked gazes has a levelling effect. Yet the move into portraiture
also establishes Herbert as a representative witness:

And then he looked at her more closely. She had on her some rag of clothing
which barely sufficed to cover her nakedness, and the baby which she held in
her arms was covered in some sort; but he could see, as he came to stand close
over her, that these garments were but loose rags which were hardly fastened
round her body. Her rough short hair hung down upon her back, clotted with
dirt, and the head and face of the child which she held was covered with dirt
and sores. On no more wretched object, in its desolate solitude, did the eye of
man ever fall. (331)

Trollope struggles to justify his protagonist's presence in this home
furnished only with straw and, in the name of pity, temporarily inscribes
social class in the metaphor of the falling eye. The Irish woman's plight
is dramatized by her position: she sits on crossed legs on the bare floor,
where Herbert looks down upon her. Trollope's favorite metaphor for a
character's predicament is "falling between two stools." Here he depicts
a life without furniture, and a dilemma that eludes aphorism; the bright
eyes, neat hair, tidy clothes, and freshness of dozens of Trollopian
heroines are obliterated by this harrowing description.

Yet the confrontation with such an image of abjection becomes more challenging when the woman rouses herself to make hospitable remarks, even as she sits, "listless, indifferent, hardly capable of suffering, even for her child, waiting her doom unconsciously" (332). Herbert's perception of her incapacity to suffer in a human way only intensifies his discomfort: "For a while Herbert stood still, looking around him, for the woman was so motionless and uncommunicative that he hardly knew how to talk to her" (332). The narrative annex alternates between abortive conversations and fragments of description that reveal to Herbert bit by bit the horror of the scene. Herbert's difficulty in perceiving the woman in human terms is explained in part by her indifference to him: "But though she cared, as it seemed, but little for the past, for the future she cared less. ''Deed, thin, an' I don't jist know.' She would say no more than that, and would not even raise her voice to ask for alms when he pitied her in her misery" (334). The woman's failure to recognize Herbert as a source of charity violates the conventional relationship between gentleman and indigent, and refuses the class positions inscribed in Victorian methods of ameliorating suffering.

In response, Herbert scrutinizes the interior of the cottage more closely:

the straw was huddled up, as though there was something lying under it. Seeing this he left the bridle of his horse, and stepping across the cabin moved the straw with the handle of his whip. As he did so he turned his back from the wall in which the small window-hole had been pierced, so that a gleam of light fell upon the bundle at his feet, and he could see that the body of a child was lying there, stripped of every vestige of clothing. (332–3)

When his own movement reveals the child's corpse in a focused spot of light, it does not occur to Herbert that he has invaded the privacy of the woman; rather, he expects her to explain voluntarily: "For a minute or two he said nothing – hardly, indeed, knowing how to speak, and looking from the corpse-like woman back to the life-like corpse, and then from the corpse back to the woman, as though he expected that she would say something unasked" (333). In this peculiar situation the fixities of life and death do not stay in their proper places and conversation fails to operate according to convention. Put at a loss by the woman's failure to respond appropriately to the presence of an "authority," Herbert explains to himself that she is practically dead herself.

Yet this scarcely animate woman rouses herself to tell a tale of official ineptitude that indicts the system that Trollope defends in the novel (and in his earlier series of letters written to the *Examiner* in the aftermath of the crisis[10]). The starving woman's experience tests Herbert's (and Trollope's) views and seriously questions the efficacy of English policy: because her crippled husband works, she and her children have been barred from the poor house where they might have obtained food. Herbert takes the side of the administrators, but balks at the evidence: "The rule itself was salutary . . . But in some cases, such as this, it pressed very cruelly. Exceptions were of course made in such cases, if they were known: but then it was so hard to know them!" (334). He almost admits the failure of policy when he sees the scraps of corn meal that have "sustained her, or rather not sustained her, since yesterday morning" (334). Within the cottage, all of Herbert's normal responses are thwarted:

He felt that he was stricken with horror as he remained there in the cabin with the dying woman and the naked corpse of the poor dead child. But what was he to do? He could not go and leave them without succour. The woman had made no plaint of her suffering, and had asked for nothing; but he felt that it would be impossible to abandon her without offering her relief; nor was it possible that he should leave the body of the child in that horrible ghastly state. (335)

Herbert contributes a few silver coins and spreads a silk handkerchief over the body of the child, quelling his disgust at "the small naked dwindled remains of humanity from which life had fled" (335) in order to reinstate himself, if not as the agent of an effective government policy, as a charitable gentleman. In the annex, Herbert experiences helplessness; making ineffectual gestures rather than authoritative decisions; and he confronts suffering in its human guise. The odd scene in the narrative annex suggests that confronting human tragedy in spite of confidence in the utilitarianism of the official response requires a separate domain and a new generic mixture – not pure fiction, not investigative reporting, but the mixed kind of docu-drama, in which the objects of study speak back to the theories of officialdom, through the mediation of the reasonable gentleman-witness.

The insights of the annex, though they have no political consequences, contaminate the surrounding primary world. The annex changes Herbert's perception of the difficulty of his situation, and also, unavoidably, trivializes his original errand. Herbert returns to the road, conscious at least that his own suffering pales by comparison with that of the starving woman and her children. When the countess explains why her daughter must break her troth to him, he listens "attentively, although he did thus think of other eloquence besides that of the countess – of the eloquence of that silent, solitary, dying woman" (338). The use to which Trollope puts the contrast between the slippery countess and the starving woman bizarrely suggests that the dying woman's eloquent indictment of the government's policy matters because it helps Herbert see through the countess's pragmatic backpedalling, exposing her dishonor. Thus the personal love plot absorbs and muffles the political challenge of the narrative annex. The resolution of the problems of fortune, position, inheritance, and engagement occupy the remainder of the novel and return the reader to familiar Trollopian territory. Yet the annex remains as an alternative realm within *Castle Richmond*, representing a view that is neither fully endorsed, nor censored, by a unifying imagination.

Trollope had been haunted by the scene of the abject Irish from the very start of his career as a novelist. Actually having witnessed the starvation of Irish people mattered to Trollope; he alludes three times to the scene of witnessing – in a descriptive set-piece[11] in his unsuccessful first novel, *The Macdermots of Ballycloran* (1847), in his letters to the *Examiner*, and finally in the narrative annex to *Castle Richmond*. In the earliest version of the scene, in *The Macdermots of Ballycloran*, the narrator takes the reader on a voyeuristic tour of the squalid cottages of Mohill: "Can that be the habitation of any of the human race! Few but such as those whose lot has fallen on such barren places, would venture in, but for a moment let us see what's there."[12] The passage emphasizes the physical near-impossibility of seeing into the cottage: "But the dark misery within hides itself in thick obscurity. The unaccustomed eye, at first, is unable to distinguish any object, and only feels the painful effect of the confined smoke; but when, at length, a faint, struggling light makes its way through the entrance, how wretched is all around" (202–3). The scene that is revealed strongly resembles contemporary engravings of the Irish poor and strikes a number of conventional notes:

A sickly woman, the entangled nature of whose garments would defy description, is sitting on a low stool before the fire, suckling a miserably dirty infant; a boy whose only covering is a tattered shirt, is putting fresh, but, alas, damp turf, beneath the pot in which are put to boil the lumpers, their only food. Two or three dim children – their number is lost in their obscurity – are cowering round the dull, dark fire, atop of one another; and, on a miserable pallet beyond

– a few rotten boards, propt upon equally infirm supports, and covered over
with only one thin black quilt, – is sitting the master of the mansion. (203)

The dirt, the turf fire, the near-nakedness, the reliance on the potato, the
immodest woman, the unmanned husband, and the obscure but too
numerous children could all be easily conjured up from the collection of
dehumanizing clichés in the air at the time. Significantly, no character
enters the cottage and no one speaks to the poverty-stricken family, who
are unaware that they are being observed. The disembodied narrator
and his tour-group of readers hover unseen at the boundary of the
home; the light and not the observer "struggles" through the entrance.
If Trollope has really seen these people, he presents them to his readers
in an image so familiar as simultaneously to verify and cast doubt on its
authenticity. Writing several years before the 1847 publication date,
with the memories of famine fresh in his mind, Trollope imagines this
scene without the examples of Charles Kingsley and Elizabeth Gaskell,
whose fictions enter the interiors of working peoples' homes, and more
sympathetically describe the wretched domiciles of the poor. The strategy of the later narrative annex, which may have been influenced by
Condition of England novelists' expanded representation of contemporary Britain, enables Trollope to rewrite *The Macdermots'* voyeuristic and
conventional digression into a narrative annex relating contact across
class barriers in *Castle Richmond.*[13]

The contrast in Trollope's use of similar materials in these two novels
underlines several traits of annexes and their consequences. Herbert's
status as the reporting and experiencing character who enters the annex
enables Trollope to present the scene as encountered by an embodied
character, not merely an ineffective beam of light. Removed from the
layer of narrator's disquisitions, the scene becomes a part of the story-
world. The generic contrast becomes striking, for the narrative annex
contains Trollope's intervention into the realm of documentary art, an
emergent form that qualifies the overt argument of the novel's "famine"
plot by bringing the protagonist inside the domicile of a family that has
not been helped by the relief effort that Trollope anxiously defends. The
opposition of document and work of art suggests the difficulty of breaking free from generic constraints without falling out of the realm of
fiction entirely. Michael Sadleir writes, "*Castle Richmond* is not in the
classic sense Trollope at all . . . It is a document, not a work of art; its
appeal is to nationalist enthusiasm, not to the literary appreciation that
knows no nationality."[14] (As we will see, contemporary reactions to

Castle Richmond anticipate Sadleir's conflation of the generic and the political.) The crossed boundary of the narrative annex in *Castle Richmond* turns out to be a topic of acute interest to Anthony Trollope, as is revealed by the elliptical references to the scene in his *Examiner* letters.

During the time that he was writing his historical novel, *La Vendée*, Trollope was working in Ireland, on Post Office business, not as a missionary of relief. He relates in his *Autobiography* that "It was my duty at that time to be travelling constantly in those parts of Ireland in which the miseries and troubles thence [from the pestilence and the famine] arising were, perhaps, at their worst" (82). Convinced that he knows Ireland and the Irish better than those who criticize the Administration's response to the disaster, Trollope attempts to enter the debate with a sequence of letters to the *Examiner*. The sense of failure that tinges this endeavor to enter the political arena is rooted in both the novelist's pride, and in the helplessness of the individual witness to a national disaster.

Unlike the letters and editorials in the *Jupiter*, which set off and sustain the action of *The Warden*, Trollope's real letters have no discernible effect. He writes that

I stated my name and official position, and the fact that opportunities had been given me of seeing the poor-houses in Ireland, and of making myself acquainted with the circumstances of the time. Would a series of letters on the subject be accepted by the Examiner? The great man [John Forster], who loomed very large to me, was pleased to say that if the letters should recommend themselves by their style and manner, if they were not too long, and if – every reader will know how on such occasions an editor will guard himself – if this and if that, they should be favourably entertained, – if printing and publication be favourable entertainment. But I heard no more of them. The world in Ireland did not declare that the Government had at last been adequately defended, nor did the treasurer of the Examiner send me a cheque in return. (*An Autobiography* 83–4)

Taking a stand on an issue of the day, of which he feels he has first-hand knowledge, seems to Trollope to be the business of a literary man, and his elaborate claims and disavowals of his place in the literary world only complicate the perceived failure of the letters. Five years after writing the letters, Trollope decries the use of novels to inspire reform and rebukes the public for being more susceptible to novelistic depictions than to "true complaints" (*The Warden* 196). Dickens' successful action against the New Poor Law earns Trollope's scorn, for *Oliver Twist* does not attempt to make a rational argument such as the sort sanctioned by "the great man," John Forster:

The artist who paints for the million must use glaring colours, as no one knew better than Mr. Sentiment when he described the inhabitants of his almshouse; and the radical reform which has now swept over such establishments has owed more to twenty numbers of Mr. Sentiment's novel, than to all the true complaints which have escaped from the public for the last half century. (*The Warden* 195–6)

Not, I think, coincidentally, Trollope's defense of the government in his *Examiner* letters praises the same bureaucracy that Dickens' novel had attacked in 1837, and his sneer at the popular novelist "who paints for the million" barely conceals the envy he feels of Dickens' sales and his power to effect change.

Within the letters, Trollope's status as a witness, not a novelist, authorizes his observations of the famine and the efficacy of relief efforts. Although he uses his experience to argue that deaths from famine were, "comparatively speaking, few," it is difficult to ascertain from his third letter to the *Examiner* (6 April 1850, on the subject of the "measures against the famine") what Trollope actually saw in Ireland.[15] His authority in refuting the sensational report of Lord Sidney Godolphin Osborne, who had published several scathing letters about government relief in *The Times*, derives from Trollope's status as an eyewitness to the misery, but his description provides few details of deprivation. Interestingly, Trollope's refutation of Godolphin's account emphasizes what he did *not* see: "During the whole period of the famine I never saw a dead body lying exposed in the open air, either in a town or in the country. I moreover never saw a dead body within a cabin which had not been laid out in some sort of rough manner" (King, "Letters" 83). This suggests that, like Herbert, Trollope entered the cottages of starving people, but that the corpses he saw had been prepared for burial. Anxious at once to defend the humanity and decency of the Irish, and to diminish the body-count, Trollope writes:

Now it may be said that if I did not enter cabins, I could not see the horrid sights which were to be met within; but such a remark cannot apply to that which is said to have been of such frequent occurrence out under the open sky. The whole period was spent by me in passing from one place to another in the south and west of Ireland. I visited at the worst periods those places which were most afflicted; and if corpses, lying exposed, unheeded, and in heaps, were to be seen, no man's eye would have been oftener offended in that way than mine. (83)

Seeing and not having seen; seeing without trying to see; and not seeing what any man's eye would have been offended to see, overlap in a perplexing passage of witness and non-witness that reminds the reader of the later, fictionalized annex in *Castle Richmond*, where we are instructed that a gentleman traveling about under open sky can expect to be sheltered within cabins. The insider's view of the famine must gaze upon the interior spaces, for the outside is unrevealing. Trollope apologizes for raising such an unpleasant subject, reminding readers that "Irish newspapers of the time teemed with the recital of such horrors" – reports of heaps of corpses by the roadside, reports that made their way into English newspapers, where such "horrid novels" (83) were picked up by gullible readers such as Godolphin. However, seeing people dead of starvation inside their own homes is bad enough. The speech of the Irish woman in the narrative annex of *Castle Richmond* represents the sort of "true complaint" Trollope holds up against the imaginings of fiction. Compelled to represent what he knows of the Irish famine, despite the fact that the scene wrought into a narrative annex disturbs the unity of his fiction with an interior version of "horrid novels," Trollope lays bare his own uneasiness about the useless gestures that may be all that remains to the gentleman-witness.[16]

"IMPATIENT OF AN EPISODE": TROLLOPE AND HIS CRITICS

The narrative annex, in which Herbert confronts the brute facts of starvation, is flanked by two narrative excursions into the problems of policy. Each of these sections is interrupted by the narrator's self-censoring remarks: "But again; *Quo Musa tendis?* I could write on this subject for a week were it not that Rhadamanthus awaits me, Rhadamanthus the critic; and Rhadamanthus is, of all things, impatient of an episode" (*Castle Richmond* 311). After the annex, the narrator interrupts himself again, having included a jibe at the hypocrisy of the Protestants in the area: "But this is an episode. And nowadays no episodes are allowed" (371). The self-consciousness of these remarks shows that something dictates a different art than that which will please the critics, that the critic "nowadays" exercises a prohibitive prerogative, like one of the judges in Hell, and that the novelist strays from the path of straight-ahead narration at his own peril. The germ of Trollope's later prohibition of episodes arises in response to his imaginary, internalized critic's disapproval of both formal deviance and political content. To varying degrees, generic and formal evaluations also mix in other critics' responses to the novel's political stance, entangling judgments of technique and subject matter.

The review of *Castle Richmond* in the *Spectator* provides the most positive response to Trollope's self-censoring management of the political content of the novel:

Mr. Trollope's new novel has its scene in the south of Ireland, in the year of the Famine; but none of its main issues are evolved out of that great calamity. Their connexion with it is casual, and just close enough to furnish in a suitable manner the secondary machinery and incidents of the story . . . The author's management of this portion of his materials is exceedingly judicious. He was in Ireland during the famine, travelling over its highways and byways in all directions, seeing everywhere the misery of the time, almost with the same fullness of opportunity as if he had been sent on a mission for its relief, but with a freedom of judgment which hardly any one could have retained amidst the distracting exigencies of such a position. Being, as everyone knows, not only a graphic writer but a man of approved administrative faculty, he must have a great deal to say about the terrible event of which he was so close an observer; but he is too good an artist to say it all in the wrong place. What he has said is eminently worthy of perusal, and will obtain it the more readily, and with the better effect, in consequence of the author's judicious reticence.[17]

This reviewer may be remembering Trollope's *Examiner* letters, or he may be familiar with the author's life and opinions in another way. His emphasis on Trollope's restraint ("he is too good an artist to say it all in the wrong place") underlines the decorum of separation that governs the realms of political analysis and novel-writing.

Among contemporary reviewers, only a few thought that Trollope had managed his material effectively, that is by limiting its exposure in the novel.[18] Instead, to most critics, some life is *too* real to be part of a novel. The *Westminster Review*'s response to *Castle Richmond* deprecates the significance of the historical setting to the plot: "The Irish famine has but little to do with the story; it furnishes, or rather Mr. Trollope's notebook has supplied, one or two good stories and a few very graphic descriptions, but these have the feeblest connexion with the story itself, which might as well have been accommodated with the general scenery of any other period of quasi-contemporary history."[19] The contrast between the plot of betrothal and the scenes of famine are too great for this critic, especially since the "graphic descriptions" appear to have been deposited directly from an eyewitness's notebook into the fiction. The critic's discomfort with the emergent form of "very graphic descriptions" emphasizes the disjunction between the Irish famine and "the general scenery" required for the plot. Drawing a distinction between the famine itself and Trollope's writing, even his on-the-spot note-taking, subtly discredits the accuracy of Trollope's description.

In the *Saturday Review*, where Trollope's fiction was often favorably reviewed, the critic discerns the author's compulsion to relate his observations on the famine: "It is impossible not to feel that [the most curious part of the book] was the part of it about which Mr. Trollope really cared, but that, as he had to get a novel out of it, he was in duty bound to mix up a hash of Desmonds and Fitzgeralds with the Indian meal on which his mind was fixed as he wrote."[20] Referring to the generic admixture of the novel, the critic writes with a bizarre insensitivity to the subject matter that "pastry and roast-beef should not be served on the same plate."[21] Roast beef here signifies the strong meat of reality, preferable to the confection of romance, but never to be presented alongside it. The distastefully trivializing image of food ruined by improper presentation turns into a covert complaint about the goryness of Trollope's novel: "The roast-beef is far the better thing of the two, but, if possible, let us have it neat" (643). Criticized in his own time for showing too much, Trollope suffers unfairly at the hands of recent critics who think he shows too little. Ross Murfin writes that in Trollope's political novels, "truth is lost even as it is gained by a relatively democratic system of political representation. By analogy, verity would be lost as well as gained by the novelist (or historian) who sought to represent a reality – say the reality of poor Ireland – rather than the games played in London by its 'representatives.'"[22] To Trollope's credit, in *Castle Richmond* he moves past the image of outdoor relief to depict the stripped-down misery of the indoor scene in a narrative annex, qualifying his own argument in defense of the government's actions by representing exactly the sort of scene that Murfin misses in the Palliser novels. However, it is not at all surprising that Trollope's self-censorship should prevent such "an episode" from appearing in the later political novels, the earliest of which, *Phineas Finn: The Irish Member* (1869), appeared nearly a decade later.

Trollope's theory of the novel,[23] laid out in *An Autobiography*, emphasizes the importance of characters and the responsibility of the novelist to dwell with those "fictitious personages" (233) until they can be made into the intimates of the reader. He asserts that the greatest fault in fiction, next to the creation of wooden characters, is the filling out of pages with what he calls "episodes" (237). Trollope's condemnation of episodes in his chapter "On Novels and the Art of Writing Them" provides an interesting contrast with his one use of a narrative annex and reminds us of the strictures of Rhadamanthus. He describes in a commonsense manner the motivation for the practice of episodical fiction-making – extension of the length:

In writing a novel the author soon becomes aware that a burden of pages is before him. Circumstances require that he should cover a certain and generally not a very confined space. Short novels are not popular with readers generally. Critics often complain of the ordinary length of novels, – of the three volumes to which they are subjected; but few novels which have attained great success in England have been told in fewer pages. The novel-writer who sticks to novel-writing as his profession will certainly find that this burden of length is incumbent upon him. How shall he carry his burden to the end? How shall he cover his space? (237)

Though the great novelists may carry off this stretching with episodes, there is hardly a greater risk to the young novelist, to whom Trollope addresses the prediction: "if you are very successful in the telling of that first story, [you] will become ambitious of further storytelling, and will look out for anecdotes, – in the narration of which you will not improbably sometimes distress your audience" (230). Trollope's warning to young authors urges the separation of exigency and imagination. In imagining a fiction, Trollope advises, these extraneous, disconnected, added-in pieces of narrative should be avoided:

There should be no episodes in a novel. Every sentence, every word, through all those pages, should tend to the telling of the story. Such episodes distract the attention of the reader, and always do so disagreeably. Who has not felt this to be the case even with *The Curious Impertinent* and with the history of *The Man of the Hill?* And if it be so with Cervantes and Fielding, who can hope to succeed? Though the novel which you have to write must be long, let it all be one. (237–8)

The admission of the temptation to stretch a fiction with anecdotes might seem damaging to Trollope's reputation, marred for half a century by the matter-of-fact way in which he describes his daily work habits (118–22), but his novels are in fact relatively free of extraneous anecdotes. Similarly, his novels rarely employ interpolations or episodes after *Castle Richmond*; instead he ordinarily creates multiply plotted, elaborated and densely populated fictions out of small suggestions of plots.[24]

Trollope's own description of his method for stretching the subject matter to fit the canvas explicitly justifies the multiplot form of the novel:

This undoubtedly must be done by the novelist; and if he will learn his business, may be done without injury to his effect. He may not paint different pictures on the same canvas, which he will do if he allow himself to wander away to matters outside his own story; but by studying proportion in his work, he may teach himself so to tell his story that it shall naturally fall into the required length. Though his story should be all one, yet it may have many parts. Though the plot itself may require but a few characters, it may be so enlarged as to find its full development in many. There may be subsidiary plots, which shall all tend to the elucidation of the main story, and which will take their places as part of one and the same work, – and there may be many figures on a canvas which shall not to the spectator seem to form themselves into separate pictures. (238–9)

The metaphor of a striking visual image, separate and discrete from the rest of the painting, combined with Trollope's condemnation of the anecdotal and the interpolated "episodes," gives us a good idea of what he seeks to avoid: difference, boundedness, separation, and especially "wander[ing] away to matters outside his own story." Having with some hesitation marshalled these qualities of the narrative annex to the task of representing a scene, in *Castle Richmond*, that defiantly breaches the craftsman's contract, Trollope resolves never again to present a separate picture before the reader's eye. What Terry Eagleton describes as Trollope's "self-consistent, blandly undifferentiated ideological space"[25] is the product of Trollope's self-disciplined avoidance of painting different pictures on the same canvas, of eschewing narrative annexes.

None the less, it is vital not to miss the variety of fictional worlds created by Trollope. The contrasts among them become evident between plots of the multiplot fictions, and between novels. Although Trollope's novels may strike the reader as being quintessentially English in their scenes and settings, in fact he conveys his characters all over Europe, to Ireland, and as far away as Australia. He brings characters into the English scene from these and other far-flung places, including the theatrical world of New York City, and he locates several of his fictions entirely outside England: other than the "Irish" novels, *La Vendée* (1850), *Nina Balatka* (1866–7), *Linda Tressel* (1867–8), *The Golden Lion of Granpere* (1872), and *The Fixed Period* (1881–2) take place in foreign settings, the last in an imaginary "Britannula." When Trollope's characters make drastic changes of location, their actions are explained in rational terms. A duel cannot be fought on English soil, so the combatants take a trip to Belgium. The arena for political intervention is Parliament, so Phineas Finn leaves Ireland for London. Dissolute young men who cannot live in England for fear of imprisonment fly to Europe, leaving their debts behind. Movements from place to place in Trollope's novels are invariably justified, deliberate, and rarely transformative. Yet alternative settings make other genre choices possible. Foreign locations in particular permit a different Trollope to emerge. Trollope writes in his *Autobiography* that his anonymously published novels, set in Prague and Nuremberg, effected a change in his "manner of story-telling . . . English life in them there was none. There was more of romance proper than had been usual with me. And I made an attempt at local colouring" (205–6).[26] Robert Tracy observes that "the novelist himself seems to undergo a change of personality and of basic attitudes when he settles to an Irish subject"[27] and L. J. Swingle argues that "Trollope saw Ireland as an opportunity to deliver his English reader, a civilized Grecian, into a Gothic place where the phenomenon of fundamental difference could be explored."[28]

Trollope's proud quotation of Nathaniel Hawthorne's description of his worldmaking underlines the virtues of vastness and consistency. Hawthorne writes that Trollope's world seems "just as real as if some giant had hewn a great lump out of the earth and put it under a glass case, with all its inhabitants going about their daily business, and not suspecting that they were being made show of" (144). No part of that great lump of earth is invisible to the Trollopian narrator. The giant stays on hand, pointing out and interpreting the goings-on under the glass, self-consciously remarking his own meddlesome role in the business. Even when he experiments with the first person as in *The Struggles of Brown, Jones, and Robinson, By One of the Firm* (1861–2), Trollope's narrative voice pervades the terrain of his fiction. Despite its prevailing psychological realism, Trollope's fiction is riddled with anti-conventional gestures.[29] Although he avoids annexes, he does employ embedded texts, such as the satires of Dickens and Carlyle in *The Warden* (1855). The parodies present alternative modes of dealing with social problems, exemplifying two forms of manipulation employed by the world of opinion, as broadcast by the *Jupiter*. The caricatures of Carlyle (Dr. Anticant) and Dickens (Mr. Popular Sentiment) draw attention to the rift between fiction and reality, as do Trollope's frequent narratorial interruptions. Although all readers may not share Henry James' disgust with Trollope's habit of stepping forward and rending the veil of illusion to chat, predict, chide, or caution them, they will certainly notice that this practice is as characteristic of Trollope's fictional worldmaking as is his orderly, chronological narration of events, his frequent use of almost allegorical names, and his unembarrassed repetition of a small set of proverbs and sayings.

Yet the characteristic sound of Trollope's narrative voice may disguise the variety of topics treated in his novels.[30] While many of Trollope's novels revolve around the basic problem of a love choice, this theme includes the Woman Question; jilting and troth-breaking; illegitimacy; and love matches across boundaries of class, religion, and nationality. Lost wills; disinheritance; struggles with faith and doubt; forgery; perjury; and the evils of gambling, murder, theft, bigamy, madness, suicide, euthanasia, prostitution, and private detection also find their places in Trollope's capacious fictional worlds. The social problems Trollope depicts are unfailingly located in a human example, with whom the omnipresent narrator exhorts his readers to sympathize.[31] Thus Trollope guards against the estrangement from his subject that a brief wandering encounter, like the narrative annex in *Castle Richmond*, can create.

To draw the boundaries around the regions of Trollope's fiction, then, is to attempt to delimit an interlinked and expansive set of fictional worlds. Main characters become part of the background social scene in other novels, even in novels disconnected from the series in which the characters were introduced.[32] Trollope's fictional world merges and blends at the joins and edges of his novels, despite the distinctive clerical, Parliamentary, city, and country arenas in which individual plots are located. The individual stories seem to spill over their own borders, into multiple plots, into other novels, and into series (novels in series may also discourage annexing, since there is always room in another fiction to develop what cannot fit in an already replete fictional world). Yet there are limits to Trollope's representation. John Kucich has written of the way Trollope creates and upholds a "middle-class moral hierarchy," by creating "a space of cultural exceptionality" that allows novelist and reader the luxury of transgression, without actually depicting lower-class subjects.[33] In his multiplot fictions, Trollope works out different variations of a given problem in parallel plots, but he never invests a whole plot line in a character poorer than the Reverend Josiah Crawley, who is, after all, a gentleman.

THE CAPACITIES OF "LOOSE BAGGY MONSTERS"

Ever since Henry James remarked on the lack of pictorial fusion and the "queer elements of the accidental and the arbitrary"[34] in the great multiplot novels of Thackeray, Hugo, and Tolstoi, this quintessential Victorian form has been known, if not celebrated, for its capacity to contain divergent plot strands, eclectic groups of characters, digressions, and embedded narratives. Examples of the form include Thackeray's *Vanity Fair* (1847–8); Dickens' *Bleak House* (1852–3) and *Little Dorrit* (1857); Gaskell's *Wives and Daughters* (1864–6); Trollope's *The Last Chronicle of Barset* (1866–7) and *The Way We Live Now* (1874–5); and Eliot's *Middlemarch* (1871–2) and *Daniel Deronda* (1876). Peter K. Garrett has observed that the inclusiveness of multiplot novels are at once their strength and their weakness, for "to multiply plots is to divide the fictional world, to disrupt the continuity of each line in order to shift from one to another, to disperse the reader's attention."[35] The double action of interrupting and including is repeated each time a plot strand is dropped in order to attend to another. Yet the benefits of the technique include the creation of "large and densely populated fictional worlds," "generalizing effects" created by similarities or analogies in parallel strands, and expansive effects "produced by differences of situation and mode between . . . narrative lines" (*Multiplot Novel* 2). In such a complex bundle of narrative lines, encouraged, as Garrett notes, by serial publication and the demand for triple-decker novels, narrative annexes are infrequently employed to cross boundaries, to shift genres, to carry a character into a new realm for action, or to introduce unlikely topics into the fictional world. If in Anthony Trollope's case we can see the development of a multiplot novelist out of a writer hoping to avoid the strictures of an external or internal Rhadamanthus, in his contemporaries we find more positive formulations of their aims in adopting techniques that at once expand and fracture their fictional worlds.

Aristotle decrees that "it is necessary . . . for the well-constructed plot to have a single rather than a double construction,"[36] but Victorian novelists did not obey. The comments of Dickens and Eliot on the subject of multiple plots reveal contrasting theories of the novel, neither of which conforms to an Aristotelian model. In *Oliver Twist*, Dickens identifies the alternation of plot strands in terms of popular drama and defends the practice by recourse to life:

It is the custom on the stage, in all good murderous melodramas, to present the tragic and comic scenes, as in regular alternation, as the layers of red and white in a side of streaky bacon . . . Such changes appear absurd; but they are not so unnatural as they would seem at first sight. The transitions in real life from well-spread boards to death-beds, and from mourning weeds to holiday garments, are not a whit less startling; only there, we are busy actors, instead of passive lookers-on, which makes a vast difference.[37]

The "streaky bacon" model imports the techniques and the topics of melodrama into the novel. Unlike Trollope's spatial metaphor of a unified canvas, Dickens' image depends on a time-bound, experiential set of transitions, resembling life in their unexpectedness, although "all good murderous melodramas" present contrasting scenes by custom. Dickens' defense of his craft rests on a self-conscious anti-Aristotelian joke: "As sudden shiftings of the scene, and rapid changes of time and place, are not only sanctioned in books by long usage, but are by many considered as the great art of authorship: an author's skill in his craft being, by such critics, chiefly estimated with relation to the dilemmas in which he leaves his characters at the end of the chapter" (*Oliver Twist* 169). For Dickens, the critics who matter are the audience of popular drama, and the readers of inexpensive serialized fiction. Thirty years later, after Thackeray and Trollope had exploited the expansive form of multiplot novels, George Eliot takes the high ground in her defense of a fiction with numerous plots and perspectives:

Your pier-glass or extensive surface of polished steel made to be rubbed by a housemaid, will be minutely and multitudinously scratched in all directions; but place now against it a lighted candle as a centre of illumination, and lo! the scratches will seem to arrange themselves in a fine series of concentric circles round that little sun. It is demonstrable that the scratches are going everywhere impartially, and it is only your little candle which produces the flattering illusion of a concentric arrangement, its light falling with an exclusive optical selection.[38]

With the eminent philosopher dignifying the shift in perspectives and the housemaid doing the manual labor, multiplot fiction rises in the world. The respectable site of this experiment in optics is the furniture of a middle-class household. Unlike the furnishings of Anodos' bedroom in *Phantastes*, or Alice's looking-glass, the pier-glass leads to no other world, but grounds Eliot's parable about individual egoism in a realm of infinite actions. A scientific view of life justifies the narrative form, even as Dickens' defense of melodramatic alternation draws on the startling juxtapositions of experience.

The manifestly artificial breaks and juxtapositions of the multiplot novel become the vehicles of a more life-like rendering of the social world, its various realms, and its representative consciousnesses. Paradoxically, fiction obeying the unities, such as Edwin Muir's "dramatic novel," appears by contrast manipulated and limited by art:

Only in a completely shut-in arena can the conflicts which [the dramatic novel] portrays arise, develop, and end inevitably. All the exits are closed, and as we watch the action we know this. There is no escape into other scenes, or if there is we know that they are false exits bringing the protagonist back to the main stage again, where he must await his destiny. The scene here is the framework within which the logic of the action can develop unimpeded, and shut off from the arbitrary interferences of the external world.[39]

The novel of character, by contrast, has room for "arbitrary interferences," since it unfolds "in space, socially" (*Structure* 63). Thus the multiplication of plots – temporal constructs – makes more room in a form, in which, strictly speaking, there is no space at all.[40] As a critic of Trollope's multiplot fiction puts it, "time is not important. For what matters is not the succession of events, but the accumulation of them, and the grouping of events and characters."[41] In narrative fiction that operates inclusively – by means of parallel plots, contrasted realms, genres, and places – narrative annexes all but disappear against the diversified background of the normative fictional world.[42]

By quoting Edwin Muir, I anticipate one of the tasks of the conclusion to this study, which shows how the Trollopian or Thackerayan "loose baggy monster" comes to stand for Victorian novels in general, creating a contrast with modern psychological realism (Muir's "dramatic" fiction). According to early twentieth-century evaluations of the previous half-century's fiction, the Victorian novel not only lacks technique, but also fails to achieve the range of representation found in French and Russian fiction. Paradoxically, to early twentieth-century reappraisers, the panoramic Victorian novel also suffers in contrast to the sleeker modern novel because it is so often long and capacious: "The English novel in the nineteenth century had been like a hold-all into which anything could be stuffed."[43] Over fifty years after Henry James' condemnation of multiplot Victorian fiction, modern theories of the novel still depend upon envisioning their predecessors as formally chaotic vehicles filled with unsorted rubble. It is therefore useful to see that Victorian practitioners developed the techniques of the multiplot novel precisely to permit a broader and more expansive canvas for representation. Writing more rigorously formal fiction than that with which modernist critics credit them, and seriously limited by edicts on what could in probability be carried by their "hold-alls," Victorian novelists also create narrative annexes to make workspaces within fictions, without permanently disrupting the useful construct of a coherent fictional world. The next chapter explores one Victorian novelist's effort to establish her authority over the lines of separation that divide the normative and the improbable by manipulating space and genre in narrative annexes.

CHAPTER 3

Norms and narrow spaces: the gendering of limits on representation

VICTORIAN NORMS: THE PLACES OF NOVEL AND ROMANCE

In the Victorian novel, norms of representation and standards regarding genres are often embodied in spatial metaphors of "realm" and "region," and both Victorian novelists and critics contribute to the sense of separation keeping "novel" and "romance" and their respective plots and subjects of representation apart. Although the fictional worlds of Victorian novels are more heterogeneous than this dichotomy suggests, the terms "romance" and "novel" refer to opposite kinds of fictional worlds, related to the actual world and its probabilities to a lesser and greater degree. Nathaniel Hawthorne articulates the opposition in his preface to *The House of The Seven Gables* (1851), writing in an often-cited passage:

When a writer calls his work a Romance, it need hardly be observed that he wishes to claim a certain latitude, both as to its fashion and material, which he would not have felt himself entitled to assume, had he professed to be writing a Novel. The latter form of composition is presumed to aim at a very minute fidelity, not merely to the possible, but to the probable and ordinary course of man's experience. The former – while as a work of art, it must rigidly subject itself to laws, and while it sins unpardonably so far as it may swerve aside from the truth of the human heart – has fairly a right to present that truth under circumstances, to a great extent, of the writer's own choosing or creation . . . The point of view in which this tale comes under the Romantic definition lies in the attempt to connect a bygone time with the very present that is flitting way from us.[1]

The term "latitude" suggests a geographical location, as well as the "fashion" and "material" that a romancer assumes. The definition, like romance itself, posits antinomous zones where possibilities and "laws" differ, and the reclamation of the kinds of fiction subsumed by the category "romance" adopts a tactic intrinsic to romance to describe opposed generic realms. Hawthorne contrasts the romance zone of "the clouds overhead" with "the actual soil of the County of Essex" (*Seven Gables* 2). Here, the novel adheres to the ground, to the "probable," the "ordinary," to "local manners" and "the characteristics of a community" (2). The elegiac urgency of Hawthorne's task, "to connect a bygone time with the very present that is flitting away from us" (2), overlaps with the novel's tasks of representing, criticizing, and altering the social world which has come, or appears to be coming, into being.

It is axiomatic that the Victorian novel represents social worlds, and that a belief in the normality of middle-class[2] experience pervades and shapes this representation. Whether the fictional world attempts to mirror an identifiable place or not, social and experiential norms combine in the Victorian novel to invest in a highly wrought convincingness that readers can enjoy even when they recognize its impossibility. So, for instance, Doctor Plarr of Graham Greene's *The Honorary Consul* (1973) describes his father as belonging, "by right, and not simply by passport, to the legendary island of snow and fog, the country of Dickens and of Conan Doyle."[3] In Plarr's view, foreigners and exiles invest fictional worlds with such value, "taking it all for contemporary truth for want of any other evidence, like a Russian who believes that the bailiff and the coffin-maker still follow their unchanged vocations in a world where Oliver Twist is somewhere imprisoned in a London cellar asking for more" (Greene, *Honorary Consul* 10). Reading Victorian novels, we are those credulous foreigners, particularly in our expectation that the novel conjures up a realizable middle-class experience. The habit of surrendering to the imagined worlds of Victorian novels trains readers in worldmaking that forgets itself. A prerequisite of the Victorian novel's most effective cultural work and play, then, is a represented world in which characters can exist and act, in which the imagined consciousnesses of these word-masses can perceive relationships, make discoveries and choices, and indirectly report back to the reader.

To make this possible, Victorian novels surround characters with spaces: places, homes, and geography depicted in a variety of ways, from the elaborate social maps of Trollope, Margaret Oliphant, or Elizabeth Gaskell, to the imaginary or far-away locations of H. Rider Haggard, Robert Louis Stevenson, or R. M. Ballantyne's adventure fiction. Pickwick, Jasper Petulengro of Borrow's *Lavengro* (1851), and Gerard of Reade's *The Cloister and the Hearth* (1861) perpetuate the special relationship between the *picaro* and the road, in narrative situations that require frequent changes in place. Similarly, the *Bildungsroman's* structure depends on the protagonist's movement through homes, institutions, and distant places. Multiplot fictions such as Eliot's *Middlemarch*, Trollope's *The Way We Live Now*, and most of Dickens' major novels deploy plots from a variety of different locales, some of these being subject to changes, as when the Dorrit entourage, freed from debtors' prison, takes its grand tour on the Continent. The role of houses and landscape in gothic fiction, and in the related kinds of sensation, detection, and female *Bildungsroman*, add to the variety of uses to which place is put in Victorian fiction. Walter Scott's romances; Charles Kingsley's and George MacDonald's fantasies for children (revealing underground and underwater realms); and Condition of England exposés, which allow readers to "enter" the dwellings and factories of the exploited working poor, all contribute to the diverse and eclectic imaginative geography created by the Victorian novel. Each of these subgenres of the novel sets up its own relation to place and changes in place, only sometimes adhering to the supposed "laws" of novel or romance.

The heterogeneity of the Victorian novel's places complicates a simple opposition of territories in the clouds and on the ground; more serious problems for a Victorian theory of the novel occur as novelists renegotiate the boundaries of representation. Embodied most notoriously in the imposing person of Mrs. Grundy, the female gender is held responsible by many contemporary critics for necessitating the most immovable barriers to representation.[4] However, as I show in this chapter, the association of women with limits takes a variety of forms, including Charlotte Brontë's oppositional assertion of authority over boundaries, in her female characters' sojourns through narrative annexes, marked at least once in each major novel by a boundary figured as an aperture permitting passage from world to world.

In 1851, the *North British Review* comments on the recent attention of writers to "contemporary human life, as overspreading the rural earth, or pent up in masses within the walls of cities."[5] The location of these subjects on the ground or inside walls constitutes a new field for representation. Not everyone appreciates the shift; in 1854, R. H. Hutton laments in the *Prospective Review* the loss of the "universal interest" of romancers such as Scott and Shakespeare.[6] Hutton complains that women writers of domestic fiction contribute especially to this deprivation: "the result of their so closely 'hugging the land' in their small cruises on the ocean of imagination, is that they delineate narrow specimens of humanity" (472). Here the depiction of contemporary life by women writers who stick to what they know paradoxically results in less convincing representation than in the "universal" romancers. Between romance and what was called the "literature of social reference," as well as between fiction and the non-fiction kinds incorporated into novels, lay boundaries or barriers that were imagined in terms of geography and genre. So for instance, George Henry Lewes expresses the expectation (in a review of Charlotte Brontë's *Shirley*) that the reader ought to be conveyed appropriately to the region that represents a particular genre: "we are by no means rigorous in expecting that the story is to move along the highway of everyday life . . . but we demand that into whatever region it carry us, it must at least be consistent: if we are to travel into fairy-land, it must be in a fairy equipage, not in a Hansom's cab."[7] Failure to negotiate successfully the boundaries between realms results in charges of "improbability," the most common criticism levelled against novels departing from a single consistent generic standard.

Though Lewes' complaint does not outlaw sojourns in fairy-land, the standard for Victorian novels was increasingly associated with "the novel of daily real life . . . of which we are least apt to weary."[8] The *Westminster Review* proclaimed in "The Progress of Fiction as an Art," that:

It has been the tendency of modern writers of fiction to restrict themselves more and more to the actual and the possible; and our own taste would be offended were they greatly to overstep these limitations, for a scientific, and somewhat skeptical age, has no longer the power of believing in the marvels which delighted our ruder ancestors. The carefully wrought story, which details events in orderly chronological sequence; which unfolds character according to those laws which experience teaches us to look for as well in the moral as in the material world; and which describes outward circumstances in their inexorable certainty, yielding to no magician's wand, or enchanter's spell, is essentially the production of a complex and advanced state of society.[9]

The terms "actual," "possible," "limitation," "law," "order," and "experience" suggest a regulation of fictional practice more restricted than that reflected by the novels of the period. The language of law and order attempts to reinforce the relationship between norms of fictional representation and social codes of behavior in an "advanced state of society," for "improbability" also functions as a term deploring inappropriate behavior (the ejaculation "Impossible!" conveys shock). The overlapping languages of disapproval and literary criticism allow these meanings to be applied simultaneously, in a fashion that would delimit representation in fiction. When Lewes writes in his review of Charlotte Brontë's second novel, "The manner and language of Shirley towards her guardian passes all permission . . . the two ladies talk at each other, in a style which, to southern ears, sounds both marvellous and alarming" ("Currer Bell's 'Shirley'"161), he arrays realism against the marvellous; real ladies against Caroline and Shirley; southern ears against northern tongues; and the novelist's license against the critic's permission (which is in this case withheld). The combination in *Shirley* of an elliptical and indirect method of storytelling (as opposed to the orderly detailing of events in chronological sequence) with the representation of shocking events affronts Lewes in both literary and social ways: "The attack on the Mill, too, instead of being described in the natural course of the narrative, is told us in snatches of dialogue between the two girls; who, in utter defiance of all *vraisemblance*, are calm spectators of that which they could not have seen" (168). Although Lewes is conscious of the value of a woman writer's point of view,[10] he is bound by a sense of probability that will not permit him to imagine female characters talking about violent political action, let alone witnessing it.

The episode to which Lewes objects is one of Charlotte Brontë's narrative annexes, and the terms of Lewes' reaction (to the "utter defiance" of likelihood, to the "girls" who could not have seen the mill riot, to the discourse of these errant female characters) suggest both the capacities of a narrative annex to alter the terrain and content of a novel, and the reaction of a critic who hopes to influence the future work of a novelist he admires. However, unlike Anthony Trollope, Charlotte Brontë does not regard the critic as a Rhadamanthus. Neither capitulating to his demands, nor defying them outright, Brontë responds to Lewes and to her other reviewers by asserting her control over the critics' territory, and by writing narrative annexes that demonstrate her power over boundary-lines and limits. The purpose of this chapter is not, however, to retell the tale of Brontë's literary relations, but to focus through an account of Brontë's three major novels on the language of a regulated representation, diffused through Victorian culture, that encourages the use of narrative annexes and imbues annexes with their capacity to test limits and challenge convention.

In the sections that follow I describe some of the most explicit prohibitions on and prescriptions for representation, by examining the criticism of a representative mid-Victorian critic, Walter Bagehot,[11] and the fiction of an exceptional mid-Victorian woman novelist, Charlotte Brontë, who employs narrative annexes in each of her major novels, *Jane Eyre*, *Shirley*, and *Villette*. Brontë manipulates the language of norms and boundaries, so often used prescriptively by literary critics, to signal

her border-crossings, daring excursions, and representation of impossibilities as necessities of action and self-discovery. Brontë's narrative
annexes not only include, in Lewes' words, "that which they could not
have seen" ("Currer Bell's 'Shirley'"168), but they call attention to the
urgency, for her characters, of defying such proscriptions. Charlotte
Brontë understands that critics' exhortations have generic, spatial, and
social registers; her narrative annexes vividly show that neither generic
proscriptions nor gendered limits on experience ought to prevent the
novelist from entering the realm of Imagination and representing what
she sees there. Although this chapter does attend to reviews of Brontë's
novels, Walter Bagehot represents for me not a critic of Currer Bell's
work, but a representative contemporary voice on the purposes and
limitations of Victorian fiction.[12]

To strikingly different ends, Bagehot's criticism and Charlotte
Brontë's fiction both employ imagery of gendered human bodies. Their
contrasting uses of this imagery, in combination with language of genre
and geography, suggest the important roles played by the woman writer
and the female reader in altering Victorian boundaries of representation. Bagehot's criticism, like R. H. Hutton's, attributes a narrowed
sphere of representation to women's fiction, particularly that written for
young girls. Charlotte Brontë's fiction acknowledges and challenges
these gendered limits, as her female protagonists and narrators contribute to the need for and the use of narrative annexes.[13] In Brontë's
annexes, female characters traverse zones of altered place and genre
and escape from the ordinary and permissible into forbidden, hazardous, and transforming realms. Each of Brontë's female protagonists gets
into the narrative annex neither in realism's hansom cab, nor in romance's fairy equipage, but on her own two feet. Walking into a world
within a world, what might such a character observe? And why would
she have to enter an annex to see it?

Women writers such as Jane Austen, George Eliot, and Charlotte
Brontë resort to annexing in order to work on narrative cruxes generated simultaneously out of contradictory or overtly prescriptive social
conventions, and out of the demands of their plots.[14] For instance, Jane
Austen sets up Fanny Price's family home, the Portsmouth household,
as an annex to the world of *Mansfield Park* (1814).[15] In the Portsmouth
annex Fanny reverses her normal role as recipient of others' gifts, giving
a knife to her younger sister, cutting herself free from the position of
dependent, and creating her own replacement. In George Eliot's novels,
annexes provide places for illicit actions and the introduction of modes

that turn plots towards their (often) tragic resolutions, as in the Red Deeps episode (Book v, chapter 1) in *The Mill on the Floss* (1860). Clearly, annexes do not always work in the service of progressive ideals and do not necessarily function as utopian devices. Nor do women writers alone feel the pressure to depict (or not to depict) prohibited subjects, as is shown by my prior discussion of Trollope and subsequent chapters on a range of novelists. All novelists' fictions are to some extent shaped by what is, according to the surrounding social world, conceivable, probable, and allowable. Even when novelists fashion topsy-turvy, fantastic combinations of the materials of fiction, the crisscrossing bindings of generic and social conventions can be felt beneath the fabric. Feminist criticism of the novel has described some of what has been omitted from fictional worlds and it has drawn attention to the work women writers have done in representing otherwise implausible materials, events, characters, and behaviors in the novel.[16] While acknowledging and drawing on that work, I suspend the assignment of particular genres and representational strategies to writers of one gender or the other, hoping rather to read the representations within novels to complicate my description of the work that narrative annexes can accomplish.[17] My examination in this chapter of the negotiation of the bounds of the normative focuses on both a masculine and feminine perspective on gender, transmuting decorum into constraint; shadowing the figuration of boundaries and border-violations; and highlighting the relationship of sexuality to reading and writing in the Victorian imagination.

VICTORIAN NORMS: WALTER BAGEHOT'S HEDGEROWS

Victorian critics writing in periodicals, while no ordinary readers, preserve a set of commonplaces about fiction and its realms. Better known for his writing on economics, politics, the English constitution, the money market, and the depreciation of silver, Walter Bagehot describes in his essays on contemporary fiction the boundaries of representation and articulates quite clearly the standards of appropriateness held in common by mid-Victorian critics, Mudie's Circulating Library, to whom publishers hoped to sell the largest number of books from a print run, and many readers.[18] Although he is only one of a constellation of critics contributing to this prescriptive discourse, Bagehot represents a frequently assumed stance in metaphors and figures of speech simultaneously conveying the clichés of conventionality, and resonating strangely with the fictional worlds of contemporary novelists. His terminology is social and spatial; it fosters the illusion of a universal set of assumptions, depending on separate spheres. The limitation of representation in accordance with a social code coincides not only with Bagehot's sense of genres, but with alternative spaces for discourse, which he differentiates in terms of gender.

Bagehot's essays on literary subjects include a number on novels and novelists and I refer here especially to "The Waverley Novels" (April 1858), "Charles Dickens" (Oct. 1858), and "Sterne and Thackeray" (April 1864). These articles for the *National Review* incorporate Bagehot's judgments and prescriptions, which I select in some detail to convey one Victorian's sense of representational norms exterior to novels, what Bagehot referred to as "the received rules" ("Lost and Won" 154). To imagine that Victorian novelists wrote in defiance or in complete ignorance of these standards would be to forget that most of the major novelists wrote, at least in part, to earn money. Since selection for Mudie's Library guaranteed both sales and the goodwill of a novelist's publisher, a novelist flouting convention risked not only the critics. Novelists producing their work in parts for serials could circumvent Mudie's Library, but as Thomas Hardy's and Anthony Trollope's experiences with periodical publication suggest, editors enforced decorum. Monthly numbers perhaps permitted the greatest freedom, but few novelists could carry off this form of publication, and dipping sales (for any reason) could result in the cancellation of the serial. (*Vanity Fair* nearly met this fate.)[19] Bagehot's essays do more than promulgate the Grundyism associated with the desire to protect the vulnerable young person (who must be able to pick up a book from Mudie's without fear of being offended, shocked, or instructed about certain subjects); they also meditate on the changing standards of appropriateness in the past century.

Writing about George Eliot, whom he regarded as "the greatest living writer of fiction," Bagehot praises Eliot's "logical style" and her "natural way" of avoiding the seemingly random, the jarring, and the improbable. In Eliot's fiction, Bagehot finds "not a space of incoherency, – not a gap" ("Sterne and Thackeray" 289–90).[20] Eliot's natural way "of telling what happened, produces the consummate effect of gradual enchantment and as gradual disenchantment" (290). In achieving this, Eliot is the most accomplished practitioner of "ubiquitous" fiction, Bagehot's idiosyncratic label for a narrative art that "aims at describing the whole of human life in all its spheres, in all its aspects, with all its varied interests, aims, and objects" ("Waverley Novels" 46).[21] In fact, no ubiquitous fiction was entirely successful in representing human life, since some spheres were prohibited – indeed, forbidden by Bagehot himself.

Bagehot sees the normative and the inappropriate as zones separated by a visible line, but he concedes that the location of that line has shifted in the century since Sterne's *Tristram Shandy* (1759–67). The reason for the shift, in Bagehot's account, lies in the popularity of the novel with female readers and the impossibility of sequestering novels to a masculine realm:

> It is quite true that the customary conventions of writing are much altered during the last century, and much which would formerly have been deemed blameless would now be censured and disliked. The audience has changed, and decency is of course dependent on who is within hearing: a divorce case may be talked over across a club table with a plainness of speech and development of expression which would be indecent in a mixed party and scandalous before young ladies. (290)

In his description of an altered audience, Bagehot makes a telling choice of topic. A divorce case, at the time of this essay, would have entailed discussion of adultery, desertion, bigamy, incest, and cruelty (physical violence) in order to obtain a true divorce, as opposed to a separation. These were not private matters. According to the Divorce Act of 1857, a husband could divorce his wife for adultery, but a woman would have to demonstrate that, in addition to committing adultery, her husband had deserted her, battered her, committed incest, or married another woman. To mention these topics before ladies, Bagehot considers indecent or scandalous, although as recently as 1847 Charlotte Brontë had treated some of them with frankness in *Jane Eyre* (while her sister Anne dealt with the others).

Despite the existence of these works by the Brontë sisters (and the more lurid offerings of lesser novelists), in imagining that the female audience for the novel forbids discussion of "the notorious facts of the world, as men speak of them to men" (290), Bagehot attributes the change not only to the broadening of the audience for fiction, but to women writers: "Much excellent and proper masculine conversation is wholly unfit for repetition to young girls; and just in the same way, books written – as was almost all old literature – for men only, or nearly only, seem coarse enough when contrasted with novels written by young ladies upon the subjects and in the tone of the drawing room" (290). The realms of club table and drawing room are associated not only with men and with women, but with "books written for men" and "novels written by young ladies," respectively. Bagehot's praise of George Eliot, however, shows not only that he regards one woman's novels as the most successful realistic fiction of the day, but that he *can* imagine the exceptional woman reader who knows the old literature written for men alone. None the less, his vision of contemporary fiction's readership admits the necessity of censoring the facts of life.

Bagehot sees that an audience of younger readers cramps the "ubiquitous" mode he prefers, but he can see no way out of the impasse:

> As soon as works of fiction are addressed to boys and girls, they must be made fit for boys and girls: they must deal with a life which is real so far as it goes, but which is yet most limited; which deals with the most passionate part of life, and yet omits the errours of the passions; which aims at describing men in their relations to women, and yet omits an all-but universal influence which more or less distorts and modifies all these relations. (291)

Bagehot also expresses this sentiment in "Lost and Won" and "La Griffe Rose." In the former essay, a review of a novel by Georgiana M. Craik, Bagehot recommends the adoption of a young woman's point of view as a safeguard to the novelist: "The obvious remedy is, that the writer should throw himself once for all into the position of a young lady in the story – hear only what she hears, see only what she sees, know only what she knows. His dramatic instincts will then preserve him even from wishing *to overstep the prescribed boundary*" ("Lost and Won" 154, my emphasis). Although Bagehot approves of the limitation on representing sexuality and desire, he worries that those persons acquiring their moral educations through novel-reading will be seriously misled and possibly endangered by a self-censored literature:

> A young-ladies' literature must be a limited and truncated literature; the indiscriminate study of human life is not desirable for them, either in fiction or in reality. But the habitual formation of a scheme of thought and a code of morality upon incomplete materials is a very serious evil: the readers for whose sake the omissions are made cannot fancy what is left out. ("Sterne and Thackeray" 291)

Here, "cannot fancy" obviously means cannot imagine. These young female readers, in Bagehot's world, cannot imagine their peril, for desertion, bigamy, incest, and sadism have been left out. (In actuality, sensational fiction provided a steady diet of such topics for young readers with library subscriptions.) Yet that phrase also contains Bagehot's worry that these readers will not learn to desire (to fancy) men as sexual beings, a "very serious evil" indeed. Bagehot becomes un-characteristically incoherent when he expands on the consequences of this situation: "Even if she admits in words that there is something beyond, of which she has no idea, she will not admit it really and in practice: what she has mastered and realized will incurably and inevitably overpower the unknown something of which she knows nothing, can imagine nothing, and can make nothing." In this bizarre circumlocution we are invited to imagine fictions of the drawing room and society acting as a sort of mental chastity belt, with an overpowering sterility that not only repels but annihilates that "unknown something" that ought to be an "all-but universal influence" on relations between the sexes (291).

When sexuality and bodily functions are represented, as in Sterne, Bagehot cannot help his fascination: "At first such things look so odd in print that you go on reading to see what they look like; but you soon give up, – what is disenchanting or even disgusting in reality does not become enchanting or endurable in delineation" (293). The body, "disenchanting" and "disgusting," threatens the experience of reading and bewilders Bagehot by menacing the purer world of fiction:

You are more angry at it in literature than in life: there is much which is barbarous and animal in reality that we could wish away, – we endure it because we cannot help it, because we did not make it and cannot alter it, because it is an inseparable part of this inexplicable world; but why we should put this coarse alloy, this dross of life, into the *optional* world of literature, which we can make as we please, it is impossible to say. (293)

Here Bagehot veers from prurience to revulsion and insists on a different separation of spheres, in which the "dross of life" is kept out of the "optional" realm of fiction. Yet the religious fervor of this outburst is balanced by Bagehot's condemnation of those persons he regards as pagan, because they are obedient to social norms in an unthinking, cowardly way:

They are pure because it is ugly to be impure, innocent because it is out of taste to be otherwise; they live within the hedge-rows of polished society, they do not wish to go beyond them into the great deep of human life; they have a horror of that "impious ocean" yet not of the impiety, but of the miscellaneous noise, the disordered confusion of the whole. (282)

The "ubiquitous" form of fiction Bagehot values takes on the challenge of this disorder, but with a crucial reservation that severely compromises his desire to enter imaginatively "the great deep of human life." The ubiquitous "searches through the whole life of man . . . or if there be any lineaments which it forbears to depict, they are only such as the inevitable repression of a regulated society excludes from the admitted province of literary art" ("Waverley Novels" 46). The "lineaments" which fiction "forbears to depict" echo Blake's lineaments of gratified desire and reinforce the effect of Bagehot's account of the change from the eighteenth-century fashion of representing life in literature.

In the mid nineteenth century, "the inevitable repression of a regulated society" divides the whole life of man into an "admitted province" and a forbidden zone. Despite his endorsement of this regulation, Bagehot's interest in the interdicted realm, beyond "the hedge-rows of polished society" comes through in his discussion of the work of Thackeray:

No one can read Mr. Thackeray's writings without feeling that he is perpetually treading as close as he dare to that border line that separates the world which may be described in books from the world which it is prohibited so to describe. No one knows better than this accomplished artist where that line is, and how curious are its windings and turns. The charge against him is that he knows it but too well; that with an anxious care and a wistful eye he is ever approximating to its edge and hinting with subtle art how thoroughly he is familiar with and how interesting he could make the interdicted region on the other side. He never violates a single conventional rule; but at the same time, the shadow of the immorality that is not seen is scarcely ever wanting to his delineation of the society that is seen, – every one may perceive what is passing in his fancy. ("Charles Dickens" 98)

We have seen how Bagehot's ubiquitous fiction depends upon an effect of sustained enchantment, though its task is to depict the whole life of man. Rather than opposing romance with realism (a term which had been current for a decade[22]), Bagehot values a fictional worldmaking that takes the reader away from the dross of life. Thackeray's fiction excites Bagehot by suggesting that there are worlds within worlds of potential representation. Approaching the boundary that separates a depicted world and a forbidden region, Bagehot's attention falls on the boundary itself. On the one hand, this line marks a gerrymandered district – "how curious are its windings and turns." Yet the active writhing of the line and the action of the novelist, sidling up to its edge, echoes the temptation of Eve in Milton's endangered Eden (Book ix, *Paradise Lost*). The novelist and the limiting, fascinating boundary mirror each other's actions and suggest the ultimate border violation of Satan, the first trespasser.[23]

Thackeray's restraint in forbearing to depict the forbidden world only heightens its attractions, as its shadow sharpens the edges of the society he does represent. For Bagehot, entering the worlds of fiction always reminds him of the virginal young lady reader whose existence represses representation and creates an intriguing boundary beyond which lies the "something" of sexuality. That she can safely look upon Thackeray's depiction of society, while Bagehot and his male compeers ("every one") can see in the shadows "what is passing in his fancy," only increases Bagehot's excitement, as her perception of "nothing" and the unrepresented but omnipresent "something" overlap, and almost touch.

Each of Charlotte Brontë's novels dramatizes in a narrative annex the passage of a female protagonist through an aperture that marks the boundary of an alternative realm. This peering, squeezing, and slipping through tight passages, such as the hedge-rows that mark the edge of a respectable realm for representation, Brontë repeats in narrative annexes that emphasize a woman writer's authority to depict prohibited subjects, to convey discomforting opinions, and to move her female protagonists (and by proxy, all of her readers, including young girls) out of conventional stations. Brontë's combination of a critique of gender roles with an exposé of the abuses of power, hypocrisy, cant, and prejudice depends upon her protagonists' capacity to explore and observe, and her narrative annexes emphasize the work that must be done to get female characters out of constraining positions. Brontë's annexes each demonstrate the difficulties a female character has in undertaking independent action, even as they enable those actions. Brontë meditates on the barriers that have been thrown up by circumstance and convention, and emphasizes the crossing of these barriers by her protagonists in precise, logistical terms. Muslins are torn; disguises worn; inhibitions discarded. As with all narrative annexes, genre shifts in tandem with place, as Brontë's protagonists enter realms where their previously limited ranges of experience radically expand. By leading her protagonists through the apertures they discover, Brontë challenges both social and fictional conventions, and enables her surrogates to see and experience things on the other side of the "line of separation." There is no evidence that Brontë attends to Bagehot's criticism, but as the subsequent discussion shows, the reaction of critics such as G. H. Lewes to the improbabilities ensuing from such a norm-violating strategy does not dissuade Brontë from altering place and genre within her fictional worlds. After *Jane Eyre*, Brontë increasingly relies on narrative annexes to package these actions of her protagonists most likely to draw charges of unreality, melodrama, or impossibility.

THE LINE OF SEPARATION IN *JANE EYRE*

> No two people could agree in their opinion of it, so full was it of contradictions. Miss A. was delighted with it, Miss B. as much disgusted – Miss C. heard it so talked of, that she was most anxious to read it; but her married sister, Mrs. D., said, "No woman under thirty ought to open it. Then, it was such a strange book! Imagine a novel with a little swarthy governess for heroine, and a middle-aged ruffian for hero."
>
> *Sharpe's London Magazine* on *Jane Eyre* [24]

In writing novels with female protagonists, Charlotte Brontë faces logistical problems, created by the standards of decorum for respectable women, in moving her characters around. Jane Eyre is taken to school and conveyed to her position as governess at Thornfield. The narrative annex beginning with her voluntary departure from Mr. Rochester's house, and leading to a sojourn in the wilderness, demonstrates some of the practical difficulties faced by a middle-class woman who leaves home on her own. Without money, friends, possessions, or food, Jane Eyre cannot even beg effectively because she does not look and sound the part. In Brontë's second novel, the eponymous Shirley acts the part of a gentleman in order to get herself and Caroline into the narrative annex, outside and across the fields at night, where they witness a riot at Robert Moore's mill. In *Villette*, the most extreme case, Lucy Snowe acts under the influence of an opiate when she leaves the *pensionnat* for the night streets. Even in *Jane Eyre*, Brontë relies on supernatural summonses to effect the departure and return to the primary world of the novel.[25] These promptings of an inward ear, like the transformation of an ordinary city into a fairy-realm in *Villette*, signal a generic as well as an actual departure. In the remaining three sections of this chapter I discuss Charlotte Brontë's use of narrative annexes to figure the boundaries between realms and genres, boundaries she delineates in order to transgress.[26] For from the very start of her career as Currer Bell, Charlotte Brontë flirts with the transgressive, and elicits responses to perceived overstepping in matters of religion, politics, sexual conduct, and conventionally gendered proprieties.

That not all of this reaction can be laid at intention's door does not mean that Brontë stumbles into the use of narrative annexes. Rather, we see from early in her career a deliberate assertion of authority over the boundaries of representation. The hint of scandal that spiced *Jane Eyre*'s popularity was (notoriously) exacerbated by Charlotte Brontë's preface to the second edition of her novel, in which she praises Thackeray's satirical truth-telling. Because Thackeray was known to have a mad wife, Brontë inadvertently instigated a rumor to the effect that "Currer Bell" was the psuedonymn of Thackeray's governess.[27] "There is a man in our own days whose words are not framed to tickle delicate ears,"[28] Brontë writes admiringly, dedicating the second edition to a man who was in fact a stranger to her. *Jane Eyre* was already controversial, without this additional scandal-fodder. Stimulated by "timorous or carping" critics who found *Jane Eyre* impious,[29] Charlotte Brontë amplifies her position on boundaries:

Conventionality is not morality. Self-righteousness is not religion. To pluck the mask from the face of the Pharisee, is not to lift an impious hand to the Crown of Thorns.

These things and deeds are diametrically opposed: they are distinct as is vice from virtue ... There is – I repeat it – a difference and it is a good, and not a bad action to mark broadly and clearly the line of separation between them. (*Jane Eyre* 3–4)

Brontë sees herself as the very creator of the boundaries that critics such as Bagehot regard as pre-existing features of a civilized world. Her role as a novelist is not to stay safely within the permitted area, but to depict freely, as Thackeray does, to scrutinize, and to expose. None the less, because her vehicle for observing and judging is in each major novel a young woman, Brontë does not employ an omniscient, distant narrator's perspective on the realms between which the author would draw the line of separation.

Though Brontë's preface declaring her control over the line between conventionality and morality, self-righteousness and religion, impiety and prophetic opprobrium appears with the second edition of *Jane Eyre*, the novel in its first edition announces Brontë's interest in re-drawing the boundaries that social and literary convention lay down around the main character, who also plays the role of narrator. Brontë presents Jane Eyre's possibilities and constraints at each stage of the novel in terms of the places she occupies, and the narrative trajectories offered to her. In the narrative annex, when Jane leaves the road at Whitcross to flee Rochester and civilization, Brontë breaks with this pattern to place her protagonist outside domestic life, and strip her of self-sustaining narratives. Crossing the boundary of the annex makes Jane into a socially suspect character who can peer through an aperture into the realm of respectable life from the outside, and can pass judgment on the behavior of comfortable insiders who serve as figures for middle-class readers. The annex's sojourn in the wilderness not only relocates Jane Eyre outside, but dignifies her observations as the utterances of a prophet.

The distinctive struggle of the fictional autobiography *Jane Eyre* takes place on the contested ground of Jane's life-story and the stories others tell about her – and to her. As Rosemarie Bodenheimer has shown, the stories of the secondary narrators (John Reed, Mrs. Reed, Rochester, Mrs. Fairfax, and St. John Rivers) act as standards, negative and positive, for Jane's construction of her own story.[30] Beginning with the opening clash in the Reed household, conflicting stories (John Reed's lies; Miss Abbot's narrative of God's wrath; the apothecary's pragmatic cover-story; Bessie's supernatural ballads; and Mrs. Reed's self-justifying misrepresentation) lay out the territory through which Jane must chart her course. The underlying narrative of a pilgrim's progress, rescripted to end in marriage and not in Heaven, is thus only one of the possible plots governing Jane's movements.[31] In this self-narrated text, other characters' representations and misrepresentations make up the terrain of Jane's fictional world; they differ from the stories Jane tells to herself (such as the ghost story she remembers in the Red Room) by leading to persecution and punishment. We rely on Jane's ability to expose the hollowness or hypocrisy of others' versions, even Rochester's vision of his dressed-up bride. When the wedding fails and Rochester's past comes out, the knowledge of Bertha Mason afflicts Jane grievously, for this narrative leaves only a kept-woman plot open. Brontë dramatizes the boxing-in of her independent character, as potential plot-lines fail her. Rather than submit Jane to the consequences of her seriously compromised situation, Brontë carries her character out of the social world of others' stories, across the boundary between civilization and wilderness, into a narrative annex. The story that erupts in Rochester's analeptic narration drives Jane into a textual space free of domestic secrets, an elemental zone without its own stories. So while the generic contrasts of different kinds of stories make up the fabric of the primary fictional world, the shift to the narrative annex presents a new situation, in which generic markers announce a dark night of the soul, and a saint-like retreat into the wilderness. Within the changed geographical locus of the annex, others are simply indifferent to Jane's story, and her own actions and intentions lead to persecution and punishment, as she starves and suffers insult and rejection.

Place marks each of the stages of the action as distinctively as the subgenres associated with each house or institution. Jane's location conditions and reflects her social function at each stage; as Jane's position changes, her reactions to solitude and the vicissitudes of group life also alter, and the reader accumulates a progress of Jane's self-images leading finally to the confident narrator. Jane the oppressed and abused child is replaced by Jane the skeptical observer in the schoolroom, and so forth: a good girl in the kind teacher's room; a witness to martyrdom in bed with Helen Burns; a sprite on the icy road; a lover in the garden; a compromised governess at Thornfield; a schoolteacher in her classroom; a courted cousin at Marsh End; a wife at Ferndean. From Gateshead to Lowood to Thornfield, through the narrative annex (the days and nights of flight, related in chapters 1 and 2 of the third volume) to the doubly named location of Marsh End/Moor House, and finally to Ferndean, Jane moves.

In her flight from Thornfield at the end of the first chapter of part III, Jane frees herself of the locations that define her situations. When she departs the road at Whitcross into the annex, she begins to make possible the reinvention of her own story by stripping away the roles that have contained her and shaped her experiences, a process that ends with the conclusion of the annex when she crosses the threshold of Marsh End. Re-entering a social and domestic world, Jane exits the annex bereft of a tellable story and divested of a social role; after two days and nights of hunger and homelessness, she refuses the opportunity to account for herself. When she begins to establish new relationships with the members of the household at Marsh End, the accomplishment of stripping-down in the narrative annex, so strange in the telling, is revealed as a necessary step in her homeward-bound plot. This process of reintegration not only enables Jane to claim her own independent self-worth, without the markers that would identify her class, position, and moral status, but also leads her to recognize the value of all other human beings, even the most incompetent and recalcitrant student in her classroom. The doubled experience of worthlessness and hopelessness represented in the annex makes possible Jane Eyre's subsequent radical recuperation of worth. Literally she finds her way through the narrative annex, in a bizarre coincidence, to the home of her nearest relations. Symbolically, the divesting of Jane's person in the narrative annex relocates the narrating protagonist firmly outside a middle-class world. The consequences of this move are political as well as practical, for in the sequence of events after the annex, Jane finally finds a way to tell the appropriate story about herself, rejecting the respectable but passionless union proposed by the missionary St. John Rivers.

Though these consequences of the narrative annex make plain the necessity of the "kernel" plot events that occur in the altered zone, a reader encountering the realm and mode off the road at Whitcross will register the difference and strangeness of both Jane's consciousness and the events Brontë arranges for her. Dropped off by the coach at Whitcross, nook-loving Jane finds the heath more welcoming than civilization: "Not a tie holds me to human society at this moment – not a charm or hope calls me where my fellow creatures are – none that saw me would have a kind thought or a good wish for me. I have no relative but the universal mother, Nature: I will seek her breast and ask repose" (327). Jane explicitly breaks her social ties with her fellow creatures and becomes a starving child of nature on the moor. Between Thornfield and the Rivers household at Marsh End, Jane endures both deprivation in the wilderness and ritual rejection, when she appears to others as a human being without a proper position, a perplexing ladylike beggar-woman. The narrative annex of flight from Thornfield entails Jane's rejection of a regulated, constraining society that would put her in an impossible position. Having narrowly escaped a bigamous marriage, an adulterous liaison, and the rage of the madwoman, Jane first attempts to surrender herself to the heath, a metaphorical return to the womb: "Beside the crag, the heath was very deep: when I lay down my feet were buried in it; rising high on each side, it left only a narrow space for the night-air to invade . . . a low mossy swell was my pillow" (328). Yet she wakes to realize that nature may lodge her for a night, but cannot sustain her. She wishes "that this weary frame, absolved by death from further conflict with fate, had now but to decay quietly, and mingle in peace with the soil of this wilderness" (329), replacing a bed (and womb) with a desire for the grave and total disintegration. The place she is born into could not be less hospitable to a human seeking warmth, food, and shelter.

Nature fails to provide and impels Jane to seek sustenance among other people again. Still in the alienated state of the annex, Jane's approach to the house of her rescuers emphasizes the extent of her departure from the social world. To take up Bagehot's phrase, she has removed herself to the region beyond "the hedge-rows" of society. To reenter that world, Jane follows a light that shines over the moor, coming to a "high and prickly hedge" (336) that she must pass:

there shot out the friendly gleam again, from the lozenged panes of a very small latticed window, within a foot of the ground; made still smaller by a growth of ivy or some other creeping plant, whose leaves clustered thick over the portion of the house wall in which it was set. The aperture was so screened and narrow, that curtain or shutter had been deemed unnecessary; and when I stooped down and put aside the spray of foliage shooting over it, I could see all within. (336)

The barrier between Jane and the world of warmth, light, cleanliness, and useful labor takes the form of a half-natural, half-architectural wall with an "aperture" so narrow that she can only glimpse the social world and feel the impossibility of reentering it: "And how impossible did it appear to touch the inmates of the house with concern on my behalf" (339). Yet through this impossible aperture she will pass, marking her departure from the alternate realm of the annex.

Brontë employs in each of her major novels a narrative annex marked by a version of this aperture, through which her protagonists move. In each case the passageway from realm to realm is narrow, half-natural, but encouraged by human hands, and appears first as a barrier. In *Jane Eyre* a domestic scene lies beyond; in *Shirley* and *Villette*, the protagonists squeeze through into realms of political action and heightened sexuality. Brontë's narrative annexes include these vivid images of permeable barriers in order to enact the passing-through to an otherwise inaccessible world: either the annex itself, in *Shirley* and *Villette*, or, in *Jane Eyre*, the primary fictional world that has been rendered uninhabitable for her protagonist.

For Brontë's characters, who undergo excruciating tests of identity throughout their stories, the space of the narrative annex allows stripping, masking, and switching of roles. The shedding of identity Jane enacts in order to get inside the door at Marsh End – she pretends to be a nobody – rapidly changes into a conscious masking of her former position. Inside the Rivers household, deprivation of human warmth replaces hunger and joblessness; even the person who takes most interest in her, St. John Rivers, is characterized as a figure of ice, chill Calvinist fervor, and sexual abstinence. Yet St. John *Eyre* Rivers reconstructs Jane's relationship to her uncle, procures her fortune for her, and provides her with three cousins in himself and his two sisters. These coincidences function as counter-offers to the possibilities of the rest of the novel, following the annex with its triad of rejections, and seem more like justice for Jane and less like impossibilities because of the transforming journey she has made. Ultimately, St. John's refusal to accept Jane's radical proposition that they journey to India as fellow-missionaries, rather than as husband and wife, suggests that he is perfectly willing to manipulate proprieties in order to get what he really wants: Jane in thrall, rather than Jane as a partner. Jane has learned the lessons of the annex well enough to recognize the hazards of St. John's proposal and scorns his idea of a self-sacrificial, yet sure-to-be-consummated love. Retrospectively, the aftermath of the annex reveals a pattern of trials endured for the sake of a marvellous reward, a pattern that cannot function in the primary narrative of insult and injury, of the relentless piling-up of difficulties and obstacles.[32] In short, the swerve from *Jane Eyre*'s primary plot towards the narrative of resolution is almost magically accomplished by the narrative annex.

By the time Jane hears the mysterious call from across the hills, she has discovered herself and her own version of faith, one which leads her back to Rochester and marriage. While the fairy-tale ending of the novel includes the recovery of Rochester from his punishing blindness, Jane's final transformation of the marriage plot founds a female *Bildungsroman*,[33] which takes up and discards stories until it reaches the position of self-narration. The conclusion with a marriage plot's ultimate reward can distract readers from the radical breaks Charlotte Brontë makes in her narrative of fulfillment, just as those challenges to the normative can lead readers to expect – ultimately – a more subversive novelist than Charlotte Brontë ever becomes.[34] Despite the conventional closure of her plot, in narrating her story Jane Eyre claims an unusual position from which she challenges both the pulpit and civilized society.

The combination of a doctrine of self-determination with the recognition of equal worth leads critics such as Elizabeth Rigby (Lady Eastlake) to reject the novel as anti-authority and anti-Christian:

There is throughout it a murmuring against the comforts of the rich and against the privations of the poor, which, as far as each individual is concerned, is a murmuring against God's appointment – there is a proud and perpetual assertion of the rights of man, for which we find no authority either in God's word or in God's providence – there is that pervading tone of ungodly discontent which is at once the most prominent and the most subtle evil which the law and the pulpit, which all civilized society in fact has at the present day to contend with. We do not hesitate to say that the tone of mind and thought which has overthrown authority and violated every code human and divine abroad, and fostered Chartism and rebellion at home, is the same which has also written Jane Eyre. ("*Vanity Fair* – and *Jane Eyre*" 173–4)

Driven in part by the crossing of class boundaries in the love affair of a gentleman and his governess, this objection responds to the urgent claim of self-worth that must express its discontent with injustice, persecution, double standards, and double dealing. Although Lady Eastlake is remembered primarily as a carping critic of *Jane Eyre*, she correctly perceives the political dimension of Jane's progress, in which the condition of woman refigures the rights of man. If Victorian novels often depict middle-class explorers who report on the squalor of homes and workplaces, Jane in the annex makes herself into the opposite, a homeless nobody who can report on the true state of charity for the poor and displaced. Jane's position alters so significantly that she may peer into a respectable and comfortable home with the same critical eye that so often, in Victorian fiction, observes the haunts of the poor. Brontë's ostensible rejection of "God's appointment" in fact makes a plain point about the contamination of Christian virtue by class-conscious notions of respectability. Her implicit plea for sympathy for the innocent but compromised woman also attacks those who collude in her punishment by upholding social standards when they ought to practice charity. In the annex the patrollers of the boundaries of respectability are revealed to be women, even middle-class Christian women, and the natural world takes shape as a rejecting mother who cannot, or will not, sustain her daughter. The transformation of Jane Eyre, in the narrative annex, into the witness who can convey this negative message hits home especially with female readers. "Lydia," a representative female voice in a review, comments, "I never can forget her passage across the heath, and her desolate night's lodging there,"[35] and Lady Eastlake (otherwise disapproving) singles out the annex's "wanderings and sufferings" as "the most striking chapters in the book" (166).

Critics more sympathetic to Brontë's critique react more specifically to the generic swerve of the narrative annex, but in this area, too, gender plays a part in distinguishing acceptable and unacceptable modes of narration. While Brontë employs an interpolated melodrama (Rochester's narrative) to drive Jane out onto the heath, the transformation she works on her protagonist in the annex makes a revolutionary shift in perspective, as Lady Eastlake perceives. Some critics could not imagine that Jane Eyre's mind and experiences could have been created by a woman writer (many remembering the joint production of the "brothers" Currer, Ellis, and Acton Bell).[36] The American critic Edwin Percy Whipple imagines that only a brother–sister collaboration can account for the generic mixture, for the "autobiography" points to "a powerful and peculiar female intellect,"[37] but the "clear, distinct, decisive style of its representation of character, manners, and scenery . . .

continually suggests a male mind" ("Novels of the Season" 356). Particularly masculine is the "daring peep into regions which acknowledge the authority of no conventional rules," of which Whipple snidely remarks, "we are gallant enough to detect the hand of a gentleman in the composition" (357). A woman ought not to be able to imagine animal appetites; hot, emphatic scenes of passion; profanity; brutality; or a man's slang.[38] Although he correctly identifies the sex of the author, G. H. Lewes, too, distinguishes her experience and imagination in terms of genre and gender. Lewes regrets that the residual form of melodrama exists within the psychological novel he so much admires in *Jane Eyre* and admonishes the author to avoid the imaginary: "Persevere; keep reality distinctly before you, and paint it as accurately as you can: invention will never equal the effect of truth."[39] Pointing to the episodes instigating the annex ("the mad wife and all that relates to her"), and the annex itself ("the wanderings of Jane when she quits Thornfield"), Lewes complains that the novel contains "too much melodrama and improbability, which smack of the circulating-library" ("Recent Novels" 692). Here the purported weakness of a genre arises from traits associated with women's fiction, since triple-deckers written for the circulating library cater to female readers' appetites.

Pleasing the libraries was a tricky business. Over a decade later, George Meredith's *The Ordeal of Richard Feverel* failed on moral grounds to win the approval of Mudie's, and he claimed that his career suffered for years.[40] Yet writing a blandly inoffensive text guaranteed nothing. Brontë's response to Lewes' criticism in a letter of 6 November 1847[41] reminds him that the demands of the circulating libraries influence publishers' decisions: *The Professor*, in which she "restrained imagination, eschewed romance, repressed excitement" had met rejection at six publishers because it lacked the "'startling incident' and 'thrilling excitement'" needed to attract the circulating libraries.[42] More importantly, while maintaining the disguise of her pseudonym, Brontë attacks Lewes' distinction between "invention" and "truth" in terms underlining the limits on experience imposed by her gender:

You advise me too, not to stray far from the ground of experience as I become weak when I enter the region of fiction; and you say "real experience is perennially interesting and to all men . . . "

I feel that this also is true, but, dear Sir, is not the real experience of each individual very limited? and if a writer dwells upon that solely or principally is he not in danger of repeating himself, and also of becoming an egotist?

Then too, Imagination is a strong, restless faculty, which claims to be heard and exercised, are we to be quite deaf to her cry and insensate to her struggles? (*1829–1847* i. 559)

The risk of weakness that the author runs in straying from the "ground of experience" is nothing to the danger of being limited, repetitious, and selfish. If the writer listens to Imagination, she must cross into the region of fiction to act and aid her outside the bounds of limited experience, as Brontë aids Jane Eyre in her distress by taking her out of Thornfield into the imaginary territory of the narrative annex.[43] For Brontë, imaginative sympathy claims the moral high ground, as the rights of a female imagination command the attention of the writer, and by extension the critic, in political terms.

As we will see in the subsequent section, Brontë once again employs a narrative annex in her next major novel. In *Shirley* the imaginary territory entered through Brontë's characteristic aperture takes an explicitly political form. Yet as her contemporaries realized, Brontë's first novel presages the more overt gender politics of *Shirley* and *Villette*. In 1855, Margaret Oliphant looks back on the change heralded by Brontë's 1847 novel: "Such was the impetuous little spirit which dashed into our well-ordered world, *broke its boundaries*, and defied its principles – and the most alarming revolution of modern times has followed the invasion of *Jane Eyre*."[44] The rights of woman declared in *Jane Eyre* radically challenge order, authority, and romantic love itself, as Jane "turn[s] the world of fancy upside down." In the prosperous and calmer year of 1855, when there is no threat of revolution at home, the critic sees quite clearly the political implications of Brontë's critique of gender:

Yes, it is but a mere vulgar boiling over of the political cauldron, which tosses your French monarch into chaos, and makes a new one in its stead. Here is your true revolution. France is but one of the Western Powers; woman is half of the world. Talk of a balance of power which may be adjusted by taking a Crimea, or fighting a dozen battles – here is a battle which must always be going forward – a balance of power only to be decided by single combat, deadly and uncompromising. ("Modern Novelists" 557–8)

Only half-mockingly, Oliphant recognizes the political significance of Jane Eyre's love affair as a challenge to the "reverent, knightly, chivalrous true-love which consecrated all womankind" (557). The gathering of a formidable power, "half of the world," is figured in terms of a generic shift initiated by *Jane Eyre*. Brontë's revision of a comfortable, domestic middle-class perspective is nowhere more radically imaged than in the privations and revelations of the narrative annex. Yet as we will see, Brontë uses the passage through the narrative annex in her following novel to rebuild the barriers that Jane Eyre, temporarily, overcomes.

REBUILDING THE BARRIERS IN *SHIRLEY*

Charlotte Brontë's second novel was written during the years when revolution in Europe was mirrored by social unrest in Britain. In *Shirley*, Brontë attempts to avoid the pitfalls of improbability, drawn to her attention by G. H. Lewes and others, by writing a historically based, explicitly political fiction on the Condition of Woman. She sets the fiction at the time of the Luddite disturbances, when displaced workers destroyed the machines that threatened their livelihood.[45] If she eschews the generic dissonance of *Jane Eyre* (she writes to Lewes, "I think I will have nothing of what you call 'melodrama'"[46]), she creates a new contrast between primary fictional world and narrative annex in order to convey her female characters into the realm of political action that imagination strains to enter. Unlike Elizabeth Gaskell, Charlotte Brontë has little first-hand experience from which to render her account of engagement. Preoccupied with the problem of women's work raised in *Jane Eyre*, and brought to its fullest expression in *Villette*, *Shirley* takes a very different tack than Gaskell's *Mary Barton* (or Gaskell's later novel *North and South* [1854–5]).

The "industrial" element of *Shirley* is limited to the events of a narrative annex, in which a journey across the space of the night fields leads to a vantage point from which Shirley and Caroline (paired protagonists of the novel) witness a riot at a mill yard. As in the annexes in Brontë's *Jane Eyre* and *Villette*, the passage from a predominantly interior, civilized and bounded setting to a place off the path, in the dark, and outside of town allows female characters to experience a temporary freedom from their normal roles. Yet in *Shirley* the overt challenge to gendered restrictions mixes with conservative horror at social unrest, and Brontë firmly reins in the implicitly liberating plot-trajectory of the narrative annex.

As *Jane Eyre* juxtaposes Jane's flight with Rochester's story of his marriage to Bertha Mason, *Shirley* pits a narrative annex against the interpolation of embedded texts (introducing secondary story-tellers' language), in a staged contest between emergent and residual forms of action for female characters.[47] Brontë makes an association between embedded texts and old-fashioned narrative outcomes, but not before she sets up a narrative annex that suggests a more emancipated plot. The narrative annex, "A Summer Night," alters both Caroline's and Shirley's plots, but not necessarily in the ways that its heroic intervention suggests. Brontë uses the journey into the hazardous, forbidden zone to establish Shirley's radically "masculine" decisiveness and her power over Caroline Helstone. The transformation of Caroline's story into a subplot begins in the annex, as transactions of violence and disobedience, including the shift of focus to the more daring and domineering Shirley, are covered by a troubling scene of female friendship. Brontë then employs alternative techniques, adding narrative levels in the form of embedded texts, to steer the diverging plot back in a more conventional direction.[48] Shirley's interpolated adolescent school essay (inserted into the narrative by her former teacher Louis Moore) establishes Shirley's desire to be mastered. Louis Moore has hoarded Shirley's essay, which he introduces in an attempt to place her, retroactively, in her own outgrown allegory of desire. Whereas the interpolated tale related by Rochester impels Jane to leave his house and enter the annex, interpolation in *Shirley* functions to correct and redress the consequences of the narrative annex.[49] The capacity of female characters to gain experience and to act in a male realm can extend only so far, as Brontë attempts to mitigate the freedoms of the narrative annex.

Meeting Shirley gives Caroline not only a companion, but a source of information about Robert Moore, for he is Shirley Keeldar's "gentleman-tenant." Shirley has reason to be in contact with Robert; she also possesses a remarkable self-image that allows her access to realms normally forbidden to women:

"I have been obliged to see him: there was business to transact. Business! Really the word makes me conscious I am indeed no longer a girl, but quite a woman and something more. I am an esquire: Shirley Keeldar, Esquire, ought to be my style and title. They gave me a man's name; I hold a man's position: it is enough to inspire me with a touch of manhood; and when I see such people as that stately Anglo-Belgian – that Gerard Moore before me, gravely talking to me of business, really I feel quite gentlemanlike." (*Shirley* 213)

Yet Shirley's "touch of manhood" does not suffice as a passport into the whole realm of gentlemen's endeavors. Realizing that he can entrust his niece Caroline to her care, Mr. Helstone encourages Shirley to play the role of gentleman-protector. He flatters Shirley as he hands her the guns that signify her exemption from danger, like the magical talisman of fairy tale: "'It is paying you a great compliment, captain, to lend you

these: were you one of the awkward squad you should not have them'"
(326). Helstone means to get both Shirley and Caroline out of harm's
way, but he underestimates Shirley's devotion to her role; once she
realizes that the mob is on its way to the mill in the Hollow, she decides it
is her "duty and wisdom" to beat them there, taking the route over the
fields, in order to warn Robert Moore. In their departure across the
fields, Shirley and Caroline position themselves (respectively) as leader
and follower. Caroline justifies her numb acquiescence to Shirley's
suggestion that they embark across the fields, despite her fear: "she felt
she could not abandon Shirley" (331). Shirley correctly reads Caroline's
response as gender-bound:

And are you so obedient to a mere caprice of mine? What a docile wife you
would make to a stern husband. The moon's face is not whiter than yours at this
moment; and the aspen at the gate does not tremble more than your busy
fingers; and so tractable and terror-struck, and dismayed and devoted, you
would follow me into the thick of real danger! (331)

Shirley mocks Caroline's feminine obedience in order to emphasize the
ostensible purpose of the journey: to enter the masculine realm of
action, to warn, to take part. Brontë also makes it clear that Caroline's
blind and meek response increases Shirley's pleasure at leading and
taking the strong role. Yet Brontë does not mean to make Shirley into a
man, but rather an extraordinary woman (Shirley is in part a portrait of
Emily Brontë). Throughout the novel, Shirley and Caroline stake out
alternative versions of ideal womanhood: Shirley's "heaven-born" Titan-Eve (315); Caroline's "gentle human form," her unknown mother
(316). Despite these ideals, Shirley does not seek a proselyte in Caroline
and Caroline does not imagine Shirley as a surrogate mother.

The way Brontë draws the boundary around the interdicted realm
the women enter together both underlines the strong resemblances to
the Whitcross annex in *Jane Eyre*, and suggests the potentially greater
empowerment of the protagonists of *Shirley*. Having overcome the fear
of impropriety, the women pass a physical border, labelled with the
word that signifies the passageway between worlds of possibility for
Brontë. The hedge, an unmistakable boundary, marks and merges the
two women as they pass through it: "A quickset hedge bounded the last
field: they lost time in seeking a gap in it: *the aperture, when found, was
narrow*, but they worked their way through: the long hair, the tender
skin, the silks and the muslins suffered" (332, my emphasis). Like the gap
between the heath and the warm lit room at Marsh End in *Jane Eyre*, an

aperture in a hedge that bars the way also suggests a way through. The two women, distinguished up until this point by their contrasting gender roles, merge synecdochically (and paradoxically) into one female penetrating force, onto whose undifferentiated body the effects of penetration are inscribed. Shirley and Caroline share the long hair, the skin, and the clothing that suffers as they squeeze through the narrow gap, in this vivid picture of the physical results of crossing the boundary into the narrative annex, and of women passing through an emblem of their difference. Before passing through the hedge, Shirley is "surefooted and agile," whereas Caroline, "more timid, and less dextrous," falls and gets bruised. On the other side of the boundary, however, the weaker Caroline rejects Miss Keeldar's offer to carry her across a wobbly plank bridge: "Caroline, without pausing, trod forward on the trembling plank as if it were a continuation of the firm turf: Shirley, who followed, did not cross it more resolutely or safely. In their present humour, on their present errand, a strong and foaming channel would have been a barrier to neither" (332). This passage suggests Caroline's growth into a temporary equality with Shirley, draws attention to the physical strength of both women, and merges the two into a single boundary-crossing adventurer, quite unlike the solitary, exhausted, starving, and rejected Jane.

By the time they actually arrive at the Hollow, Caroline and Shirley are too late to warn the millowner, so instead they witness the riot they have hoped to forestall. Shirley restrains Caroline in order that they may watch, unobserved: "'At this moment, Moore would be both shocked and embarrassed, if he saw either you or me. . . . We shall see what transpires with our own eyes: we are here on the spot, and none know it'" (333–4). In Shirley's words, Brontë anticipates the problem of representing women witnessing the things that they can see only because they have left their proper sphere. Intervention proves impossible; but knowledge of their very presence would prove both shocking and embarrassing. As if to emphasize the transgressive nature of the annex's border-violation, Brontë makes the thrill of witnessing erotic: "Caroline rose; Shirley put her arm round her: they stood together as still as the straight stems of two trees . . . Both the girls felt their faces glow and their pulses throb: both knew they would do no good by rushing down into the melee: they desired neither to deal nor to receive blows; but they could not have run away –" (335–6). When the wounded have been taken up and doctors sent for, Shirley advises Caroline on their return to the primary realm of the novel, in a fashion that acknowledges the impropriety of their action: "'We will steal in as we stole out: none shall know where we have been, or what we have seen to-night: neither taunt nor misconstruction can consequently molest us'" (340). The evocation of trembling limbs, throbbing pulses, expostulation, taunts, and molestation underlines the eroticism of the scene, at the same time that it emphasizes the location of the gaze in the two women. Yet by representing what they see, Brontë opens herself to the very taunts and misconstructions that Shirley seeks to avoid through secrecy. Shirley teaches Caroline self-discipline and restrains her from humiliating herself by rushing to Robert Moore. The women enter the realm of political action, if only to observe, and repudiate the feminine role of caring for the wounded. An act of persuasion akin to seduction has also transpired, a seduction of woman by woman, in which the domineering Shirley forces Caroline to confront her desire, and then to renounce it. Taking advantage of her power to prevent Caroline from going to Moore, Shirley offers her own strong arms as a substitute. "Friendship" seems rather a weak term to describe the hierarchical bonding that occurs in the annex, as the nonviolent position of "friend" masks the mastery which Shirley, armed and dangerous, achieves over the woman in her arms. When G. H. Lewes quarrels with the witnessing of the mill riot by the "two girls," as I relate in the beginning of this chapter, he recognizes that the conversation of the two women occludes and replaces the conflict between the millowner and the protesters.

Though the novel does finally return to Caroline's love plot, when it becomes clear that Shirley has only a "businessman's" interest in Robert Moore (and when Moore's business problems are resolved, allowing him to think of acquiring a wife), the text's attention to Caroline has been subdued by the narrative annex. Caroline's story of renunciation and self-denial, of squeezing the scorpion that stings, gives way to the work of feminizing Shirley and of making plausible the attraction of a man to a woman who is determined to be read as a gentleman, or alternatively, as a daughter of the monumental Titan-Eve. That Shirley, who masters the weaker woman in the annex, must relinquish her fluctuating gender-identification, requires the rebuilding of the barriers that have been breached in the annex. Significantly, both plots return to indoor spaces and civilized daylit grounds as the subversive locus of the annex dissolves into the double marriage plot. The novel remains de-centered, set-off balance by the shift from Caroline to Shirley and further disturbed by the attempt to remake Shirley in Caroline's weaker image.

Brontë's decision not to carry through the more progressive plot suggested by Shirley's action in the narrative annex does not mean that she tempers her criticism of the limitations placed on respectable females. During the first third of the novel, when Caroline is the sole heroine of the story, there is no question that she will hear about conflict second hand (information matters to Caroline because she fears for the safety of her cousin Robert Moore, whom she loves). When Caroline's uncle and guardian Mr. Helstone, who disagrees with Robert Moore's politics, forbids her to visit her cousin's cottage daily, Caroline obeys. Comprehending that she can have nothing to do with Robert's life because she has no way of participating in the business at its center, Caroline tries when she sees him in church to understand the "perplexities, liabilities, duties, exactions" of business and to "realize the state of mind of a 'man of business'" (188). At the same time, she attempts to reconcile herself to living as an old maid, a state which will limit her to visiting, receiving visitors, and doing charitable work. (Her uncle forbids her to seek a position as a governess and she will not consider any of the ludicrous young curates whose company she endures for his sake.) Caroline's struggle to come to terms with her confining circumstances, as she passes through levels of crisis whose signs are misunderstood by the people who surround her, emphasizes her desperate isolation. In this way, Brontë sets up an equation between lady-like deferential behavior and a painfully narrowing sphere. In her authorship, Brontë attempts to earn the rights of Shirley and to avoid the fate of Caroline.

Having breached the barrier that normally conceals the site of information from surveillance by female eyes, and defied the decorum that would keep gentlewomen inside at night, Brontë boldly announces her intention to carry her characters over whatever lines of separation convention lays down. Her reaction to G. H. Lewes' negative criticism of the scene picks up on his emphasis of gendered plausibility and propriety. As I mention earlier, Lewes objects that "the two girls . . . in utter defiance of all *vraisemblance*, are calm spectators of that which they could not have seen," protests that Shirley's language and behavior "passes all permission," and cavils at the women's "marvellous and alarming" talk ("Currer Bell's 'Shirley'" 161, 168). Brontë feels betrayed by Lewes' response because she has implored him, in a letter of 1 November 1849, to treat her as an ungendered, or (implicitly) as a male, writer. Brontë's plaint shows that, by remaining incognito, she anticipates the censure that Shirley seeks to avoid when acting in a masculine realm: "I wish you did not think me a woman. I wish all reviewers believed 'Currer Bell' to be a man; they would be more just to him. You will, I know, keep measuring me by some standard of what you deem becoming to my sex; where I am not what you consider graceful you will condemn me" (Spark, *Letters* 171). Ten weeks later, Brontë had read Lewes' unsigned piece in the *Edinburgh Review*; its meditation on the proper sphere of woman (maternity) exacerbated its charges of vulgarity and improbability. Referring to the narrative annex's account of the attack on the mill, Lewes betrays his prejudice as he hangs fire: "It is scarcely worth while to point out the several details in this scene, which betray a female and inexperienced hand" ("Currer Bell's 'Shirley'" 168).[50] To this Brontë plainly reasserts her point to Lewes:

I was so hurt by that review . . . because after I had said earnestly that I wished critics would judge me as an *author*, not as a woman, you so roughly – I even thought cruelly – handled the question of sex. I dare say you meant no harm, and perhaps you will not now be able to understand why I was so grieved at what you will probably deem such a trifle; but grieved I was, and indignant too. (Letter to Lewes on 19 January 1850 [Spark, *Letters* 105])

Brontë believes that the gentleman-like woman (Shirley, Currer Bell) who enters the masculine realm draped with its symbols of power ought to be treated better; Lewes wounds her by identifying her as a member of "the awkward squad."

It is, of course, vital to acknowledge that Lewes' and other critics'[51] negative reactions to *Shirley* took the form of legitimate complaints about the novel's formal awkwardness. From the earliest reviews to recent evaluations, assessments of *Shirley*'s failures almost always loop back to the problem of form. As Joseph Boone notes, the collapse of the feminist plot back into the marriage plot does not occur unprecipitatedly at the moment of Shirley's consent to marriage.[52] The vacillation of Brontë's attention and intentions can be observed earlier. Brontë casts *Shirley* as a third-person narrative, whose title character does not even show up until chapter 11. During the second third of the novel, the reader is left to wonder whether to root for Caroline Helstone, or for the newly introduced Shirley, whose independence and energy make her attractive even to the cautious Caroline. Since *Shirley* takes the form of an erratically omniscient account, rather than a fictional autobiography, and since the narration is not focalized consistently on one character alone, the novel becomes responsible for narrating the inward experience of characters, including its heroes – the potential husbands – whom it has hitherto observed from the outside. Formal awkwardness reaches its height when Brontë introduces the passages from Louis Moore's "little blank book" in the penultimate chapter of the novel. These sections of unmotivated interiority attempt to transform the bossy schoolmaster into an appealing lover and appropriate mate for Shirley. They double the effort, through interpolation, to justify Shirley's marriage plot, demarcating the space into which Shirley will be forced by the novel's conclusion, that is, the limited space next to Louis Moore's "I." Taken as a sequence, the transactions made in the narrative annex and the counterweighted interpolations call attention to the disconcerting changes in the novel's focus. The narrative annex in *Shirley* thus causes more problems than it solves, but Brontë does not abandon the technique. Though she vows to her publisher George Smith that her next novel (*Villette*) "touches on no matter of public interest," handles no "topics of the day," and contains no "moral" or "philanthropic scheme,"[53] she continues to struggle with ways to combine changes of genre and changes of place in order to validate the extraordinary actions of her female protagonists.

THE LAST APERTURE: NARRATIVE ANNEXES IN *VILLETTE*

In *Villette*, Charlotte Brontë returns to the form of fictional autobiography and again represents the border-crossing actions of her protagonist in narrative annexes that serve to engineer encounters and introduce information barred from the primary world of the fiction in brief, bounded, generically altered episodes. In this novel, as in *Jane Eyre*, Brontë moves her heroine through a sequence of different locations, but Lucy Snowe's pilgrimage ends in a centered, solitary self, not in marriage. Brontë's ultimate use of narrative annexes is striking for three related reasons. First, in *Villette*, Brontë uses not one narrative annex, but a sequence of *three*: in chapter 15, "The Long Vacation"; in chapter 34, "Malevola"; and, climactically, in an annex spanning chapters 38 and 39, "Cloud" and "Old and New Acquaintances."[54] While the primary fictional world from which Lucy Snowe departs into each of these annexes is nominally the same (Madame Beck's *pension-nat*), and while each annex independently represents a contrasting place and genre (fragments of the surrounding foreign city), their differences from one another, and the changes in Lucy's perceptions of her primary world after returning from each annex, underline Brontë's interest in using annexes to represent a psychological process that moves in stages. Lucy's understanding of difference and otherness is complicated by the sequence of annexes, because they do not cohere generically or spatially, nor come together into a discrete plot strand, though they do feature, as the chapter title suggests, an identifiable set of "old and new acquaintances." Brontë's evident reluctance to use the annexes as zones through which her protagonist passes in order to achieve a rewarding resolution (as in *Jane Eyre*) presages the chilling denial of a conventional conclusion at the end of the novel. Like *Shirley*, Villette entices the reader into a misleading set of interests, and endeavors to revise those interests later in the novel. In *Shirley*, this correction disappoints when it returns to a conventional love plot that diminishes its heroine. In *Villette*, Lucy Snowe's narration makes explicit the necessity of interpreting and reinterpreting, by forcing the reader first to judge situations with an incomplete set of facts, and then to reevaluate when the missing information surfaces. Creating not one but three annexes is symptomatic of the complications and qualifications of *Villette*. To see why the entire novel is not just a long series of annexes, unfolding episodically, and making encounters with difference into a norm, we must first consider the ways in which Brontë builds a primary world intricate and flexible enough to maintain coherence and sustain the three departures of the annexes. This leads to the second and third ways in which *Villette*'s annexes are striking, for the novel presents a primary fictional world already diversified spatially and generically.

The contrast in setting that a narrative annex uses (with a boundary and changed genre) is more difficult to perceive when a novel employs changes in place normatively. Even more than Jane Eyre, Lucy Snowe is already the most mobile and resourceful of Brontë's protagonists. She emigrates to Villette voluntarily. The deliberate choice to change her location, undertaken in ignorance but in hopes of finding employment, marks Lucy as a different variant of Brontë's questing protagonists. According to Lucy Snowe, an English woman can be trusted to travel by herself. (Ruth Yeazell points out that Lucy's freedom depends on her Englishness and her Protestantism, as opposed to the suspicious regulation and surveillance of Catholic European women.[55]) If her protagonist can leave England, embarking alone for a destination guaranteed to be different from what she has known, for what would Brontë need the specialized, heightened, and bounded changes of place created by narrative annexes? The answer to this pragmatic question lies in the concomitant alteration of genre, the possibilities for plot, and the attractions – and repulsions – of a zone of difference more alien even than the new setting of a foreign place. For Charlotte Brontë, that zone can be labelled "Roman Catholicism." The settings contained by the three annexes – church and confessional, private home, and public space – represent fragments of a monolithic influence on, but not an explanation of, the character of M. Paul Emanuel. Brontë uses the annexes' contrasting places contrarily, to demonstrate how character (Lucy's and her lover's) cannot be adequately interpreted simply by being contextualized, or thrown into relief, by an external setting.

Similarly, a schematic generic contrast alone will not satisfy the demands of Brontë's exploration of character under acute external and internal pressure. As many critics have noted, *Villette* is permeated by fragments of an alternative genre, undermining and undergirding its psychological realism – gothic.[56] Gothic themes, figures, and occasions for paranoia are not confined to narrative annexes, but coexist with the homelier details of life and work in the *pensionnat*. When the narrative annexes in *Villette* shift genre, they present fragmentary scraps of a middle ground between the autobiographical mode and the gothic, enabling Lucy to encounter and ultimately debunk the subplots that threaten her own successful self-narration.[57] The sequence of generic shifts to confession, fairy tale, and altered-state spy story serves as a conduit to encounter the threats and promises of Catholic plotting.[58] Even as the kernel plot elements present in the annexes contribute to Lucy's psychological "heretic narrative," they playfully rearrange the counters of gothic and Catholic subplotting. Though she presents the first encounter (in the confessional) oppositionally, Brontë uses the transition into a world of enchantment in the second annex ("Malevola") to expose her heroine to Catholics in a positive light, despite the prevailing anti-Catholicism of Lucy's world view.[59] The annexes in *Villette* bring antithetical realms of experience (Lucy's private walled-off Protestant world, and M. Paul's predominantly social existence as a Catholic) into contact, without confirming the apparent opposition of realistic and gothic plotting. When in the third and last annex Lucy adopts Madame Beck's *modus operandi*, surveillance, she discovers and is temporarily taken in by widely shared misapprehensions, not private truths, about M. Paul.

For Lucy never renounces the activities that bring her, like Madame Beck, the most pleasure and power: observation and interpretation.[60] Lucy remarks when she formally introduces herself that watching leads to over-interpretation: "I, Lucy Snowe, plead guiltless of that curse, an overheated and discursive imagination; but whenever, opening a room-door, I found her [Paulina] seated in a corner alone, her head in her pigmy hand, that room seemed to me not inhabited, but haunted" (69). Lucy's reaction to the presence of another's potential subjectivity within her restless first-person fiction suggests a pattern. She diverts herself from the discomfort of her own consciousness by reading others as alien, doubled, and haunting. Exorcising the specters of a haunted imagination will be a crucial task of Lucy's narration, which literalizes encounters with gothic doubles on the one hand, and projects figuratively a psychomachic struggle between Reason and Imagination on the other.[61] The disciplinary figure of Reason, both associated with a workaday world of humdrum realities and yet as "envenomed as a step-mother," governs a nightmare household: "her stint, her chill, her barren board, her icy bed, her savage, ceaseless blows" (308). Yet Reason also threatens to drive Lucy out, "by night, in midwinter, on cold snow, flinging for sustenance the gnawed bone dogs had forsaken" (308). Here the places of *Jane Eyre* are internalized as figures of Lucy's mental agonies. Pure space provides the only relief in the temple of Imagination: "A dwelling thou hast, too wide for walls, too high for a dome – a temple whose floors are space – rites whose mysteries transpire in presence, to the kindling, the harmony of worlds!" (308). Between Reason and Imagination, Lucy moves, fearful of the "terrible revenge that awaits our return" (308) after breaking bounds.

Lucy declares "we shall and must break bounds at intervals" (308), but first Brontë establishes the process by which a character comes to belong in the place that will imprison. In the opening chapters of the novel, Lucy relates the procedure of observation, testing, and judgment which a newcomer entering a house undergoes. The beginning of *Villette* introduces Lucy Snowe as an observer and interpreter in the house of her godmother, and the rest of the novel is structured around Lucy's entrances into strange houses. That the last one is a real home, Lucy's own, and a house empty of judgmental observers demonstrates that Lucy's awkward and discomforting arrivals have in fact made up a progress. Before she can arrive at that place, out of surveillance and in charge of herself, Lucy must depart from the *pensionnat* where she teaches. This school fixes Lucy not only in her public, professional role, but in her private, self-defined position as a Protestant surrounded by deceitful Catholics. For although Lucy's vivid picturing of storms of despair and depression make the outside world seem particularly threatening, images of shelter are also tainted by the fear of scrutiny by others.

By chapter 4, Lucy has centered her story uneasily in the self-scrutinizing narrative that makes up the remainder of the novel. She establishes her authority by introducing and despatching with her elderly employer, Miss Marchmont, in the space of one chapter; though she may not control the external circumstances of her life, she certainly governs her story and its metaphors. When Lucy arrives in Villette, her relation of her own story becomes cautious to the point of unreliability, as her life becomes more susceptible to the agendas and methods of unfathomable strangers.[62] Madame Beck hires Lucy, despite her lack of references and experience, on the recommendation of M. Paul, who reads her countenance. Luckily Lucy's face passes: "by God's blessing I was spared the necessity of passing forth again into the lonesome, dreary, hostile street" (129). M. Paul will prove to be Lucy's best reader, who recognizes in her a willful and skillful manipulator (although Lucy undergoes a prolonged hopeless crush on Dr. John [Graham Bretton] before she can reciprocate M. Paul's knowing gaze). Here M. Paul acts as a judge of character who rescues her from the uncertainties of the outside world. Yet in order finally to connect with him, she ventures in *Villette*'s three narrative annexes into the very realm she hopes to escape: the "lonesome, dreary, hostile street."

The revelation of the identity of Dr. John (Graham Bretton/"Isidore") provides the most significant example of Lucy misleading the reader. The narrative annex in chapter 15 ("The Long Vacation") produces this revelation, calling Lucy's reliability into question, problematizing Lucy's role-playing, and demonstrating that Lucy needs to pass out of her bounded world in order to correct the misleading narration she governs there. In a novel so dependent on the assumption of roles (and so explicit about the benefits and hazards of assuming these roles), depicting both a character's inner life and her social life is fraught with difficulties. Though the masks Lucy assumes protect her in a crowd, they fail her when she is left alone with herself. By coming to Villette, where she is alien in language, nationality, and religion, Lucy Snowe places herself in a position that demands role-playing and self-restriction. She must not be too friendly with her students; she must not leave clues that could reveal her to the spying Madame Beck; she must restrict herself to the relatively safe enclosure of the *pensionnat*. For Lucy's protective coloration to succeed, the community within the walls must read and interpret her according to her own plan. Madame Beck, after all, affirms Lucy's self-definition as an outsider and a potential danger by spying on her, and the surveillance parodoxically brings Lucy into a community which derives its coherence from being watched. The risky times for Lucy occur when her community of interpreters departs, when she must fall back on her own inner resources. The outside world so frantically entered and interpreted by Lucy in the narrative annexes provides an alternative to self-examination in solitude.

The long vacation empties the *pensionnat* of everyone but Lucy, a servant, and "a poor deformed and imbecile pupil, a sort of cretin whom her stepmother in a distant province would not allow to return home" (227). For some weeks Lucy cares for Marie Broc, a degrading and exhausting job that falls to her because even the servant is absent. If Lucy's flight from England represents an escape from menial labor (for many educated dependent women, working as a governess came perilously close to being a servant), she is warranted in feeling threatened by the way this responsibility falls onto her. Yet the distraction of caring for the cretin (who is not identified by name until later in the novel) protects Lucy from the terrible prospect of being alone with herself. The weeks with the cretin separate Lucy from her audience and introduce her painful mental state. Her experience forces her back into herself, for "It was more like being prisoned with some tameless animal, than associating with a human being" (229). When the cretin is taken away, Lucy begins a series of daytime excursions, compelled by "a want of companionship" experienced as "the cravings of a most deadly famine" (229–30). In her attempt to lose herself, Lucy tests the limits of her emotional stability. During her solitary walks, she imagines Ginevra's love for Dr. John, which is so different from her own alienated experience: "I conceived an electric chord of sympathy between them, a fine chain of mutual understanding, sustaining union through separation of a hundred leagues – carrying, across mound and hollow, communication by prayer and wish" (230). Lucy is no Jane Eyre, attuned to supernatural communications, but an observer who realizes that such sympathy exists – and excludes her. The figure of a chain of connection draws a line between two lovers; Lucy's excursions cross this and other lines of separation.

Exhausted and ill, Lucy goes out into the stormy night streets, entering the narrative annex. Oppressed by her safe haven, she imagines that her desire to be loved and owned "would shine clearer if I got out from under this house-roof, which was crushing as the slab of a tomb" (232). Instead of going to the open fields, however, Lucy enters a Catholic church, where she clumsily confesses to a priest. Here the encounter with a Catholic form of self-narration leads Lucy to claim instead the territory of her own "heretic narrative" (235). Despite Lucy's rejection of the invitation to further conversation (and conversion), the priest treats her kindly and takes her affliction seriously. Lost in an unfamiliar part of the city, Lucy gets hit by the full force of a storm, and passes out, "pitch[ing] headlong down an abyss" (236). She has crossed through two alien territories in order to lose the consciousness that torments her. In this excursion Lucy faces her mental instability, and, in trying to avoid madness, breaks through the borders she has drawn around herself. Having moved through the "lonesome, dreary, hostile street," Lucy mimics M. Paul's pilgrimage to Rome, but she moves beyond the confessional to a reconstituted (surrogate) family.

When she wakes up from her descent into the abyss, Lucy finds herself back in the Bretton household. Unlike Jane Eyre's experiences at Marsh End, in the household of her cousins, which serve the ends of plotting through a discovered inheritance, the revelations of this episode reveal more about Lucy's reticence and her anxious relationship to plots. Here Dr. John's identity is revealed to the reader, for he is the son in that familiar home. Lucy has known all along that Dr. John is Graham Bretton, but he has not recognized her. Temporarily, Lucy imagines being "loved and owned," although the renewed relationship between Lucy and Dr. John resumes on an unequal footing. (M. Paul, on the other hand, sees the "real" Lucy beneath the role-playing and audaciously forces her to play roles of his devising. Ultimately, M. Paul will insist on loving Lucy *without* owning her, when he sets her up to be independent.) Dramatizing the dangers of independence, this annex makes Lucy's renovation necessary. In the two annexes of the third volume, Lucy resituates herself in relation to an alien social world, so that she may be herself among the residents of Villette.

When Lucy Snowe runs her errand to Madame Walravens in the chapter "Malevola," she leaves her usual world of school and shops to enter a fantastic realm, peopled by fairy-tale creatures and covered by transforming weather. From the earliest pages of the novel, Lucy reflects upon her dread of literal and metaphorical (e.g. emotional) storms. The crisis of the first annex apparently confirms her fear. On the verge of entering the second annex, however, she changes her mind: "I rather liked the prospect of a long walk, deep into the old and grim Basse-Ville; and I liked it no worse because the evening sky, over the city, was settling into a mass of black-blue metal, heated at the rim, and inflaming slowly to a heavy red" (479). Lucy's description shows that she willingly walks under a sky like a smelting furnace, whose vivid "inflaming" suggests a metaphorical body. Lucy welcomes the storm because she desires to relinquish herself to her fate (falling in love with M. Paul) and she relishes the anticipated transformation, which she figures in emotional, generic, and geographical terms:

I fear a high wind, because storm demands that exertion of strength and use of action I always yield with pain; but the sullen down-fall, the thick snow-descent, or dark rush of rain, asks only resignation – and the quiet abandonment of garments and person to be drenched. In return, it sweeps a great capital clean before you; it makes you a quiet path through broad, grand streets; it petrifies a living city, as if by eastern enchantment; it transforms a Villette into a Tadmor. (479)

Lucy believes her torpor can be alleviated by violent weather and she craves release from herself. Brontë represents resignation to an elemental seductive force, enabling "the quiet abandonment of garments and person," as Lucy's fundamental desire. The image Lucy reads in the sky promises her not only passive drenching, but privacy, for, "in return," the rainstorm also sweeps away grime and people, emptying the city. On her path away from the *pensionnat*, Lucy perceives that Villette has been petrified, made ancient, and transformed into another place entirely, as by "eastern enchantment." The exotic suggestion of Tadmor, one of the cities Solomon built in the wilderness, emphasizes the vehement Protestantism of Lucy's imagination, just as she steps out into a completely Catholic world. For the first time in the novel, Lucy dares to imagine the transformation of her surroundings without jeopardizing her security and emotional stability.

Crossing the boundary created by the storm, Lucy enters a part of Villette that she does not know. In this unfamiliar zone she encounters the individual Catholics whose points of view and stories she accepts with surprising openness. Up until this point, the novel has described encounters with Catholics and Catholic culture as fraught with peril to Lucy's spirit and personal property alike.[63] Lucy defies a witch (Madame Walravens) and a wolf (Pere Silas, the priest) and tarries to hear a story. The enchanted city's genre shifts to accommodate these potentially threatening inhabitants. As Lucy draws near Madame Walravens, she registers the change:

Yet, was it actual substance, this appearance approaching me? this obstruction, partially darkening the arch?
   It drew near, and I saw it well. I began to comprehend where I was. Well might this old square be named quarter of the Magii – well might the three

towers, overlooking it, own for godfathers three mystic sages of a dead and dark art. Hoar enchantment here prevailed; a spell had opened for me elf-land – that cell-like room, that vanishing picture, that arch and passage, and stair and stone, were all parts of a fairy tale. (481)

From a transformed outer world, Lucy enters a spellbound building that strikes her as a fairy-tale setting. The storm that rages outside reinforces the generic shift: "The tale of magic seemed to proceed with due accompaniment of the elements. The wanderer, decoyed into the enchanted castle, heard rising, outside, the spell-awakened tempest" (482). Not until the end of the storm, when Pere Silas has related the fabulous tale of Paul Emanuel's devotion, a contemporary saint's life, does Lucy leave the house and the realm of fairy tale.

In the narrative annex the canny narrator travels through a fictional place that disables her commonsensical, matter-of-fact descriptions. Temporarily spellbound, Lucy "accidentally" learns the history of M. Paul. Thus the annex solves a practical problem of a first-person narrative in which the narrator is confined by custom and regulation: as a respectable woman, a foreigner, and an employee of Madame Beck, Lucy is triply bound. Where else could she learn about Paul? Certainly not from Madame Beck or from Paul himself. Yet the shift to a fantastic and sinister world outside of the *pensionnat* unleashes into the novel more than just information about a character; it also provides a (false) gothic explanation, in the priest's story of Justine Marie, for the appearances of the spectral nun who haunts the school. Lucy's return to the normal world is managed by a meditation on the dangers of Romanism, but the annex enables her to reflect that "this man, Emanuel, seemed of the best; touched with superstition, influenced by priestcraft, yet wondrous for fond faith, for pious devotion, for sacrifice of self, for charity unbounded" (488–9). The second annex mitigates the simple suspicion of Catholics that has allowed Lucy to position herself as a skeptical outsider caught in a hostile environment.

Each of the three annexes sets up different versions of a middle ground on which Lucy and the Walravens faction convene: confessional; Catholic home; and finally, public fête. The counter-narrative of the apparitional nun, who haunts Lucy's home-territory, the *pensionnat*, heightens the stakes of these external encounters with Catholics, as gothic, saint's life, and (ultimately) farce compete to explain the events that Lucy has observed. "Malevola" provides a supernatural possibility for explaining the apparition, in the story of Justine Marie; but at the close of the third and final annex, when Lucy returns from her drugged wanderings, the nun is revealed as a mere disguise, a costume covering Ginevra's and M. de Hamal's banal affair. Yet until the small group of Catholics have been revealed to be ordinary people, with self-interested reasons for meddling with the affair between Lucy and M. Paul, Lucy cannot get beyond her sinister characterization of their motives. This debunking and "renovation" from fantasy to reality paradoxically requires the most elaborately imagined annex in the drug-induced excursion into the night streets of Villette, a phantasmagoric and yet all too concrete middle ground in which the characters from mundane and gothic realms mix.

The pressure from within and without Lucy to keep private and social worlds separate accounts for Brontë's extravagances in conveying her protagonist into the annexes, for in *Villette*, as in *Jane Eyre* and *Shirley*, the boundary-crossing itself is recounted in detail, in terms that announce the erotic nature of the narrator's action. When Lucy Snowe presses herself through an "aperture" in the final annex in *Villette*, Brontë rewrites both the conclusion of *Jane Eyre*'s annex, and the entrance into *Shirley*'s mill riot annex. The friends, "Freedom" and "Renovation," with whom Lucy bonds on the other side of the aperture, are allegorical figures of her own solitude, and, instead of surrender to death or to an exciting sisterhood, we find Lucy's half-disguised voyeurism underlined by autoerotic sexual imagery.[64] If in *Shirley* the narrative annex configures a female's will in a way that must be quelled by the remainder of the novel, *Villette* writes the tale of a self-quelling excursion that stridently reneges on the fairy-tale promises of *Jane Eyre* (suffering in the annex will not guarantee domestic bliss), and combines Shirley's bold direction with Caroline's masochistic renunciation of pleasure. Lucy's placement of her own mind and body in the physical world, in a community, in friendship, and in a loving relationship with a man requires the enactment of a spiritual, social, and sexual self-renovation.

Towards the end of the novel, when M. Paul has replaced Dr. John in Lucy's love plot, she gets the news that M. Paul must leave on a trip to Basseterre in Guadeloupe. As the hour of M. Paul's departure arrives, Lucy waits in vain for him to bid her goodbye. Perceiving Madame Beck's interference, Lucy confronts her rival without fear: "in some stimulated states of perception, like that of this instant – her habitual disguise, her mask and her domino, were to me a mere network reticulated with holes; and I saw underneath a being heartless, self-indulgent, and ignoble" (544). Seeing through Madame Beck's mask emboldens Lucy to put on her own disguise, although she has dressed parts reluctantly in the past. Hoping to knock her rival out, Madame Beck administers an opiate to Lucy. The drug stimulates instead of inducing sleep, however, and Lucy embarks on her final journey into a narrative annex.

Flanked on both sides by sections of present-tense narration, the narrative annex emphasizes Lucy's urgency and her trance-state as she exits and reenters the primary world. Her hand on the lock, she feels as if she is being propelled into the night streets, where she can seek the park:

> It yields to my hand, yields with propitious facility. I wonder as that portal seems almost spontaneously to unclose; I wonder as I cross the threshold and step on the paved street, wonder at the strange ease with which this prison has been forced. It seems as if I had been pioneered invisibly, as if some dissolving force had gone before me; for myself, I have scarce made an effort. (548)

The sensations are the result of the opiate, of course, but the "dissolving force" brings to earth the powers of the rainstorm to release and transform, emanating from Lucy herself as she breaks out of her prison.[65] Lucy projects allegorical figures to explain the prompting by her own desires; "Imagination" shows her a strange vision of the park, an image that is also a vision of her sexual self, "with its long alleys all silent, lone, and safe; among these lay a huge stone-basin – that basin I knew, and beside which I had often stood – deep-set in the tree-shadows, brimming with cool water, clear, with a green, leafy, rushy bed" (547). Lucy's trip into the night would enact an entrance into that desired and forbidden place; she imagines she can sneak into the park through a gap in the paling, "a narrow, irregular aperture visible between the stems of the lindens" (547). Here Brontë's "aperture" recurs as an image of a boundary that will be crossed, a boundary that also provides an unmistakable image of Lucy's person. Where Jane Eyre finds on the moor the embracing womb of Nature, and Shirley and Caroline pass through an image of their own gendered boundedness, Lucy Snowe reads in the exterior world an image of her own desiring body.

Yet the annex contains not a private place, but a complicated and crowded social scene, where most of the characters from the novel congregate and pass in front of Lucy. All Villette has turned out for a fête on the occasion of the deaths of patriotic martyrs. The park has been transformed with lights and architectural amazements, but Lucy debunks the decorations and the martyrs as pasteboard and apocrypha. She imagines she has disguised herself, with her straw hat bound around her face, but a bookseller recognizes her and guides her to a seat. Lucy discovers that she sits near the Brettons, the Beck party, and finally, "the whole conjuration, the secret junta" (558) – Madame Walravens, Madame Beck, and Pere Silas. Out in the lit-up midnight, Lucy finds herself within eavesdropping distance of her antagonists. Her description of this sequence of events emphasizes the chance in these positionings, but the way in which she half disguises herself and fails to look away suggests that desire has guided her here, as well.

Earlier in the novel, Lucy avoids invisibility by wearing labels: teacher; Protestant; Englishwoman. With the promptings of her desiring body made manifest, Lucy enjoys in the annex the benefits of a self-assumed, if not efficacious, invisibility. Unlike Shirley and Caroline, she does not shrink from the embarrassment of being caught witnessing something she ought not to see. Brontë turns the erotic game of seeing and being seen to Lucy's advantage, as she turns away from Dr. John when he nearly (or surely) recognizes her, "failing" to acknowledge him as he has often failed to see her. The sight of Dr. John prompts Lucy to meditate on the imaginary places each of them keeps furnished for the other: "I believe that in that goodly mansion, his heart, he kept one little place under the skylights where Lucy might have entertainment, if she chose to call . . . I kept a place for him, too – a place of which I never took measure, either by rule or compass: I think it was like the tent of Peri-Banou" (555). Lucy's description of this compartment suggests how a character's unnarrated possibilities might expand: "All my life long I carried it folded in the hollow of my hand – yet, released from that hold and constriction, I know not but its innate capacity for expanse might have magnified it into a tabernacle for a host" (555). This telling image moves from the Arabian Nights to Catholic architecture in miniature. As strange as the stage inside Dr. John where Lucy may be entertained is the monstrance embedded in Lucy's relentlessly Protestant imagination. Brontë sets the vast domeless temple Imagination against her figure for hopeless fantasy, a fairy's magic tent that might be converted into a tabernacle for a (false) host.

Of course, unbeknownst to Lucy, M. Paul has been busy furnishing an actual apartment and an actual school that will not magically expand but will provide real shelter and real employment for her. Unaware of Paul's renovations, Lucy remakes her desire and despair into a matter-of-fact acceptance in the annex. She learns through eavesdropping that mercenary interests motivate M. Paul's journey and that he is only a tool of the Walravens/Beck faction. Then she assumes, seeing the young girl

Justine Marie and M. Paul together, that a marriage has been planned as a reward. She does not suspect that M. Paul has delayed his departure for her own sake. In a manner reminiscent of Caroline Helstone's "squeezing the scorpion," she reacts:

I hastened to accept the whole plan. I extended my grasp and took it all in. I gathered it to me with a sort of rage of haste and folded it round me, as the soldier struck on the field folds his colours about his breast. I invoked Conviction to nail upon me the certainty, abhorred while embraced, to fix it with the strongest spikes her strongest strokes could drive; and when the iron had entered well my soul, I stood up, as I thought renovated. (566)

Although Lucy discards her allegorical companions shortly after the close of the annex, Renovation and Conviction gird her up from within to endure a centered and unmasked existence. The masochistic process works. M. Paul establishes her in a home with a schoolroom and asks her to marry him. Then he disappears from the novel, for three years and then forever, lost at sea. The last annex teaches Lucy (if not all readers) to accept these excruciating facts, for the vivid depiction of desire in the narrative annex leads uncompromisingly to solitude. Brontë postpones the loss of Paul, but she has already taught Lucy Snowe how to lose him, and in fact the three years of Paul's initial absence become Lucy's happiest time.

In *Jane Eyre*, the solitude endured on the moor leads Jane to the reward of a marriage plot, but, in *Villette*, the emancipatory direction of the annexes ends with a centered, independent, abandoned self. Walter Bagehot relishes the thought of the interdicted realm that lies on the other side of the line of separation; Brontë shows in *Villette* that although desire may impel the crossing, loss – not gratification – lies on the other side. Conveying this unpleasant message requires Brontë to challenge conventionality, as her contemporary critics noted. One reviewer marvels that

Currer Bell can bring off her heroine in triumph . . . can find her a respectable shelter, without the slightest previous prospect, the first day that an unknown stranger sets foot in a foreign land, – can pilot her home through illuminated Brussels on a gala night without a rough word said to her . . . But we fear that such sequences are to be found rather in the artist's chambers of faery imagery than on the pages of Reality's record.[66]

Deploring the unreality of the residual form ("faery imagery"), the same reviewer also recognizes that Brontë's depiction of "the strange, pathetic, painful, revelation of Woman's nature . . . may – and possibly does – belong to our times" ("Villette" 186). The uneasy reaction suggests that the critic recognizes an emergent form in Brontë's novel, one that may "belong to our times" despite its failure to adhere to "Reality's record." From the contest of genres staged in the narrative annexes, Brontë creates a new kind of psychological fiction, a "heretic narrative" revealing woman's nature, instead of her socially sanctioned plot. This troubles the *Athenaeum* reviewer, who writes that "There are other ways for a woman of squaring accounts with trial than that of rushing about the world when the homeland becomes wearisome – of taking midnight rambles through a city when the sense of agony drives off sleep" (186). The alarming consequence of admitting that Brontë's psychological portraiture may accurately depict something about contemporary women's states of mind, for this reviewer, lies in the message female readers will absorb from this discomforting novel: "Her books will drive many minds out among the breakers, – they will guide few to sure havens" (186). Described in a negative way (as it often is by contemporary reviewers), the progression from the improbable and improper action – "of taking midnight rambles through a city" – leads to a disturbing boundary-breaking image of its own, as the very minds of readers are taken offshore and away from "sure havens" into dangerous and unpredictable zones. Not M. Paul, nor Lucy alone, but the vulnerable female reader is endangered by the departure of the narrative annex.

Though she eschews in this novel the topical material approached in *Shirley* (as we have seen, Brontë herself wrote to her publisher that *Villette* "touches on no matter of public interest. I cannot write books handling topics of the day; it is of no use trying. Nor can I write a book for its moral"[67]), Brontë succeeds in forging a new variation of the novel by means of these departures from conventional depiction of "Reality's record." Though fewer contemporaries appreciated her accomplishment, G. H. Lewes found in the novel "a moral carried in the story – not preached, but manifested." He celebrates the effect of Brontë's emergent psychological novel: "From its pages there issues an influence of truth as healthful as a mountain breeze. Contempt of conventions in all things, in style, in thought, even in the art of storytelling, here visibly springs from the independent originality of a strong mind nurtured in solitude."[68] Here at last Brontë's departures from convention earn Lewes' approval as the work of an original imagination.

From her early writings, Brontë imagines generic departures in terms of entrance into another imaginary place. She writes, at the conclusion of her Angrian apprenticeship, "I long to quit for awhile that burning clime where we have sojourned too long – its skies flame – the glow of sunset is always upon it – the mind would cease from excitement and turn now to a cooler region where the dawn breaks grey and sober, and the coming day for a time at least is subdued by clouds."[69] In *Villette*, Brontë gives Lucy Snowe the experiences that she describes in her own authorship, "departing" from the characters who have become her intimate acquaintances: "When I try to conjure up new inmates I feel as if I had got into a distant country where every face was unknown and the character of all the population an enigma which it would take much study to comprehend and much talent to expound" ("Farewell" 230). That the character Lucy perceives her border-crossing excursions as necessary steps at moments of psychological and spiritual crisis suggests that in *Villette* Brontë revises her authorial supervision of boundaries to serve psychology. Rather than providing a thrilling plot, *Villette* relates the story of a woman who comes into possession of her inner self, gradually and haltingly revealing the stages in that process of self-inhabiting. Lucy may be capable of travelling by herself, but the work of *Villette* is devoted to reconstructing its protagonist until she can be trusted to be alone. A shifty and not-entirely-divulging narrator, Lucy does not cultivate her reader's sympathetic identification in the way that Jane Eyre does, and the annexes of Villette do little to win readers over to a fictive personality.[70] Instead, the annexes seem especially strange, as Brontë uses generic and physical changes to make spaces for Lucy Snowe's flights and escapes from her own tormented mental condition. Ultimately, the revelations and encounters of the annexes lead Lucy to a renovated interior, where she escapes surveillance and in which she centers her unmasked self.

While Brontë's use of narrative annexes to append alternative places and the genres they contain reveals a dynamic of constraint and liberation, her novels do not always follow through the altered trajectories of their annexes. Her heroines sometimes find freedom in the alternative space and mode of annexes, as Lucy Snowe does in her escape into the world outside the *pensionnat* and as Jane Eyre does in her sojourn on the moor, but Brontë also uses annexes to suggest a startlingly liberated plot in *Shirley*, although the novel reneges on this direction. Both *Jane Eyre* and *Villette* chart a heroine's pilgrimage through a varied landscape. In these novels, annexes enable escapes from and renegotiations of the boundaries of repressive settings. *Shirley* uses an annex to free characters temporarily from the restricted fictional world in which they move, but later employs interpolation to redirect those characters, building back up the barriers that have been breached. In *Shirley* an emancipatory fiction about the possibility of a woman's agency in the economic, political, and sexual realms loses the contest of outcome to a tidy but disappointing double marriage plot, as the dominant form defeats the possibilities of the emergent form. Yet even if Brontë's annexes do not necessarily serve feminist ends, her figuration of the boundaries crossed as characters enter annexes emphasizes the gendered nature of limits on representation and experience. For Brontë, as for Victorian critics, the image of a human body underlies the geography of permitted and interdicted realms. In Brontë's case, however, this body belongs to a monumental Titan-Eve, a universal mother, or an image of the female sexual self whose presence in the textual world confutes conventional ideas of woman's dependency on man. Although Brontë's ambiguous pseudonym led early critics to speculate about her gender, there can be no doubt that her experience of authorship is reflected in narrative annexes that challenge gender roles, figure female sexuality, and demonstrate her power to cross the hedgerows that, according to contemporaries whose views resemble Bagehot's, ought to keep the woman writer on the safe side of the "interdicted realm."

CHAPTER 4

Narrative annexes, social mobility, and class anxiety

SOCIAL FICTION AND THE BOUNDARIES OF REPRESENTATION

Any account of the social restrictions on representation in the Victorian novel would be incomplete without acknowledging the importance of the mythical figure Mrs. Grundy. Her person represents most plainly the gendered limits on representation, for it is she, on behalf of novel-reading young ladies, who forbids frank depiction of adult sexuality. If, as we have seen, some prominent Victorian critics held women writers and female readers to blame for a constricted realm of representation (even as they enforced those limits when responding to novels by women), to these same critics Mrs. Grundy embodied the worst of a "maternal" impulse to protect the vulnerable young person from the effects of fiction-reading. Her genesis can be traced to the early nineteenth-century evangelical reaction to the dangers of novels, promulgated in warnings such as this one from an 1824 issue of the *Lady's Magazine*:

One great foremost evil of novel-reading is generated and established in its tendency to banish simplicity and nature from the mind, and to form artificial, imitative character; to fashion and confirm a practised mind; to seduce the frank and honest disposition from its native ingenuousness, and to teach the art of acting perpetually upon plan; to be frivolously busy in analysing what never can be analysed, except by that power which formed it – the human heart.

Novel-reading leads to a fondness of making experiments on the affections of others toward ourselves.[1]

In fighting a losing battle against the reading of fiction, particularly by girls and young unmarried ladies, the evangelical proscribers in subsequent decades target, instead of all novels, particular areas of representation of human life. The availability of a more licentious French fiction makes the task of Mrs. Grundy clearer. In contrast to the "almost unbounded latitude allowed the French novelist,"[2] for the English, according to R. H. Hutton, "there are whole portions of thought in which our minds run in an entirely distinct channel."[3] Mrs. Grundy's job at mid-century is to keep the English novel from breaching the walls of that channel and running in the direction of the permissive French novel. Yet by the 1850s, when critics such as Walter Bagehot accept the idea of an interdicted realm, others chafe against the restrictions associated with Mrs. Grundy. The limits on representation enforced by institutions such as Mudie's Library are figured in terms of a maternal repressiveness that fails to educate in its eagerness to protect:

Oh, Grundy . . . What a noble English matron thou mightest have been, with children and grandchildren at thy knee, looking up to thee lovingly, trustfully, reverently, for advice, teaching, true education, the educing, bringing out, and developing of their latent faculties, nascent aspirations, instead of sneaking about as they do now to all manner of forbidden bookshops in fear of the perpetual "You musn't!" – conceiving of a parent's function as merely that of thwarting and stunting – like wretched snails, never putting out a feeler without expecting it to be rapped back into the shell again by Mrs. Grundy's maternal ferula.[4]

Yet if Mrs. Grundy can be blamed, in effect, for the corruption of an ignorant reading public driven to "all manner of forbidden bookshops," this anonymous critic makes a more serious charge, alleging that the imaginary middle-class Christian woman's insistence on a blinkered representation betrays her willful ignorance of poverty and exploitation:

It was very disgusting, no doubt; but perhaps it may do Mrs. Grundy good now and then to know how the pictures which she admires at the Exhibition get painted, just as it may to know how the cheap clothes which she prides herself on buying get made, and the cheap "Society Bibles" which she distributes get bound, at the price – we assert it solemnly as a fact – of the starvation and prostitution of the workwomen. ("Mrs. Grundy" 101)

Representing the "horrible" may in fact be better for readers than leaving it out, this critic suggests, for it may serve both as a warning and as a stimulus to charity. The combination of a gendered image of the limits on representation with an equally powerfully gendered image of those (the starving and prostituted workwomen) who exist in the interdicted realm makes it plain that more than depiction of sexuality is at stake, despite the emphasis on women. The prudery and censoriousness of Mrs. Grundy, according to this mid-century voice, inhibits readers from discovering the worlds of social fiction.

Sexuality was only one of a number of subjects that drew the fire of critics attempting to keep the English novel in its proper channel. Indeed, as Richard Stang writes:

Every important novelist of the period . . . was attacked, most novelists more than once, for lowering the standards of "purity" of the English novel: Dickens and Bulwer for their treatment of crime and extramarital unions; Thackeray for his fondness in general for "unpleasant" subjects, especially the suggestion of incest in *Henry Esmond*; Mrs. Gaskell for dealing with such social questions as the plight of the unmarried mother in *Ruth*, prostitution in *Mary Barton*, and the condition of the Manchester factory hands in both *North and South* and *Mary Barton*; and George Eliot for allowing Maggie Tulliver to run off with Stephen Guest, and for her portrayal of the seduction of Hetty Sorrel. Even the Reverend Charles Kingsley, chaplain to Queen Victoria, who avowedly wrote didactic and improving novels that were always in danger of becoming tracts, had several of his novels branded as immoral. (*Theory of the Novel* 217)

As Stang's examples suggest, it is difficult to disentangle class and gender in the subjects that rouse critics' ire; clearly, representation of improper sexual behavior accounts for only some of the negative reactions of Mrs. Grundy. I show in this chapter how narrative annexes to social fictions overtly represent desire, illicit sexuality, and responses to impropriety in a diversionary fashion. The story lines arising out of annexes may at first seem permissive, liberating, or pleasingly transgressive, but their punitive sides reflect the anxieties of progressive novelists about the consequences of class mobility and the extension of the franchise.

Kathleen Tillotson points out in *Novels of the Eighteen-Forties* that contemporary reviewers describe authors of social fictions as explorers or anthropologists who venture into alien worlds that all too alarmingly exist near or within the realms familiar to middle-class readers.[5] For despite the protests of critics who dislike or disapprove of social fiction, many novelists of the Victorian period take it as their primary mission to bridge the gulf that lies between their readers and the worlds of the working poor, the exploited, and the criminal underclass. Social novels present unpleasant pictures to readers, pictures based on the authors' first-hand experiences, on parliamentary investigations, contemporary journalism, and on topical issues filled in by the novelists' imagination. Associated with the development of mid-century realism, "social fiction" is the broadest of the terms encompassing industrial novels, Condition of England novels, social problem novels, novels-with-a-purpose, and the *roman à thèse*.[6] Stimulated variously by the examples of William Godwin, Thomas Carlyle, and by religious tracts, the social novel as a genre does not espouse a consistent or fixed political position.[7]

Early practitioners include Harriet Martineau, in her *Illustrations of Political Economy* (1832–5), Mrs. Trollope, in *Michael Armstrong, The Factory Boy* (1839–40), and Charles Dickens, in *Oliver Twist* (1837). In the Hungry Forties the social problem novel becomes the vehicle of Disraeli's Tory "Young England" movement, in *Coningsby, Sybil* (1845), and *Tancred* (1847). Kingsley offers a Christian Socialist version in *Yeast, A Problem* (1848)[8] and *Alton Locke*; and Elizabeth Gaskell's *Mary Barton* and *North and South* present a more nuanced Christian consideration of the Condition of England. By most accounts, the social problem novel of the 1830s, 1840s, and early 1850s loses impetus when the Chartist moment passes, but the long process of enfranchisement initiated by the first Reform Bill and the Chartist agitation continues through the 1880s, and late Victorian novels such as Hardy's and Gissing's still grapple with social problems. While the explicitly "industrial" novel fades out after the 1850s, the Condition of England remains a topic for British novelists throughout the century and up to the present day.[9]

The attitudes towards change in social novels vary widely, though they are conventionally regarded as attempting to elicit sympathy for their subjects. Raymond Williams has influentially argued that industrial novels have a contrary effect on their readers, transforming sympathy into withdrawal,[10] and novels about working-class characters have been criticized for failing to represent their subjects accurately. Victorian critics and readers were the first to question the accuracy of social fiction, recognizing its ideological thrust, and, as often as not, registering distance from the characters and situations not through an excess of sympathetic identification, but through an understandable distaste for social fiction's characteristic lecturing and sermonizing. While W. E. Aytoun, reviewing for *Blackwood's Edinburgh Magazine*, attacks Kingsley's veracity in the way that critics often attacked Elizabeth Gaskell,[11] Tom Taylor's assessment in the first number of the *National Review* regrets that the material worked up from "blue books and direct visitings, from reports of Morning Chronicle commissioners, and intercourse with individual artisans" cannot be regarded as genuine because it was not written by a real working man.[12] Regardless of the source of the information, the *Fraser's* review of Charles Kingsley's *Alton Locke* judges that "the writer who attempts in this way to steal a march upon his readers, by insinuating grave theories in the shape of popular stories, as nauseous drugs are sometimes wrapt up in jam and administered to children, has no right to complain if his sinister dose should be cast up the moment its flavour is detected."[13] These readers react as much to the packaging of the improving "sinister dose" as to the contents of social fiction. Their assessment of the novelists' accuracy and effectiveness in getting readers to swallow the didactic pill of "grave theories" (whether they approve or disapprove of the messages embedded in the fictions), suggests that Victorians believed in the potential of fiction to influence readers. Thus, however ineffective or distorted it may appear to twentieth-century readers, Victorian social fiction does represent the novel's part in the reform movements of the period.

Rather than attempting to evaluate the effects of social fiction on social change, however, in focusing on the narrative annexes in Charles Kingsley's *Alton Locke* and Thomas Hardy's *The Mayor of Casterbridge* I explore instead evidence of mixed feelings. For while the 1850 and the 1886 novels might be seen as marking distinct stages in the development of social fiction from problem novel into mainstream realism, and reflecting real progress in the representation of lower-class characters, both Kingsley and Hardy betray in their narrative annexes anxieties about the consequences of social change. The narrative annexes in *Alton Locke* and *The Mayor of Casterbridge* figure the difficulties of imagining emergent fictional worlds in which working men and ordinary people make judgments and act on their desires. Both Hardy and Kingsley sympathise with the plight of the poor; and both novelists write biting critiques of responses to social problems. Yet both are hampered by conventionality, fear, and failures in empathy. Their narrative annexes make passageways into alternative realms where changed genres and places make residual or emergent forms that enable plot lines to develop, but the same narrative annexes undermine the progressive directions of their novels. The annex in *The Mayor of Casterbridge*, which enables the plots of changing social position to come to fixed conclusions, paradoxically relies on residual forms and customs to enforce conventional Victorian morality, while uneasily figuring emergent enfranchisement in the common people's action. In Kingsley's *Alton Locke*, the problem of a rising man's place in a society that ought to be transformed by Christian Socialism is resolved with some ferocity by the emergent evolutionary narrative of the annex.

In both novels, the narrative annex reveals the entanglement of social mobility with overt (improper) sexual behavior. In *Alton Locke*, Kingsley considers the boundary-crossing desire of the rising tailor–poet, uneasily representing his protagonist's aggressive masculinity, which is conveniently tamed by Christian conversion and death. This conclusion bespeaks the wish-fulfilling solution of the patronizing middle-class pastor, but also reminds us of Kingsley's unusual willingness (in private correspondence) to fantasize about his own sexuality.[14] While the English novel from *Pamela* (1740–1) and *Moll Flanders* (1722) represents female sexuality both as a device of social mobility and as the source of female susceptibility to male predation, male sexuality is less often figured, as it is in *Alton Locke*, in terms of a fatal or life-endangering vulnerability.[15] In Kingsley's novel, a repressive mother's crushing influence teaches her son not to eschew sexual desire, but to imagine its consequences in fatal terms. Hardy's novel represents an alternative source of social control: the lowest and most marginal characters in Casterbridge punish those who would rise from their ranks. Here the threat of repressive surveillance comes from below, as Hardy uses the punitive reaction to sexual transgression to suggest the hazards of enfranchising the lower orders. In both novels, a ferocious Grundyism emanates not from the middle class, but from below. By this displacement Kingsley and Hardy mean not to extend the circle of respectability, but to underline the negative consequences of allowing members of the lower orders to act on their desires.

These two novels describe opposite views of Victorian morality and employ their annexes in a revealing chiasmus. While Kingsley uses the annex "Dream Land" to represent vividly the desires and fears of the educated and endangered working man, Hardy's annex describes Mixen Lane, a zone of sexual transactions and the locale of an underclass, whose actions represent conventional condemnation of sexual and social transgression. Each of these social fictions sheds light on the anxiety with which Victorians regarded social mobility and the formation of character.[16] Kingsley writes at a time when the Chartist agitation (and failure) would have been fresh in his readers' minds, as would have been the knowledge that the author had supported some aspects of Chartism. In 1838, the People's Charter demanded universal manhood suffrage; secret ballots; annual parliaments; equal electoral districts; no property qualifications for Commons; and the payment of members of Parliament. This movement represented the popular radicalism (political democracy) of working men, mainly small craftsmen. In the same year, the Anti-Corn Law League and the Royal Agricultural Society were founded, events of importance to the background of Hardy's novel. In the 1880s, Hardy writes in *The Mayor of Casterbridge* of an earlier generation, which suits his elegiac evocation of a disappearing provincial culture, but he also alludes to contemporary worries about the role common people, "Dorsetshire labourers," play in community life.[17] For

Kingsley, the Chartist movement of the 1840s, and for Hardy, the conditions leading up to the repeal of the Corn Law,[18] serve as backgrounds for their rising characters and motivate their use of plots of sexual transgression, worked out in narrative annexes, to cover the novelists' ambivalence about the consequences of social mobility.

THE TAILOR–POET'S NEW CLOTHES

In Charles Kingsley's 1850 novel *Alton Locke*,[19] the working-class poet's crossing into a fantastic dream world within his fictional autobiography draws attention to the remaking and unmaking Kingsley resorts to in dispensing with his narrating protagonist. Alton's visions and revisions of his evolving self in the annex (the chapter "Dream Land") provide an opportunity to examine one version of Victorian masculine self-fashioning, set against the alternative, revolutionary refashioning of the political novel. The events in "Dream Land" have been seen as a preparation for Alton's conversion, as a prophetic depiction of human evolution, and as an exploration of Alton Locke's psyche.[20] The fashioning in the annex, however, leads to dissolution rather than to the new solution that the setting of the novel (at the time of the Chartist revolution) seems to promise. The narrative annex not only provides the bounded alternative space that Kingsley requires to fulfill Alton's narrative of vocation as a (dead) poet, but makes explicit the replacement of class with sexuality, and draws attention to Kingsley's need to make the working-class poet into a dead poet before he procreates (even in distant America).

In *Alton Locke*, the chiasmic narratives of conversion and revolution intersect and overlap with the tragic *Kunstlerroman* into which the narrating poet writes himself. The apprentice Alton Locke is preoccupied with self-making and the social forces that interfere with this project. No sooner does he ascend the stairs into the tailors' workroom, where "the combined odours of human breath and perspiration, stale beer, the sweet sickly smell of gin, and the sour and hardly less disgusting one of new cloth" (23) mingle, than he discovers the world of books. Books, particularly poetry, suggest to him a way into "a life of action and excitement" (31). Yet the book that sets the pattern for Alton's narration and for the trajectory of the tailor's self-making is a "sad history of labour, sorrow, and death" (32). In the life and works of John Bethune, cowherd and Scots poet, Alton reads "how the Highland cotter . . . educated himself – how he toiled unceasingly with his hands – how he wrote his poems in secret on dirty scraps of paper and old leaves of books – how thus he wore himself out . . . till the weak flesh would bear no more; and the noble spirit, unrecognized by the lord of the soil, returned to God who gave it" (32). Bethune's model suggests that the poet expends himself in a double labor of the hands, until expiration releases an ennobled soul, and Alton takes to heart the tragic pattern set by the cotter-poet: "I seemed to see in his history a sad presage of my own" (32). Phrenology reveals Alton's aptitude for learning to his mentor, the book-seller Sandy Mackaye, who tries to guide him away from destructive models such as Bethune. Mackaye sets the young man on the path of self-education, but, unlike the cow-herd, Alton lives in a city filled with characters such as the revolutionist Crosswaithe. Since Mackaye suggests that a poet of the people should write about what he knows, rather than coral reefs in the Pacific, he sets the boundaries of representation for Alton Locke. In order to fulfill the narrative of vocation that he borrows from Bethune, Alton (and Kingsley) breaks from what a contemporary reviewer labelled "Sandy Mackayeism," or a "Literature of Social Reference,"[21] to an alternative mode in the narrative annex.

If a strict sense of the contemporary political experience delimits Sandy Mackaye's version of Alton Locke's world, a grim representative of Mrs. Grundy – descended from the Old Dissent, and sanctioned by Evangelicalism – impels the working-class child to seek an escape route in the imaginary. Telling the story of his tailor–poet in this way complicates Kingsley's task, for he cannot allow his representative witness to avert his eyes from his immediate surroundings. Kingsley sets his novel in urban, industrial England, at the time leading up to the Chartists' uprising on 10 April 1848. Although it tells the story of a collective struggle on the part of working people, Kingsley's version of Christian Socialism requires the conversion of his skeptical protagonist and the channeling of mob violence into tightly controlled personal relations. The Chartists' attempt at revolution provides a backdrop for Alton's struggle to better himself, an effort that expresses itself in social rather than spiritual ways. He rejects the rigid sectarianism of his upbringing, escaping his dissenting mother's rules, methods, and punishments through imagination. However, the specter of the forbidding maternal figure is not evaded, but displaced into the poet's private vision of his sexual self. While success as a poet does bring greater liberty, Alton never completely escapes the Calvinist framework of his childhood. If the fittest survive and the elect are sanctified, Alton sympathizes with the reprobate, as his self-punishing dream vision emphasizes: in the annex he is crushed, devoured, and reborn to be consumed again.

The job Kingsley needs his narrating protagonist to perform requires broad experience of contemporary London, and Alton's recording consciousness bridges the modes of the social world as he collects evidence of the pernicious effects of political economy. For instance, even the communities with the most abhorrent living conditions are threatened as much by competition as by neglect:

The neighbourhood was undergoing, as it seemed, "improvements," of that peculiar metropolitan species which consists in pulling down the dwellings of the poor, and building up rich men's houses instead; and great buildings, within high temporary palings, had already eaten up half the little houses; as the great fish, and the great estates, and the great shopkeepers, eat up the little ones of their species – by the law of competition, lately discovered to be the true creator and preserver of the universe. (330–1)

Spiritual regeneration – the path towards conversion – allows for shifts from Alton's narration to the constructive criticism of an overlapping voice, a voice of social conscience. The novel accomplishes this despite its commitment to first-person narration, by suggesting from the first that Alton's selves are derived from literary sources, including those who resemble the real author. The outraged, observant Victorian, Kingsley the Muscular Christian, and Parson Lot[22] permeate Alton's discourse; Kingsley's novel is nothing if not multivocal.[23] *Alton Locke*'s many modes include a pastoral excursion; satires on undergraduate life; parodies of Emersonian sermons, revolutionary fervor, and the Old Dissent; ex-posés of inhumane working conditions in the style of Mayhew; a loving portrait of Mackaye, the Carlylean book-seller; and a painful depiction of the failure of a middle-class academic to carry through his "good intentions" regarding the educable, but hopelessly awkward, working man, who remains useful only so long as his poetry does not tell the truth about what he witnesses. Alton's escape from the tailors' workroom through the bookshop makes the mimicry of modes convincing; the tailor–poet makes himself many sets of new clothes. Alton's sardonic and world-weary tone deepens throughout the novel, as he verifies that competition inevitably works against the poor and laboring classes. His witness as a narrator and as a poet exposes the inequities he deplores, but his unusual position as a tailor–poet prevents him from ever being an actor in that world; he has risen out of his own class without becoming part of a different class. Though surrounded, he has no real place. His own survival in a world where his fellow tailor's wife and children lie dead and rat-eaten under a half-sewn coat carries a burden of guilt that drives him out of the Malthusian press into the private space of the annex, where Kingsley rewrites this competition in condensed forms.

While Alton Locke dreams, the narratives interrupted by the annex come to a standstill, for he passes into another world, a linked set of exotic places and remote times. The Christian Socialist polemic; reform of tailors' workrooms; negotiation of the Chartists' demands; the choice of the wrong or the right woman; and finding faith – all wait. The annex declares a geographical boundary between waking and dreaming, in which bedroom furniture is transformed into a Himalayan obstacle course:

A river ran from its summit; and up that river bed it seemed I was doomed to climb and climb for ever, millions and millions of miles upwards, against the rushing stream . . . Suddenly I fancied that I could pass round the foot of the mountain; and jumbling as madmen will, the sublime and the ridiculous, I sprang up to go round the foot of my bed, which was the mountain. (334–5)

Alton's narration charts the entry into the annex in a way that clearly demarcates the gap between genres, for separated by Alton's climb up and around the mountain are the genres of social realism and the place of dream vision, "Dream Land" (the chapter title). The hallucination brought on by fever transforms the bedroom into a volcanic landscape and Alton imagines himself clambering about in it. Falling to the floor, he comes to consciousness briefly, to find that he has surmounted the obstacle that bars the way into a vast wild realm of the fancy:

I recollect a doctor; and talk about brain fever and delirium. It was true. I was in a raging fever. And my fancy, long pent up and crushed by circumstances, burst out in uncontrollable wildness, and swept my other faculties with it helpless away over all heaven and earth, presenting to me, as in a vast kaleidoscope, fantastic symbols of all I had ever thought, or read, or felt.
    That fancy of the mountain returned; but I had climbed it now. (335)

In the annex, imagination takes over, freed from the constraints of circumstances, released into a fantastic travelogue. The first step of the journey takes Alton away from the real and far from London. The exotic travel narrative gives way to narratives of regeneration, continuing as Alton finds himself, freshly garbed in the clothing of a variety of creatures, in a sequence of unprecedented locations and situations, from the "lowest point of created life" (336) to early tribal humans. When the dreamer wakes, his story returns to the primary fictional world as from a detour. Yet the work of the narrative annex advances each of these plots, by making Alton "evolve" into a place in a moral world that has henceforth been inaccessible to him. It provides a structure within the novel where the community can be numbered and known; the only actors are Alton, his rival, and the woman they both love.

In the outer social world of the novel, crowds surround Alton at every stage. From the household of his boyhood, the tailor's shop, the bank of the Cam, the field in the country, to the streets where the Chartists gather to present their petition, Alton cannot escape the press of other people. Against this Malthusian backdrop, embodied particularly by the sinister slum neighborhood of Jemmy Downes, the stripped-down world of the love triangle, clothed in the shifting shapes of the dream, provides a fantastic escape, a refuge, a place where social struggle can be temporarily figured in the terms of sexual struggle.[24] After the failure of revolution on 10 April, Alton despairs of winning Lillian, the woman he loves. Having confronted his wealthy cousin George after seeing him embrace Lillian, Alton cowers like a deer under the snake's fixed eye. Alton's metaphor for his paralysis, drawn from myth and the lore of animal behavior, evades the social facts of his situation. George articulates the terms that guarantee Alton's failure: "The strong and the weak have been matched for the same prize: and what wonder, if the strong man conquers?" (327). Strength in the social world of Alton Locke comes from money, rather than bodies. Crucially, Alton has compromised his art, his body of work, at Lillian's request. He has emended the most critical, satirical sections, blunting his poetry's attack on the social order. Alton refers to the editing of his verses as "emasculation" (182). This capitulation to love results neither in wealth, nor in romantic gratification. Swept instead through revolutionary plotting and three years of imprisonment, Alton falls prey to a fever that infects the poor and finally escapes the confinement of the novel, in delirium.[25]

In contrast to the over-crowded social world, each of the dream's episodes presents a setting that is practically empty. Each location holds an Alton, a Lillian, and a George, not a swarming, struggling welter of organisms. The dream reduces competition to a triangulated form, though the familiar positioning of a desired female between two men is sometimes disguised by the costumes these players wear. The reappearance of the unattainable love-object Lillian, for whom Alton has emasculated his verses, and George, Alton's cousin and rival, ties the narrative of the dream sequence to sexual competition, and leads to the crucial recognition (for the sake of the outer *Bildungsroman*) that Eleanor is his proper mate. Significantly, Eleanor has, from the first, expounded Carlylean doctrine regarding the potential reconciliation of science with religion. The progress of Alton's dream, however, does not propose a coherent system for achieving such a goal, but jumbles science and myth into a perplexing fable of regeneration.[26] The presence of Hindu mythology and sacred locations throughout the dream sequence reinscribes evolution into religious myth, in preparation for Alton's Christian conversion; these also help to evoke the exotic locations where the work of the annex takes place.

Alton's dream enacts the struggle of the weak against natural forces. Being weak, he fails repeatedly, dying over and over. Because the dream starts again and again, however, the dreamer can survive each phase of evolution by being born into the next in a new form. The implication that a soul can make a progress from form to form shows Kingsley's struggle to reconcile the emergent structure of Darwinism with Christianity, reversing the more typical pattern in which religion loses the contest. Although the narrative does postpone the fulfillment of death to the end and the novel reprehends suicide as the ultimate failure, the annex reenacts death obsessively, in tandem with its variations on the outcomes of sexual competition. The dreams help Alton Locke realize his internalized ideal, when the plots of the actual world have failed him. It becomes clear as the vision progresses that Alton has known all along what to make of himself – a dead poet.[27]

Although he begins as a madrepore, a multiplying "crowd of innumerable polypi" (336), in fact, Alton moves from creature to creature in the sequence by means of an individuality that is distinct because it is so easily and so repetitiously exterminated. In the darkness, Alton's regeneration occurs in tenacious narratives of embodiment. Alton does not dream his dream during the three-year imprisonment that precedes his infection with fever, for Kingsley repudiates the Calvinist vision, in which Christian proves to be the fittest in Bunyan's competitive journey towards salvation and no story-time is wasted on the many characters who fall to Hell along the way. The creatures Alton Locke inhabits are crushed, squelched, gobbled up, and tossed aside – always losing the contest of evolution – yet regeneration proves to be as certain in his dream as the winnowing of the damned from the elect is in Bunyan's. Alton's consciousness locates itself both in the individual creatures he becomes and in the promise of evolution to a next stage.

The rhythmic, paratactic language of the dream narration differs markedly from the adopted language of a self-conscious working-class poet. Events are reported rather than analyzed in the dream narration, yet these events underline Alton's position in the social world he has left behind:

And I was a remora, weak and helpless, till I could attach myself to some living thing; and then I had the power to stop the largest ship. And Lillian was a flying fish, and skimmed over the crests of the waves on gauzy wings. And my cousin was a huge shark, rushing after her, greedy and open-mouthed; and I saw her danger, and clung to him, and held him back; and just as I had stopped him, she turned and swam back into his open jaws. (337)

After a sequence of dream episodes in which "Alton" suffers repeated exterminations, the dreamer is embodied as a mylodon, a gigantic (extinct) form of sloth. This incarnation marks a new phase in the evolutionary sequence, for the animal has enough strength to revenge himself on threatening figures; up until this point they overpower the dreamer. In this episode, Alton's evolving masculinity and the violence of the mylodon unmistakably overlap:[28]

intense and new was the animal delight, to plant my hinder claws at some tree foot into the black rotting vegetable-mound which steamed rich gases up wherever it was pierced, and clasp my huge arms round the stem of some palm or tree-fern; and then slowly bring my enormous weight and muscle to bear upon it, till the stem bent like a withe, and the laced bark cracked, and the fibres groaned and shrieked, and the roots sprang up out of the soil; and then, with a slow circular wrench, the whole tree was twisted bodily out of the ground, and the maddening tension of my muscles suddenly relaxed, and I sank sleepily down upon the turf, to browse upon the crisp tart foliage, and fall asleep in the glare of sunshine which streamed through the new gap in the green forest roof. (338)

The mylodon's rapacious activity creates a path through the forest, "marked, like that of a tornado, by snapped and prostrate stems and withering branches" (339). Desire to destroy occludes all other longings. The mylodon's action suggests violence against phallic forms, but the process of bringing down a tree also exposes "the black rotting vegetable-mound which steamed rich gases up wherever it was pierced" (338), in a telling expression of sexual revulsion. The dreamer pauses to reflect, in a moment calling up the Victorian audience, "Had I been a few degrees more human, I might have expected a retribution for my sin" (339). The mylodon does not repent, however; he desires the unattainable, a tall tree that rises above a plain of thistles: "A strange longing seized me to go and tear it down" (339). When the mylodon crawls to the foot of the tree, he sees the evidence, in the form of bleaching skeletons, that predatory winged ants protect the gold buried at the base of the tree. The fruit of the tree, however, most interests the dreamer: "wonder of wonders! from among the branches hung great sea-green lilies, and nestled in the heart of each of them, the bust of a beautiful girl. Their white bosoms and shoulders gleamed rosy-white against the emerald petals, like conch-shells half-hidden among sea-weeds, while their delicate waists melted mysteriously into the central sanctuary of the flower" (339–40). These disembodied female faces and torsos lack full bodies, specifically legs, feet, and genitalia. The mylodon exposes and creates gaps in the earth and in the foliage each time he tears down a tree; access to these abbreviated female forms depends upon the destruction and uprooting of the tree. When the sloth attempts to bring this tree down, an American backwoodsman – cousin George – interrupts him, stares down the flying ants, unearths the gold, fells the tree, and escapes unscathed. The falling tree strikes the self-sacrificing, self-punishing mylodon "full across the loins" (341), breaking his back-bone and pinning him to the ground. The flower-fairies shriek as they fall from their lilies and shrink from human size. In this episode, rape takes the form of dismembering and crushing, as well as of abduction. One of the dying fairies is Lillian; in the sloth's "last death-shiver [he] saw [George] coolly pick up the little beautiful figure, which looked like a fragment of some exquisite cameo, and deliberately put it away in his cigar-case" (341). Because the tension in this narrative derives its energy from the tearing down of trees and the revenge of the tree on the mylodon, the mylodon's appetite and power is evidently mismatched with his longing for a lover in human form. Here, as elsewhere in the annex, containment and death are the fruits of consummation; the deaths in the dream vision can be understood as practice for the real world, as exorcisms of Alton's own violent and frightening masculinity.

The narrative annex permits sexual struggle – against both a male competitor for the female, and the subject's own violent masculinity – to occupy the consciousness of the first-person narrator and the space of the page. At the same time, it lets Alton Locke practice dying, so that his death in the "real" world of the novel can be the dignified expiration of a poet: "If I could but write in such a metre one true people's song, that should embody all my sorrow, indignation, hope – fitting last words for a poet of a people – for they will be my last words – " (388). The narrative annex disappears without a trace when its work is done. In the following chapter Eleanor completes the work of conversion that has been set in motion by the dream. Cured, converted, enriched by an inheritance from Sandy Mackaye, and paired with the right Christian woman, Alton Locke becomes the author of the "autobiography" we read. He has eradicated the "self-indulgent habit" (80) of poetry, though his lonely death on shipboard verifies Alton Locke's vocation by fulfilling the pattern set by the cowherd–poet's life.

Kingsley uses the dream vision to depict the dark night of the soul before conversion; but to accept Alton's Christian rebirth without asking how the dream-sequence makes this un-fashioning possible is to move too quickly away from his visions. The text hurries the reader away from the dream to a Christian application to the political struggle: "'Freedom, Equality, and Brotherhood are here . . . Not from without, from Charters and Republics, but from within, from the Spirit working in each'" (386). Yet in the outer social world of the novel, victims will not be brought back from the dead; dead poets write no more poems. Alton's cure requires forgetting the struggle he has undergone to become the sexless, sacrificial victim of the novel's resolution. Although Kingsley does his best to discredit revolutionary physical force, his protagonist must work through his masculine sexual aggression in order to be fit for a brotherhood of man that he does not live to join. Evolutionary forces, or a set of lessons in dying, prepare Alton for his *dénouement*. Alton Locke's struggle to make himself a place in an inaccessible version of that imagined middle-class world leads to the annex's incorporation of emergent materials, the evolutionary sequence, into a residual form, dream vision, rewriting the progress of a soul in Darwinian terms.[29] When we see the tailor-poet in his new clothes, he has made himself a cadaver.

That a Victorian working man could be a poet, Kingsley knew from the example of Thomas Cooper,[30] but Kingsley's contemporaries regarded Alton Locke's vocation as improbable at best. In *Fraser's* the reviewer remarks facetiously that

It was an ingenious escape for much of the hot-brained enthusiasm of the political agitator to make him also a poet. The two vocations fall in well together; and afford an excuse . . . for tolerating a great deal of wild invective against established institutions, and for believing, at the same time, that under such circumstances it is not likely to be attended with much mischief. The union of poetry and Chartism is quite natural. Chartism is a sort of poetry in itself, dealing largely in those visions of human perfectibility and longings after an impossible Elysium which have afforded such innocent delights to the poets from time immemorial.[31]

The explicitly hostile review in *Blackwood's Edinburgh Magazine* opens with a tale of a Dalkeith tailor, Mansie Wauch, whose literary career had not prevented him from doing excellent work. His son Benjamin, however, is both a tailor and a poet, to the dismay of his patrons. The reviewer pronounces that "we fear it is a lamentable fact that the two trades are irreconcilable. The perpetrator of distichs is usually a bungler at cross-stitch: and there is no analogy between the measurement of trousers and the measure of a Spenserian stanza" (Aytoun, "Alton Locke" 592).[32] That a tailor, even a tailor–poet, could encounter and fall in love with a woman of a higher station is also ridiculed, but Alton Locke's autodidacticism is "the leading fault of the book" (596). Had Defoe written the story, the reviewer adds, it would have been realistic, and "we should have had no idealism, at least of the transcendental kind; and no dreams, decidedly of a tawdry and uninterpretable description" (596). This remark registers at once the disturbing mixture of genres, the unrealistic social and political aspirations of Kingsley's protagonist, and the affronting sexuality of the narrative annex's dream vision. The idealism of which this reviewer complains emanates from the represented consciousness of a character who ought to be represented realistically, that is, from the outside and according to type. In a later review, W. E. Aytoun emphasizes in hindsight the impropriety of representing sexual attraction across classes: "Richardson's Pamela, which was at one time to be found in the drawer of every kitchen-dresser, because it advocated the propriety of gentlemen marrying their maid-servants, was really mild and rational in comparison with *Alton Locke*."[33]

Critics both in Kingsley's time and afterwards have either struggled to come to terms with the dream sequence, or dismissed it. The *Blackwood's* reviewer, for instance, comments that the dreams are "ambitiously written, but without either myth or meaning, so far as we can discover" (Aytoun, "Alton Locke" 608). Many twentieth-century critics have gone no further, or have simply omitted mention of the dream sequence, even in synopses of the novel. Despite this response, Kingsley chose to use this narrative annex deliberately. By claiming the ground of the irrational in the annex, Kingsley makes space for an alternative mode whose very excesses and improprieties serve the needs of the outer plot. He carefully charts Alton's descent into delirium, describing with great care the remote places to which the vision transports his protagonist. Using the contrasting setting and genre of the narrative annex, Kingsley frames its phantasmata with insulating signs of difference. Yet these measures were not sufficient, for according to his biographers, even Kingsley's friends tried to talk him out of including the chapter.[34] In a letter to Robert Ludlow, editor of the the *Christian Socialist*, Kingsley defends the annex: "How do you know that the book from that point was not intended to take a mythic and prophetic form, that those dreams come in for the very purpose of taking the story off the ground of the actual into the deeper and wider one of the ideal, and that they actually do what they were intended to do?"[35] Kingsley's remarks make explicit the connection between a shift in mode and place, and an opening of possibilities for representation. The narrative annex in this flawed novel takes "the story off the ground of the actual" in order to represent with surprising frankness the sexual imaginings of a character escaping from a fictional world governed by rigid class distinctions, brutal economic limitations, dangerous work and living conditions, and repressive Grundyism. The narrative annex enables us to see both Kingsley's attempt to make a space for his remarkable tailor–poet's desires, and his failure to imagine a place, even in America, where Alton Locke could continue his career and have a family *on* "the ground of the actual."

LUCETTA'S LETTERS AND THE "LANE OF NOTORIETY"

Social fiction includes novels, usually set in London or the northern factory towns, investigating, exposing to view, and (sometimes) proposing solutions to social problems arising out of the reorganization of industrialization. Hardy's tragic meditation in *The Mayor of Casterbridge* on public roles and personal relationships in a changing social world adds a view of the south of England, where, as Gaskell suggests in *North and South*, folk ways contribute to social control. As in Kingsley's earlier novel, the narrative annex in this social fiction unleashes violent force to resolve the plot. Though Hardy's annex contains a higher density of population placed closer to home than Kingsley's radically displaced and condensed dream vision, Hardy, like Kingsley, imagines the narrative annex as the locus of a lethal solution to complication. Reading the secret packet of letters entrusted to Jopp by Henchard, the people in Mixen Lane plan the skimmington ride that eliminates Lucetta, frees Farfrae, and brings down Henchard. Though Thomas Hardy's contest with a censoring Grundyism, and his sympathetic depiction of members of the laboring class are axiomatic, in the annex to *The Mayor of Casterbridge* he uses a separate zone and a residual custom (the skimmington) to make his laborers and low-lifes lawlessly enforce conventional morality. The relationship between folk ways and social control suggest Hardy's uneasiness with the enfranchisement he supported, and reminds us of the historical context of the novel's composition.

Hardy writes in his preface to the Wessex Edition, "The incidents narrated arise mainly out of three events . . . in the real history of the town called Casterbridge and the neighboring country. They were the sale of a wife by her husband, the uncertain harvests which immediately preceded the repeal of the Corn Laws, and the visit of a Royal personage to the aforesaid part of England" (preface, Wessex Edition, vii). Hardy's enumeration of these three historical events has occluded his interest in the extension of the franchise in the period when he researched and wrote both the novel and his essay "The Dorsetshire Labourer," published in *Longman's Magazine* (July 1883).[36] Although the First Reform Bill (of 1832) coincides with the background of the novel, the contemporary Reform Bill of 1884 lies behind the novel's composition. In 1917, Hardy wrote to the current proprietor of the *Dorset County Chronicle*, returning issues of that local paper from the 1830s, which he had recently discovered in a cupboard. Hardy writes, "They must have been borrowed I think from a former editor for reference to something or other connected with the first Reform Bill."[37] Purdy and Millgate, the editors of Hardy's correspondence, note that from 1883 to 1885, while composing *The Mayor of Casterbridge*, Thomas Hardy combed through back issues of the *Dorset County Chronicle* from January 1826 towards the time of the passage of the First Reform Bill (*Collected Letters* v. 210n).

While thinking about the First Reform Bill and the background of his novel, Hardy made a contribution to the debate about the enfranchisement of agricultural laborers, in his essay "The Dorsetshire Labourer." Michael Millgate interprets Hardy's sending offprints to John Morley and Gladstone as a sign that he supported the Liberals' effort to enfranchise agricultural workers (Millgate, *Thomas Hardy* 236). Hardy's notebooks reveal, in the occasional fretful musing, the author's ambivalence about the consequence of "diffused political privileges," for which few nations are fit: "Our country is probably destined to become much more democratic," Hardy writes, wondering "who or what will give a high tone to the nation then?"[38] Although fundamentally sympathetic to its subjects, "The Dorsetshire Labourer" also reflects Hardy's anxiety about the movement of rural workers into the towns, an uneasiness vividly rewritten by the narrative annex to *The Mayor of Casterbridge*. In the essay Hardy writes that a natural tendency to evil, which develops to unlawful action when excited by contact with others like minded, would often have remained latent amid the isolated experiences of a village life. The cause of morality cannot be secured by compelling a population hitherto evenly distributed over the country to concentrate in a few towns, with the inevitable results of overcrowding and want of regular employment. ("Dorsetshire Labourer" 269)

In the narrative annex, Hardy depicts just such an occasion, where the concentration of idle and irregularly employed people (displaced from the surrounding country to inside the borders of the town) act illegally and violently. Yet rather than lingering on the folk's "natural tendency to evil," Hardy uses the concentrating force of the narrative annex ironically, to represent the folk's disapproval of illicit sexual behavior. As in Kingsley's *Alton Locke*, the narrative annex's overt concern with sexuality coincides with a meditation on social class. Punishment for sexual transgression simultaneously brings down those who threaten to rise above their station. The entrance to Peter's Finger, the place where the privacy of Lucetta's letters is violated, relates metonymically to female sexuality – particularly to the bodies of prostitutes. Yet the narrative annex from which the punishing mob flows to act out the residual custom of the skimmington also represents Hardy's uneasiness of 1883: what will happen when these concentrated laborers express their desires lawfully, by voting? In the public house entered through a slit (in which a collection of papers leads to the lawless exercise of censure by a judgmental mob who hold others to standards they do not meet themselves), I read a metaphor of the ballot box.

Hardy's annex enables him to worry covertly about the challenges of enfranchisement, but it also serves the needs of his complicated, generically mixed plot. In a novel that has been discussed from the first as tragedy, character study, and as a realistic[39] representation of places, practices, and "peasants,"[40] genre complicates the way that critics have regarded the novel's most striking episodes. Written for weekly serial publication[41] in the *Graphic*, the novel elicited the following comment from Hardy in his autobiographical *The Life of Thomas Hardy*:

The Mayor of Casterbridge was issued complete about the end of May [1886]. It was a story which Hardy fancied he had damaged more recklessly as an artistic whole, in the interest of the newspaper in which it appeared serially, than perhaps any other of his novels, his aiming to get an incident into almost every week's part causing him in his own judgment to add events to the narrative somewhat too freely. However, as at this time he called his novel-writing "mere journeywork" he cared little about it as art, though it must be said in favour of the plot, as he admitted later, that it was quite coherent and organic, in spite of its complications.[42]

The former part of this judgment has been attended to more than the latter, and has certainly contributed to the focus on Henchard's character as a unifying and organizing feature of the narrative.[43] I take the second part of the statement, regarding the coherence of the complicated plot as equally important. The success of the plot requires attention to Farfrae, Lucetta, Susan Newson, the sailor Newson, and Elizabeth-Jane, as well as to Henchard. When Hardy writes that "tragedy exhibits a state of things in the life of an individual which unavoidably causes some natural aim or desire of his to end in the catastrophe when carried out,"[44] he describes Henchard's individual trajectory, but does not limit the novel's plot to that single thread. The narrative annex provides Hardy with an alternative place and mode, the ritual drama of social excommunication, that makes possible the conclusions to *all* its stories, for Hardy's narrator uses a diverse set of focalizing characters, five of whom (Lucetta, Henchard, Newson, Farfrae, Elizabeth-Jane) are irrevocably affected by the work of the annex. Like *Alton Locke*, *The Mayor of Casterbridge* depicts the unmaking of a character – in this case, the first "Mayor," Henchard.[45] Unlike *Alton Locke*, *The Mayor of Casterbridge*'s narrative annex reinscribes the separate individual's story back into a knowable and knowing social world.

The narrative annex in the novel maps a marginal social space, the ancient environs known as Mixen Lane, within the town of Casterbridge. The work of the annex depends on Mixen Lane's hiddenness, and its accessibility; on its antiquity, and its presence in contemporary Casterbridge; on its forbidding borders, and their permeability; as well as on its capacity to hold and discharge characters into the outer plot. The events narrated in chapter 36 take place in a liminal location (Peter's Finger in Mixen Lane), and the small-scale social drama enacted there permits a critical, corrective solution to be forced onto the problems that have been generated in the main world of the novel – the public zones of Casterbridge, especially those arenas associated with spectacles of transaction.[46] Mixen Lane functions as the most porous boundary of the otherwise well-regulated town of Casterbridge. It provides a space where, paradoxically, sexual favors can be purchased and communal punishments for sexual transgressors can be planned. This combination of "turning a blind eye" and "pointing the finger" coexists in the annex, particularly in the carefully hidden public house,

Peter's Finger.[47] If, as Hardy's narrator comments, "the inn called Peter's Finger was the church of Mixen Lane," we enter more than an alternative social center when we follow Jopp and Mother Cuxsom as they enter. The ritual of excommunication which takes place in Peter's Finger shifts generic and social registers so people brought "to a common level" (*Mayor* 331), that is, to the lowest level, speak in a plural, choral voice. Here prostitutes and poachers invade Lucetta's privacy and choose the form of her punishment. This transgression of privacy is all the more remarkable because, other than letters, there are so few truly private places or things in the novel. (Even the originary crime of the plot, the wife-sale, takes place in full view of an almost entirely complicitous audience.) The old furmity woman in whose tent the wife-sale takes place shows up time and again in the novel to remind us of the public nature of that act and of the long memory of the witness, and this economy in the appearance and reappearance of characters gives the novel its texture of coincidence and inevitability.

The location of the action and the movements of characters through a sequence of different locales link placement and possibility in all of Hardy's novels. Although *The Life and Death of the Mayor of Casterbridge: A Story of a Man of Character* has been seen as primarily a character study,[48] Hardy's settings can take on agency more powerful and complicated even than individual characters. Few novelists so successfully convince readers that they have entered a fictional territory, a world with idiosyncratic places, landscapes, and geographical features (even as Hardy compromises the sense of actuality he evokes by employing intricate plots and coincidences). *The Mayor of Casterbridge* differs from *Jude the Obscure* and *Tess of the D'Urbervilles* in that the plot remains fixed on the stage of Casterbridge, while characters appear, disappear, and reappear within its boundaries. In *The Mayor of Casterbridge*, Hardy does not avail himself of the advantages of episodic shifts in setting. He compresses all of the symbolic and narrative functions of changed place and shifted genre into a single narrative annex.

One of the most important surprises of the novel comes when the reader realizes that Casterbridge has an area within it, Mixen Lane, where behavior impossible in any other public space not only occurs, but alters the outcome of the novel. Because Hardy demarcates the annex from the main world of the text so explicitly, the alternative place Mixen Lane heightens the significance of spaces in a fictional world already rigorously organized by locations. Geographically isolated from the rest of Casterbridge, and yet very much a part of it, the annex unleashes events that bring the linked plots of Henchard, Lucetta, Farfrae, Elizabeth and Newson to their various ends. In a novel in which characters repeatedly start over – with new vows, names, husbands, fathers, lovers, clothing, houses, and jobs – the annex allows the work of ending to begin. The archaic practices of an ancient environ erupt out of the annex to put an end to the proliferating repetitions of the middle, which have been set in motion by a striking double beginning.

The opening sequence of the novel, in which Newson purchases Susan from her husband Henchard, establishes the sale of a wife in a public marketplace as possible, though outrageous.[49] This beginning contaminates every transaction between men that follows. Though the novel in fact focuses on a series of transactions between the two Mayors of Casterbridge, Henchard and Farfrae, business transactions at the lowest end of the social scale instigate and move the plot along. Business forms the basis of political power and prestige in the world of *The Mayor of Casterbridge*, and the witnesses to and participants in business transactions believe in their efficacy and binding nature – only when Susan Newson ceases to believe in the legality of her union with her buyer does the sailor absent himself from her life and the story. Newson's reentry into the novel (through the narrative annex) provides Elizabeth-Jane with a father she can believe in – a father who can give her away – and it also underlines the presence of an illicit economy and zone of commerce within the boundaries of Casterbridge.

The fundamental problems posed by *The Mayor of Casterbridge* operate through a structure of analogy that asks its readers to see that the buying, selling, and decision-making of the lowest social stratum not only resemble, but coexist with and intervene in, the commerce, marriage, and civic behavior of the prosperous and respectable classes. So, for instance, although Hardy presents the traffic in women as an archaic survival practiced outside of Casterbridge in country fairs, and as a sinful practice that decent people abhor, the more socially acceptable forms of that traffic in fact structure the novel.[50] When Henchard remarries his wife Susan he has already bought her back for the exact amount for which he sold her: "He said nothing about the enclosure of five guineas. The amount was significant; it may tacitly have said to her that he bought her back again."[51] (The marriage realigns the characters into a family, although a false one, for Elizabeth-Jane is not in fact Henchard's daughter.) Hardy deepens the novel's critique of marriage by pointing out its symmetry with commercial exchange, anticipating Lévi-Strauss' description of matrimony as the most powerful form of exchange enforcing exogamy: "For the woman herself is nothing other than . . . the supreme gift among those that can only be obtained in the form of reciprocal gifts."[52] Although men literally sell and buy Susan Newson, her daughter Elizabeth-Jane serves as a model gift-object, transacted from man to man according to the rules of exogamy – in Gayle Rubin's terms, "a conduit of a relationship rather than a partner to it."[53] Hardy devotes part of the work of the annex to solving his overlapping puzzles of triangulation, by reintroducing the one character who has the right to give Elizabeth-Jane away to Farfrae.

To this end, the sailor Newson, presumed drowned, reappears through Mixen Lane, where the marginal space of the narrative annex permits the "dead" husband and father to be reintegrated into the living world.[54] Newson's passage from the dark field over the plank bridge, into the public house, where he participates in the planning of the skimmington, and out of Mixen Lane into Casterbridge itself emphasizes the annex's liminality. Progressing from "some one from the other side," to "the man in the moor," to "no enemy," Newson passes the porous border:

"Ahoy – is this the way to Casterbridge?" said some one from the other side.
"Not in particular," said Charl. "There's a river afore 'ee."
"I don't care – here's for through it!" said the man in the moor. "I've had enough for travelling today."
"Stop a minute, then," said Charl, finding that the man was no enemy. "Joe, bring the plank and lantern; here's somebody that's lost his way. You should have kept along the turnpike road, friend, and not have strook across here."
(333)

The very unsuitability of the entry-way, even from the point of view of those who open it, emphasizes the significance of Newson's reappearance and underlines the spatiality of Hardy's plotting. Merely a ghost, or a memory, before he shouts "Ahoy," Newson joins the furmity woman in embodying the return of the repressed. The annex provides the opportunity for Newson to take on flesh, as it were, and social connections. By the time he leaves Mixen Lane, Newson is a ghost no more; by purchasing a drink, he becomes a customer, resuming his most important role for the novel's plot. Further, he contributes a sovereign to the "performance," the skimmington ride planned by the people in Peter's Finger. Before he even makes his first attempt to find his daughter, he has linked himself with coins to the punishment that will make it possible for him to give Elizabeth-Jane away to Farfrae.

Symmetrically, the annex also eliminates a woman, Lucetta, who has attempted to give herself, sequentially, to two different men. Although Henchard, too, has relationships with two different women, his thwarted desire for Farfrae and the transformation of that love into hatred sets him up for his fall. Eliminating Lucetta, degrading and humiliating Henchard, and freeing Farfrae, the narrative annex sets up a "right" triangle that allows Elizabeth-Jane to be transacted from father to husband. The structures of these transactions call attention to the structures that bind the characters in social places, and connect social places to literal locations.

Modeled on Dorchester, Hardy's Casterbridge is remarkable for the clarity of its layout, especially for the strict border between town and country: "Casterbridge, as has been hinted, was a place deposited in the block upon a corn-field. There was no suburb in the modern sense, or transitional intermixture of town and down. It stood, with regard to the wide fertile land adjoining, clean-cut and distinct, like a chessboard on a green table-cloth" (162). The chessboard provides a particularly apt metaphor for the setting of the novel, for Hardy makes Casterbridge a remarkably public, exposed ground for action. Here observers mark every actor's every move. There is no need to imagine, as Dickens does, the removal of the rooftops in order to see into the private lives of individuals,[55] for people in Casterbridge transact their business in full view of the public.[56] Hardy makes the marketplace in the middle of the town the most important arena, where the rise of Farfrae and the decline of Henchard play out in front of and among the people whose personal and pragmatic estimations of worth make that chiasmic action possible.

This is not to imply that all the action, or even all the important action in the novel takes place outdoors, but to emphasize the importance of place in mapping social relations. Casterbridge's variety of public spaces mark characters' rises and falls in status and fortune. Farfrae not only takes over Henchard's positions as most prominent corn broker and Mayor, but he also takes the bankrupt's business place and house. Farfrae literally makes a place for himself early in the novel, when the rival entertainment Henchard plans fails because Farfrae has made one of the walks marking the border of the town into an indoor place where the fun can go on in a downpour, transforming with rickcloths in the trees the familiar walk into an outdoor ballroom. Farfrae's tent includes: everyone may come, just as everyone in Casterbridge may watch and judge the actions of their fellow citizens. However, far from inviting an eruption of carnivalesque celebration, both entertainments arise at the prompting of national authority: "Thus their lives rolled on till a day of public rejoicing was suggested to the country at large in celebration of a national event that had recently taken place" (173).

Like the tented celebration, the Ring (the second "alternate" space built into the primary world of Casterbridge) has its roots in an official past. The Roman amphitheatre has become the site for "secret" meetings, for its shape enables these encounters, technically, to take place in public:

Melancholy, impressive, lonely, yet accessible from every part of the town, the historic circle was the frequent spot for appointments of a furtive kind. Intrigues were arranged there; tentative meetings were there experimented after divisions and feuds ... pugilistic encounters almost to the death had come off down to recent dates in that secluded arena, entirely invisible to the outside world save by climbing to the top of the enclosure, which few townspeople in the daily round of their lives ever took the trouble to do. (141)

The very fact of potential visibility virtually guarantees invisibility. To avoid surveillance inside a structure that was built for the mass observation of spectacles foretells the story of the function of Mixen Lane; originally a place where crowds come together to watch entertainments, the social space has become one devoted to concealment.[57] Both the Ring and Mixen Lane are associated, in their remote pasts, with contrasting modes of entertainment, one arising from authority and the other arising from peoples' covert activities, and that association is maintained in the present time of the novel. The narrator makes it clear that the association of blood sports and executions makes the Ring too sinister a place for liaisons of happy lovers. In fact, happy love affairs and marriages have hardly a place at all in Casterbridge: the union between Susan and her "husband" Newson and Henchard's affair with Lucetta take place far away from Casterbridge and its observing inhabitants.

Long before any character enters into the place known as Mixen Lane, Hardy establishes Lucetta's bold entrance into the social world of *The Mayor of Casterbridge* in relation to it. Lucetta's apartment overlooks the central marketplace; she and Elizabeth-Jane spend hours scanning the crowd from their vantage point in the windows. High-Place Hall backs on "one of the little-used alleys of the town," Mixen Lane (210). Although the mansion (like Lucetta) puts up a fairly convincing front of respectability, Elizabeth-Jane discovers behind it the border between a world subject to surveillance and the concealed vice of Mixen Lane: "By the alley it had been possible to come unseen from all sorts of quarters in the town – the old play-house, the old bull-stake, the old cock-pit, the pool wherein nameless infants had been used to disappear" (212). This sequence draws attention to locations where people could watch performances, gamble at bloodsports, and practice infanticide without fear of censure.[58] Of course, the play-house, bull-stake, and cock-pit hold crowds who gather to watch the spectacle, crowds who have come from all parts of town. The disappearance of "nameless infants" taints the recreations in the sequence, marking Mixen Lane as a location where secrecy covers activities that would be considered sordid in the outer part of Casterbridge. In rewriting Dorchester's Mill Street, Fordington, and Colleton Row into Casterbridge's Mixen Lane, Hardy adopts their unsavory historical reputations. Historian David Underdown connects Hardy's Mixen Lane with its ill-governed counterparts, where poaching, underage drinking, and adulterous trysting were recorded in the seventeenth century.[59] In the novel, what has been a zone of carnivalesque celebration becomes a secret arena for activity that would be judged criminal were it to be drawn out into the open. Paradoxically, it is also the only place where the lowest characters, people who have fallen out of the legitimate commercial economy of Casterbridge, can exercise power as moral arbiters. Even the decrepit old furmity woman has a place in the marketplaces and courts of Casterbridge, but the people who inhabit Mixen Lane carry on commerce that official Casterbridge would not recognize. The events in Mixen Lane eventually permit a comic outcome to the novel's love plot (Farfrae will marry Elizabeth-Jane), but the resolution is achieved by the exposure and punishment of illicit sexual behavior by a mob that pours out of the annex, exercising its vengeful disapproval of Lucetta in a most old-fashioned manner.

But before Hardy allows this force to erupt out of the narrative annex, he establishes a boundary between respectable Casterbridge and disorderly Mixen Lane. The door between the mansion and the alley marks the border with a mask that forms the keystone of its archway: "Originally the mask had exhibited a comic leer, as could still be discerned; but generations of Casterbridge boys had thrown stones at the mask, aiming at its open mouth; and the blows thereon had chipped off the lips and jaws as if they had been eaten away by disease" (211–12). This gruesome syphilitic sentinel reiterates the connection of sexuality (the leer; disease), bloodsports (stoning), and acting (the comic mask) in the zone it guards. The mask indicates Mixen Lane's former use as a place where festive laughter governed action. It has become a grotesque, however, and its decay symbolises the decadence of Mixen Lane's social function. Although no character passes the mask to enter into Mixen Lane until late in the novel, the alley and its environs are established as a place that once fulfilled a role in providing certain "conveniences" to an otherwise well-regulated town. The narrator coyly reveals that this border region functions as a haven for the disreputable and down-and-out folk of Casterbridge, to provide a secret means of egress for poachers and thieves, and certain other services.

An attentive observer such as the narrator might discern the signs of these activities:

One was an intermittent rumbling from the back premises of the inn half-way up; this meant a skittle alley. Another was the extensive prevalence of whistling in the various domiciles – a piped note of some kind coming from nearly every open door. Another was the frequency of white aprons over dingy gowns among the women around the doorways. A white apron is a suspicious vestment in situations where spotlessness is difficult; moreover, the industry and cleanliness which the white apron expressed were belied by the postures and gaits of the women who wore it. (329)

The white aprons advertise the practice of prostitution. The adoption of a sign of domestic, housewifely cleanliness, rather than the trade the women practice, draws suspicion. In "The Dorsetshire Labourer," Hardy satirizes the philanthropic ladies who are misled by the color of a cottage's interior and its inhabitants' dress:

A cottage in which the walls, the furniture, and the dress of the inmates reflect the brighter rays of the solar spectrum is read by these amiable visitors as a cleanly, happy home while one whose prevailing hue happens to be dingy russet, or a quaint old leather tint, or any of the numerous varieties of mud colour is thought necessarily the abode of filth and Giant Despair. ("Dorsetshire Labourer" 255)

Yet the slovenly woman's manipulation of the sign of cleanliness antici-pates the false advertising of the prostitutes of Mixen Lane. Hardy quotes one such housewife:

"I always kip a white apron behind the door to slip on when the gentlefolk knock, for if so be they see a white apron they think ye be clane," said an honest woman one day, whose bedroom floors could have been scraped with as much advantage as a pigeon-loft, but who, by a judicious use of high lights, shone as a pattern of neatness in her patrons' eyes. ("Dorsetshire Labourer" 255)

In the annex, however, signs that normally mean "spotlessness" and "industry" have connotations that only "postures" and "gaits" can express. The novel presents prostitution as a residual form, an economic practice that adopts and taints the sign of domestic industry. Sequestered in the annex like nuns in a convent, the prostitutes' white "vestments" mark them as women who have found a marginal location within an economy that has no room for them otherwise.

In the outer world of Casterbridge, Lucetta chooses a spring outfit of red that marks her less ambiguously as one of their kind. Prophetically, Lucetta remarks on the importance of the choice of clothing: "'You are that person' (pointing to one of the arrangements), 'or you are that totally different person' (pointing to the other), 'for the whole of the coming spring: and one of the two, you don't know which, may turn out to be very objectionable.'" With an uncharacteristic and inadvertent truthfulness Lucetta chooses to "be the cherry-coloured person at all hazards" (*Mayor* 238). The cherry-colored outfit is a much more expensive way of calling attention to her person than the white aprons of the prostitutes, and the new clothes are intended to remind her observers that she is a wealthy lady, but the force of the reaction against Lucetta can be explained, in part, by her self-advertisement. Ultimately, the spectacle of the skimmity presents an unmistakable effigy of the "lady" Lucetta, to convey her disgrace.

Hardy complicates the narrative annex's connection with female sexuality in several important ways. The shape of the entrance to the inn, Peter's Finger (which serves as the social center of Mixen Lane), emphasizes the connections between that locale, commerce, and illicit sexuality: "at the corner of the public house was an alley, a mere slit, dividing it from the next building. Half-way up the alley was a narrow door shiny and paintless from the rub of infinite hands and shoulders. This was the actual entrance to the inn" (330). Here is an entrance, buffed to a shine through use, that suggests the secret that everyone knows, the customary estre or path through the neighborhood. It also serves as a second synecdoche of the white-aproned women. The slit into which Jopp edges leads to a barroom where the characters who have individually served minor choral functions in the novel gather together: ex-poachers and ex-gamekeepers, Nance Mockridge and Mother Cuxsom, the ubiquitous furmity woman, and the other regulars of Peter's Finger encourage Jopp to read the letters he possesses. Their voices have a profound effect on the community and on the plot when they make their judgment in the annex. Out of the zone marked by a corrupted mask of comedy, Hardy musters the force required to bring his tragedy to its climax and catastrophe.

Though Hardy's handling of tragedy in *The Mayor of Casterbridge* relies on scenes that could be blocked for stage performance, his plotting and character study requires the representation of interiority. Characteristically, he makes plot devices of the vehicles of characters' private expression. The public nature of domestic life in Casterbridge makes it difficult for characters to speak confidentially with one another, especially with those of the opposite sex. The one space that the novel provides for lovers, or anyone else, to make contact with any privacy at all is the "space" of the letter.[60] No fewer than sixteen notes or letters crisscross the novel. Though Hardy invariably reveals their contents to the reader, their privacy is respected within the fiction. Even when the sender remains anonymous, as Susan does when she brings Elizabeth-Jane and Farfrae together, the letters reach their intended readers. In one instance, another of Susan's letters reaches its recipient (Henchard) too soon, disrupting the relationship of "father" and daughter and indirectly undoing the courtship of Elizabeth-Jane and Farfrae. Though Henchard reads aloud from Lucetta's letters to Farfrae in an excruciating scene, Henchard does not reveal the identity of the writer. He comes close to breaking the rules of privacy that protect letters; indeed, Lucetta, who eavesdrops on part of the scene, thinks he has violated that trust. Yet technically he keeps it. In the primary world of Casterbridge, letters function as specially protected spaces where secrets, plans, and requests can be communicated in true privacy. Just as it seems that Henchard will keep his word and Lucetta's secret, Jopp carries the packet of letters into the annex, where the rules of communal knowledge and action override respect for individual privacy. In the annex, Jopp violates the norm established in the rest of the plot by reading Lucetta's incriminating letters aloud, exposing her (and Henchard) to a judgmental audience.

Though the folk are themselves of questionable character, they condemn Lucetta immediately: "'Tis a humbling thing for us, as respectable women, that one of the same sex could do it. And now she's vowed herself to another man!'" (332). Throughout the novel Hardy associates the lower-class characters with orality and memory. Yet it is Jopp's literacy that makes public the private, and rewrites the dive into the second court-room of the novel. In the liminal space of the narrative annex, the people arrive at a verdict and plan a punishment for a crime that outrages them, at least in part because they have failed to witness it. Common practice in the seventeenth century,[61] and known to have occurred within a few years of the composition of *The Mayor of Caster-*

bridge, the skimmington they plan is based on the communal right to judge other people's behavior. (According to Ruth A. Firor, skimmingtons commonly occurred in Dorset towns through 1884, despite the fact that after 1882 they were judged violations of the Highway Act.)[62] The skimmington ride itself takes place in the main world of the novel, in the public marketplace and streets. The impetus for the action, coming as it does from centuries-old tradition, takes place in the annex. That this secret part should turn out to rule over the outer Casterbridge refigures the social world with boundaries encompassing the underclass and its traditions.

Thus the annex provides an alternate story space where a solution that mingles the traditional rough justice of folk practice, the logic of a ballad's conclusion, and conventional Victorian morality can be unleashed into the fantastically regulated world that surrounds it. While Hardy's novel has contained many revelations, this one is unique in that it proves to be fatal; Lucetta will not survive the publicity that this old form of community regulation plans. (Henchard does not die immediately, but he faces the figure of his annihilation after the skimmington.) The malice of the punishment is in this case directed more cruelly against Lucetta than against Henchard (or Farfrae), and the spectacle kills the guilty woman by displaying her effigy in the unmistakable position of shame. Ultimately, though Henchard's effigy does come back to haunt him in a later scene, the skimmington's function in the plot is to get rid of the woman who has tried to give herself to two different men.

The folk of the annex remind us of the diversity of people who make up the social world of Casterbridge. That their residual practice comes from within the town suggests that the conflict in the novel has to do not only with rural values coming into conflict with cosmopolitan, modernized ways, but also with the impossibility of constructing Casterbridge as a mere backdrop to an individual's fate. Those who were safely "behind the scenes" of the tragedy erupt from the surprisingly capacious backstage, demonstrating that they were part of Casterbridge all along. Their enactment of the traditional punishment completes Henchard's and Lucetta's tragedies, but it also converts the afflicted individuals into the most recent set of figures to occupy positions in a ritual that has been repeated countless times in the past. Not as complicitous members of an audience, but as actors, the people assert their power to judge and punish, participating in the making of Henchard's tragedy, Lucetta's melodrama, and their own social drama.

When the nameless mob pours out of the dark corners of the town to stage the spectacle of the skimmington, it lasts no longer than the annex that generates it, and melts away when its work has been done: "The ideas diffused by the reading of Lucetta's letters at Peter's Finger had condensed into a scandal, which was spreading like a miasmatic fog through Mixen Lane, and thence up the back streets of Casterbridge" (341). The perpetrators of the skimmington are as difficult to lay hands on as the miasma that spreads rumor, like disease. When the tailor–poet Alton Locke falls into a fever-dream in Kingsley's novel, the entrance into the annex is precipitated by a miasma that carries cholera. According to contemporary theories of contagion, miasma was thought to induce delirium and death, as this excerpt from a poem appearing in *Household Words* suggests:

> Near a cotter's back door, in a murky lane,
> Beneath steaming dirt and stagnant rain,
> Miasma lay in a festering drain.
> . . .
> Then Miasma arose from his reeking bed,
> And around the children his mantle spread –
> "To save them from harm," Miasma said.
>
> But they sighed a last sigh. He had stolen their breath,
> And had wrapped them in Cholera's cloak of death.[63]

The malevolent "Miasma" of the poem suggests the degree to which the word itself is associated with mortality. That the real-world "Mixen Lane" should have been the site of one of England's last outbreaks of cholera, in 1854, suggests the killing power of a miasma flowing from that locale.[64] The miasmatic rumor of Hardy's novel also resonates with the fog that covers and permeates the London of Dickens' *Bleak House* (1853), for both cloudy substances are derived from the deliberations in courts. Both also destabilize genre. The fog covers London and its surroundings horizontally and is swallowed into the interiors of throats and lungs. Yet it also permits a fanciful elevation: "Chance people on the bridges peeping over the parapets into a nether sky of fog, with fog all around them, as if they were up in a balloon, and hanging in the misty clouds" (*Bleak House* 5). Hawthorne's contrast between the romance realm of the clouds and the "actual soil of the County of Essex" (*The House of the Seven Gables* 2) is here melded into one transformed and combining zone by Dickens' fog. In the fog, the "romantic side of familiar things" can be descried (*Bleak House*, "Preface" 4), but the danger of infection is also risked. Hardy's miasma wafts into the streets of Casterbridge to infect, to transform, and to disguise. Within the annex, ideas are fixed and made visible by the transfer of coins; outside, in the back streets of Casterbridge, they form the fog that occludes vision even as it communicates scandal.

When the skimmington that is planned in the annex takes place, everyone sees it, but no one is apprehended except for its objects: "Neither in back street nor in front street, however, could the disturbers be perceived; . . . Effigies, donkey, lanterns, band, all had disappeared like the crew of Comus" (*Mayor* 356). This comparison reminds us that the business of Mixen Lane has been to combine the production of spectacle with concealment. The worlds of law and order and masque overlap but cannot communicate. When the blundering constables attempt to penetrate the annex, they discover nothing because of the way they enter Peter's Finger:

The rusty-jointed executors of the law mustered assistance as soon as they could, and the whole party marched off to the lane of notoriety. It was no rapid matter to get there at night, not a lamp or a glimmer of any sort offering itself to light the way, except an occasional pale radiance through some window-curtain, or through the chink of some door which could not be closed because of the smoky chimney within. At last they entered the inn boldly, by the till then bolted front-door. (356)

After the work of the annex has been accomplished, it leaves hardly a trace in the text. The place remains, but entered the right way, by the front-door, it looks like an ordinary barroom. "The constable nodded knowingly; but what he knew was nothing. Nohow could anything be elicited from this mute and inoffensive assembly" (357). This final glimpse of Mixen Lane is particularly revealing in its failure to reveal. The constables who police the main world of Casterbridge stare into the very place where alternative folkways have permitted a crime to be planned, a crime that puts an end to plots unloosed by the original wife-sale[65] but the constables cannot see a thing. The only thing to do is to carry on with a plot that has been shaped by the work of the annex, putting it behind them: "In a few minutes the investigators went out, and joining those of their auxiliaries who had been left at the door they pursued their way elsewither" (357). The reader follows, heading for the multiple resolutions unleashed into the plot by the peculiar commerce and community action headquartered in Mixen Lane.

Ironically, the women and men who punish Lucetta are themselves people who find it convenient to live outside the reach of the law. They continue to provide some of the services of the ancient quarter, yet they also preserve a code of morality that would condemn those activities.[66] The question of how Hardy means us to take this paradoxical situation remains. Hardy's contemporaries, some of whom were to prove so intractable when it came to his frank representation of sexuality, react approvingly to the actions of the mob. For instance, although he finds *The Mayor of Casterbridge* improbable, George Saintsbury seems to concur with the judgment of this convention-upholding underclass. In the *Saturday Review* (29 May 1886), he writes, "The 'skimmington' or 'skimm-ity' ride will, we fancy, be a novelty to most readers, though the author has doubtless witnessed, or has excellent warranty for describing, this burlesque but forcible protest against what villagers regard as unseemly pre-nuptial conduct on the part of a bride" ("Mayor" 757). Does Hardy anticipate the approval of his middle-class critics, and subversively represent them as sharing the opinions of a mob, or as John Kucich suggests, does Hardy's critique of honesty subvert the common novelis-tic association of middle class and honest behavior ("Moral Authority" 223)? Which ever way we read the inhabitants of Mixen Lane, they are surely not, as John Paterson claims, an unredeemed peasantry who disturb the social order ("*The Mayor*" 105–6). Rather, as Patricia Ingham observes, they function in the plot to exact retribution for social trans-gressions.[67] One might read the women's revenge on Lucetta as com-mercially motivated, a negative advertising campaign masquerading as moral outrage.[68] Hardy uses the bounded and separated zone of Mixen Lane not to announce a contrast between modern, up-to-date literacy and the backward orality of the folk, but to show how the folk's literacy and power may be exercised to regressive ends.

Published shortly after the passage of the Third Reform Bill, *The Mayor of Casterbridge* reflects an earlier world in which the judgments of the people were confined to expression outside the political realm. The Bill that redistributed seats, regularized districts, and got rid of pocket boroughs controlled by patronage also enfranchised some farm laborers; due to the Secret Ballot Act of 1872, these new voters would cast their ballots in privacy.[69] Although other historical circumstances are suggested by the fictional world of Casterbridge, most prominently the mechanization of certain aspects of agriculture, this scene is reminis-cent of the futile investigations into election fraud that preceded the 1884 Reform Bill, the third of the great extensions of the franchise. How many times did the Parliamentary investigators peer into a pub where everyone knew that the candidate's agents had doled out coins and stood drinks for voters, only to find no evidence of wrongdoing at all?

The link between the mob and the concealing fog reminds the reader that secrecy is risky indeed. Hardy's novel imagines a world in which the common people of Casterbridge make a crucial judgment in the confinement of the annex, one that brings to final ruin the Mayor of the town. The two entrances to Peter's Finger, well-worn slit and locked front suggest that the space into which the authorities gaze, having entered through the "till then bolted front-door," can also be read as a figurative ballot box, filled with a "mute and inoffensive assembly" – people, having cast their ballots in covert demonstration. In the space of the annex, Hardy creates an alternative zone where prostitutes, poachers, and the homeless demonstrate their engagement in a social world that has habitually regarded them as conventional figures, "of uncouth manner and aspect, stolid understanding, and snail-like movement," with "speech [of] such a chaotic corruption of regular language that few persons of progressive aims consider it worth while to inquire what views, if any, of life, of nature, or of society are conveyed in these utterances" ("Dorsetshire Labourer" 252). As I have argued, the views of the individuals in Mixen Lane reinforce conventional morality, though the actions of the mob, staging the skimmington, break the law. As Kingsley does, Hardy combines the residual with the emergent in his narrative annex, figuring class conflict in terms of sexuality, and uneasily revealing the vengeful rustics in the ancient lane of notoriety, in a different light, as metaphorically enfranchised.

CHAPTER 5

Older, deeper, further: narrative annexes and the extent of the Condition of England

WHY POLITICAL NOVELS HAVE ANNEXES

If the project of political novels is to announce the presence of another world, a second nation, within the realm whose condition they investigate, narrative annexes might seem to be superfluous to them. The political novel already juxtaposes the houses and halls of power with the factory and the dwellings of the poor; it already sets the over-rationalized schoolroom against the circus; contrasts North and South; past and present; city and country; honest and vicious; clean and filthy; victim of industrial life and prosperous (sometimes even well-meaning) factory-owner. The characteristic gesture of the Victorian political novel is to expose the shocking world (Gaskell's homes of workers; Dickens' schools and workhouses; Kingsley's sweatshops and dwellings of the urban poor) and to insist that these zones of disease, degradation, and dehumanization are not only part, but the *other half*, of England. To call attention to (if not to redress) the evils that afflict the whole nation, political novels choose representative evils to stand for this other nation. These choices notoriously fail to represent working people either as convincing individuals or as diverse groups with their own elaborate social strata.[1] Furthermore, the binary structure of the two nations[2] occludes the variety of suffering endured by workers and the poor in Britain, and this effect was often manipulated to serve political ends. (The history of the Corn Law Repeal and the sequence of Reform Acts is one of alliance politics, which requires the oversimplification of losses and gains in order to consolidate support.) Condition of England novels record the desires of a culture that hopes to reconcile its material needs with both its political and its altruistic hopes. By attempting diagnosis, these novels distance themselves from the "condition" of the others they describe, even as they expose selected targets within the economic, industrial, and political establishments. As a result, they can appear

startlingly complacent about social problems beyond the ken of their
particular topic. When Charlotte Brontë addresses the Condition of
Women in *Shirley*, bringing Shirley and Caroline to the site of a mill riot,
her revolutionary impulse does not extend to the rebelling workers – it is
noted with satisfaction later in the novel that the ringleaders of the
attack on the mill have been sentenced to transportation. Yet as often as
political novels fail to carry out full examinations, or prescribe cures that
would only exacerbate, they also represent in annexes the symptoms of
conditions that cannot, in conscience, be left off the chart.

Condition of England novels are generally assumed to have reached
their peak of production in the 1850s, trickling off with the end of the
Chartist movement.[3] Yet the impulse to reform and convert, to alert
readers to the state of the nation, continues through the century. By
treating an 1844, 1854, and 1909 novel (*Coningsby*, *Hard Times*, and
Tono-Bungay), I draw out a sequence of these conditions for the repair of
the nation. The first condition, which Disraeli urges in *Coningsby*, is the
recognition of the role of Jewish knowledge, purity, and leadership in
the recovery of a threatened cultural heritage for England's new men
through alliance with its reformed aristocratic youth. Disraeli (an M. P.
for seven years at the time of the novel's publication) suggests a political
program; Dickens' and Wells' conditions take the form of evils which
must be faced, though neither author outlines clear means for their
correction. The second condition, exposed but also used by Dickens in
Hard Times, is the expendability of the materials of England, especially
its workers. The third condition, in Wells' vision in *Tono-Bungay*, is the
dehumanization of the financers and managers of entrepreneurial projects, by their victimization of the most unwitting and distant peoples.
Political, mortal, and spiritual consequences depend upon the revivifica-
tion and corruption that the encounters in these political novels' annexes promise and threaten.

In the previous chapter I argued that, in the broader category of
social fiction, anxiety about class often expresses itself in terms of the
regulation of sexuality, and Condition of England novels have been
shown to draw, in an apparently contradictory way, on courtship plots
to contain and resolve their narratives of class conflict and political
violence.[4] When political novels employ narrative annexes, however, we
find these resolutions qualified and the binary simplifications they employ exposed. The dynamic intersection of conversion narratives, plots
of class conflict, and homosocial encounters complicates the narrative
structure of the two nations. In this chapter I attend to intimate meetings

between men, staged in narrative annexes of political fiction, in which the project of bridging the great gulf is perplexed by troubled consciences and overly optimistic scenarios of conversion. If the underlying sermon of Gaskell's *Mary Barton* urges her middle-class readers to acknowledge that the parable of Dives and Lazarus makes them responsible for avoiding the sin of the rich man by converting their own hearts and reaching out to the poor, the Condition of England novels of Disraeli, Dickens, and Wells imagine different and more dangerous conversions ensuing from encounters with those on the other side, or the inside, of the gulf.

The otherness of class difference veers towards race in the annexes in Benjamin Disraeli's *Coningsby, or the New Generation*, Charles Dickens' *Hard Times*, and H. G. Wells' *Tono-Bungay*.[5] These annexes provide spaces older, deeper, and further from contemporary England, for protagonists to encounter, respectively: the Jewish financier and behind-the-scenes politician; the expiring working man; and the native black islander. The confrontations with the figures of the annexes emphasize the existence of others beyond the novels' representational range.[6] If Condition of England novels ask "what should we do about the nation?" their annexes ask, "what should we do about *them*?" The placement of these disruptive figures – Jew, dying millworker, black murder-victim[7] – in annexes suggests the interruptions of conscience, but a conscience insulated and restrained from having its full effect on the surrounding fictional worlds. The often adverse reaction of contemporary critics to Condition of England novels focuses not only, as I will show, on their generic admixture, but also on the very characters embodying an affronting difference in narrative annexes.

As my earlier discussion of *Alton Locke* suggests, the narrative annexes in Condition of England novels reveal vexed relationships with conversion narratives. Disraeli uses conversion *by* a Jew to invert the traditional figure of futurity, in a manifesto for immediate political action that conjures up an idealized feudal past. Sidonia's conversion of Coningsby reverses the Christian baptism of Benjamin Disraeli. The distressing problem of overlapping narratives of victimization and spiritual profit, unresolved by Kingsley's Christian socialism, is reactivated in the annex to *Hard Times*, a novel which plays on conventional piety to justify its most outrageous human sacrifice, the killing of Stephen Blackpool. Dickens' muddle of oppressive agency blames "systems" for most of the ills of *Hard Times*, but Stephen's death is elevated to the status of Christian martyrdom. At the end of the "long" nineteenth century,

H. G. Wells' examination of the corruption at the heart of Edwardian prosperity employs a narrative annex to convert the protagonist into a guilty man, whose self-narrated *Bildungsroman* contains a jarring confession of murder. In representing those figures who do not fit in the political novel, and by suggesting uncanny changes and wish-fulfilling consequences, annexes reveal the ambivalence of Disraeli, Dickens, and Wells towards the necessary but expendable others they depict.

As a sequence, the annexes to *Coningsby*, *Hard Times*, and *Tono-Bungay* chart the increasing distance that must be traversed to represent these troubling others. In *Coningsby*, Sidonia occupies the heart of an ancient English forest. In *Hard Times*, Stephen Blackpool falls below the surface of the earth. In *Tono-Bungay*, the criminal encounter with the other takes place far from Britain's shore on the fringes of the empire. Older, deeper, and further away, separated by boundaries that thicken from the belt of forest to the depth of solid rock to the width of the sea, these narrative annexes make distance and difference material. Confronting the alien figures within the annexes reveals doubled impulses of inspiration (or eroticism) in *Coningsby*; tragedy (or utilitarian sacrifice) in *Hard Times*; and unmotivated violence (or vengeful murder) in *Tono-Bungay*. The ever-more-remote locations of the narrative annexes suggest an anxiety about boundaries, and about who can be counted part of the England whose condition novelists investigate, for each figure of the annex exists simultaneously outside of and deep inside the worlds of the novels.

"THE JEWISH CHAMPION"

Although Christian baptism allows Disraeli to participate in public life, his fictional creation, the Jew Sidonia cannot serve in Parliament (like Rothschild, Disraeli's contemporary, who could not take his seat until the oath of office was revised in 1866). Sidonia's celebration of racial purity and ancient culture comes from a place remote from England, yet he teaches Coningsby to be more truly English in their homosocial encounter in an English forest inn, redolent of the past. Sidonia's introduction to the novel demonstrates and solemnizes England's penetrability. Not subversion but the recovery of endangered ideals, and a surrogate enfranchisement, motivate Sidonia's intervention in Coningsby's development. The Jewish figure who exerts his influence from the annex calls attention to the ineffectuality of tactics of marginalization, as they apparently lead to conversion. Michael Ragussis has shown how Disraeli's argument that "Hebraism was the foundation of English culture" leads to a "particular form of anti-Semitic representation: 'the secret Jew' who invades England through the passport of conversion in order to undermine English culture."[8] Mary Poovey's discussion of misplaced eroticism traces the pervasive homosociality of *Coningsby*,[9] attending to the way that Harry Coningsby becomes an ideal Englishman by being a passive vessel into which the interests of a "whig millowner, an apolitical Catholic, and a Jewish financier" are poured (*Social Body* 136). In Poovey's reading, Coningsby's meditation on industrial machinery in Manchester "allows Disraeli to introduce both gender and eroticism into his hero's career" (139). This displaced erotic effect has already entered the novel by the time the hero reaches Manchester, occurring when young Coningsby encounters a mysterious stranger and his beautiful horse in the narrative annex. As I will show, both the promise of eroticism and intellectual enticements to conversion underlie Sidonia's influential agency, which was to annoy critics of both novel and author.

Although in 1844 Disraeli could not have anticipated the anti-Semitic backlash to his celebration of Hebraism, he might have forseen that presenting a thinly disguised version of himself in the charismatic Sidonia would elicit hostility. There was no chance that Sidonia would go unrecognized. In *Coningsby*, Disraeli speaks from a Tory splinter group, "Young England," and attacks his leader, Sir Robert Peel. In the political world of the 1840s, a prominent little clique of youthful Tories comprised "Young England." Mainly noble in origins themselves, they endeavored to improve the lot of the poor by encouraging harmonious relations between the classes. To this end, they advocated respect not only for the Church and the monarch, but for all of Britain's time-hallowed institutions and traditions.[10] In *Coningsby*, Disraeli articulates points in the not entirely coherent program of "Young England," attacks both Whig and Tory policies and personalities, and depicts, in thinly veiled portraits, the members of the group. Disraeli himself can be readily identified with both Sidonia and the narrator of the novel. The reviewer in *Fraser's Magazine* writes: "Such a sustained interference with the private, as well as the public lives of well-known men and women, we certainly do not remember . . . there is scarce a character introduced into this tale of which the prototype is not as familiar to the mind of the reader as a household word." The reviewer goes on to identify Coningsby with George Smythe; Lord Monmouth with the late Marquess of Hertford; the Duke of Blanc with the Duke of Rutland; Lord

Henry Sydney with Lord John Manners; Mr. Lyle with Lord Surrey; Mr. Rigby with John Wilson Croker; and Sidonia, "the most sublimated abstraction of the whole, Mr. Benjamin Disraeli, accommodated, for the nonce, with the wealth and political position of Baron Rothschild."[11] In the narrative annex Disraeli's idealized Jewish mentor instructs the aristocratic protagonist in the reconciliation of interests, and inspires him, as a member of "Young England," to protect and rejuvenate Old England.

Disraeli, though not a nobleman, was attracted by the alternative to utilitarianism that "Young England"'s ideals furnished. "Young England" held out for the Corn Laws and believed that the poor should be cared for by the Church and a caring aristocracy. The group fervently expressed an alternative set of ideals in the hope of effecting political change in a practical world: "Young England" members believed that ancient customs such as May-pole dancing should be revived; they opposed centralized government, middle-class liberalism, and Peel. According to a contemporary, the self-styled "New Generation" was made up of only five or six members, who "adorn the benches of St. Stephen, and annoy Sir Robert Peel with that honorable kind of practice, which the Quarterly Review has described as 'firing shots from the rear upon their own friends in the van.'"[12] The pinnacle of "Young England"'s political life was reached on 3 October 1844, when Disraeli, Smythe, and Lord John Manners spoke at the Manchester Athenaeum. This alliance of four young MPs (counting Baillie-Cochrane) lasted only for two sessions, 1843 and 1844 (precisely contemporary with the writing and publication of *Coningsby*), but was seen at the time as a development of a trajectory beginning with the First Reform Bill.[13]

Coningsby represents not an anti-establishment broadside, but Disraeli's appeal for centrality. Disraeli believed in the vitality of institutions such as Parliament, Church, and a feudal aristocracy, but feared that England's moral civilization lagged behind its industrial development. As a young MP, he criticized the New Poor Law and was alone in supporting most of the Chartists' demands. Later he deplored their severe punishments (Braun, *Disraeli* 74). Not only a defining instance of the political novel, *Coningsby* is also one of the first Victorian novels to concern itself explicitly with the Condition of England. Disraeli sets the stage with an explicit reference to the Carlylean challenge:

Now commenced that Condition-of-England question of which our generation hears so much. During five-and-twenty years every influence that can develop the energies and resources of a nation had been acting with concentrated stimulation on the British Isles ... [causing] ... that rapid advance of material civilisation in England, to which the annals of the world can afford no parallel. But there was no proportionate advance in our moral civilisation. In the hurry-skurry of money-making, men-making, and machine-making, we had altogether outgrown, not the spirit, but the organisation, of our institutions. (*Coningsby* 96–7)

Whether Carlyle, or the authors of other Condition of England novels, could believe in the "spirit" of the challenged institutions of England as Disraeli does, *Coningsby* combines economic, political, and religious change with conservative moral values by means of a nostalgic appeal to the past. Disraeli's novel imagines the alliance to be made between industrialists and aristocrats, to form a Carlylean Aristocracy of Talent.[14] In the first novel of what was to become his Young England Trilogy, Disraeli depicts the coming-of-age of the eponymous hero in a political world where the interests of old landed money and new, entrepreneurial wealth must be reconciled. Although the novel is filled with raptures about the deliverance of England by Manchester, Disraeli does not investigate and expose the indignities of the lives of industrial workers. That task he attempts, with limited success, in the second novel of the trilogy, *Sybil, or the Two Nations*. In *Coningsby*, however, Disraeli articulates a political solution to the problems generated by social change and Sidonia – the stranger in the annex – serves as his mouthpiece.

Disraeli introduces this stranger in the annex, in a setting so out of place in the novel that it seems, according to readers such as John Holloway, entirely irresponsible and melodramatic.[15] The improbable action – the inspiration of a young leader by an unidentified Jewish traveler – requires the altered locale and mode of the narrative annex. The grounds of Eton, the dining rooms and parlours of the affluent, and the halls of Parliament provide the settings for Coningsby's growth into manhood, a path marked, as Daniel Bivona has argued, by a spiralling sequence of restorations and returns ("Trilogy" 312). The interactions of the novel take the form of conversations, meditations, or occasional heroic actions, such as the rescue of a drowning boy. Punctuated by political excurses delivered by advisors and the narrator, the novel celebrates Coningsby's maturation – the outcome never seems much in doubt, as the mysteries set up to drive the plot unravel into mere snares. Each mode contributes to the creation of a character who becomes less our hero and more a public figure as the novel progresses. The crucial transition from adolesence to adulthood is mysteriously linked to the events in the forest, where Coningsby encounters the stranger, the behind-the-scenes manipulator of peers and princes.[16]

Although the encounter in the annex may indeed strike the reader as melodramatic, the Cervantine setting creates a temporary resting place within the progress of the *Bildungsroman* to introduce inspiration and transfer an erotic charge through an unlikely medium – Sidonia's mare. Sidonia notes the literariness of the encounter, alluding to meetings in inns in *Don Quixote*, and identifies himself with romance and picaresque in this novel of public life. Sidonia's byword "adventure" overrides any anti-chivalric associations (becoming a governor is no joke in *Coningsby*). The character Sidonia embodies in a deliberate gesture the generic difference upon which contemporary readers were fixated, as it symbolized a deeper racial difference that threatened to contaminate the English novel.

As Condition of England novels came out in the 1840s and 1850s, they were often greeted with criticism for mixing the matters of fiction with instructive manifestos. For instance, Thackeray writes, in a review of *Sybil*, "We stand already committed as to our idea of the tendency and province of the novel. Morals and manners we believe to be the novelist's best themes; and hence prefer romances which do not treat of algebra, religion, political economy, or other abstract science."[17] Since it was an early example of the kind, *Coningsby*'s genre did not seem obvious to Disraeli's first critics, and the Jewishness of the author – and Sidonia – impelled some to declare the novel un-English and practically un-classifiable. Here is Thackeray:

It is the fashionable novel, pushed, we really do believe, to its extremest verge, beyond which all is naught . . . It is a dandy-social, dandy-political, dandy-religious novel. Fancy a prostrate world kissing the feet of a reformer – in patent blacking; fancy a prophet delivering heavenly messages – with his hair in papers, and the reader will have our notion of the book. The dandyism, moreover, is intense, but not real; not English, that is. It is vastly too ornamental for our quiet habits.[18]

A foreign, decorated, vain and fashionable figure stands for the unwholesome, unreal generic mixture of the novel. G. H. Lewes, writing in 1849, describes the "Young England" novels as "political manifestoes spiced with personalities."[19] The French critic Eugene Forcade, who presumably did not care whether a novel seemed English enough for English readers' quiet habits, also comments on its hybrid nature:

"*Coningsby* is really a manifesto, but we cannot deny that it is also a novel ... we could compare the attack D'Israeli had made against art, in the name of and for the benefit of political issues of the day, to the act of barbarism of introducing firearms into an orchestra."[20] Disraeli's Sidonia not only embodies generic difference, but self-consciously draws attention to it as he works to convert the youth in the annex.

Book III begins with the entrance to the annex, figured in terms of a crossing over a generically and spatially marked liminal area which contains the isolated inn. In the final scene of Book II, the reader leaves a pensive young Coningsby staring out of the window of his room at Eton. He has completed his education, but every question about its outcome remains to be answered:

He will become more wise; will he remain as generous? His ambition may be as great; will it be as noble? What, indeed, is to be the future of this existence that is now to be sent forth into the great aggregate of entities? Is it an ordinary organisation that will jostle among the crowd, and be jostled? Is it a finer temperament, susceptible of receiving the impressions and imbibing the inspirations of superior yet sympathising spirits? Or is it a primordial and creative mind; one that will say to his fellows, "Behold, God has given me thought; I have discovered truth, and you shall believe?" (134–5)

There is no chance that Coningsby will become a parson, but his conversion to political life is instigated by an encounter with just such a "primordial and creative mind." Before discovering his aptitude for politics, Coningsby passes through a liminal space that transforms him into a man, capable of forming goals and articulating both ambitions and desires. The boundary that marks the annex is described in language full of nostalgia for an older world, a green world: "There are few things more full of delight and splendour, than to travel during the heat of a refulgent summer in the green district of some ancient forest" (137). Disraeli goes to some pains to introduce the reader to the new scene in a passage that was noted by contemporaries as one of the (rare) beauties of the novel:[21]

It was a fragment of one of those vast sylvan tracts wherein Norman kings once hunted, and Saxon outlaws plundered; and although the plough had for centuries successfully invaded brake and bower, the relics retained all their original character of wildness and seclusion. Sometimes the green earth was thickly studded with groves of huge and vigorous oaks, intersected with those smooth and sunny glades, that seem as if they must be cut for dames and knights to saunter on. Then again the undulating ground spread on all sides, as far as the eye could range, covered with copse and fern of immense growth.

Anon you found yourself in a turfy wilderness, girt in apparently by dark woods. And when you had wound your way a little through this gloomy belt, the landscape, still strictly sylvan, would beautifully expand with every combination and variety of woodland; while at its centre, the wildfowl covered the waters of a lake, and the deer basked on the knolls that abounded on its banks. (137)

The reader and Coningsby alike are guided by the narrator's description through the "gloomy belt" into a shimmering zone of greenery, shadow, and unstartled, abundant fauna; into a trace of "old England"; into a tract of forest that has survived enclosure. In this place out of time Disraeli romanticizes the oppressive history of Norman hunting grounds, as the shades of Norman kings, Saxon outlaws, and dames and knights populate a locale of "wildness and seclusion." Pseudo-archaic language signals the romantic wanderer's entrance into a wildlife preserve where fowl and deer calmly display themselves. No contemporary poachers disturb the scene, as if hunger were a thing of the past in the 1840s; only the plough and imaginary "dames and knights" pass peaceably through the woods. Disraeli conjures up a faux-medieval past in a Victorian park, the perfect setting for the hero of "Young England" to contemplate his losses and anticipate his gains.

For the "traveller" who throws "himself under the shade of a spreading tree" (137), poised for reverie and in no Spenserian danger, is of course young Coningsby. Alone in the wild, romantic setting, Coningsby's thoughts turn to the losses that come along with maturity. He leaves behind a world (Eton) where his emotional life is based on boys' affection for one another:

And those friends too, so fond, so sympathising, so devoted, where were they now? Already they were dispersed; the first great separation of life had been experienced; the former schoolboy had planted his foot on the threshold of manhood . . . They would meet again with altered mien, with different manners, different voices. Their eyes would not shine with the same light; they would not speak the same words. The favourite phrases of their intimacy, the mystic sounds that spoke only to their initiated ear, they would be ashamed to use them. Yes, they might meet again, but the gushing and secret tenderness was gone forever. (138–9)

Coningsby's consciousness that "his had been the inspiring mind" (139) among his schoolfellows tempers his lament. The orphan "sighs" for a mentor to fill the role of a paternal advisor: "Often, indeed, had he needed, sometimes he had even sighed for, the companionship of an equal or superior mind; one who, by the comprehension of his thought, and the richness of his knowledge, and the advantage of his experience, might strengthen and illuminate and guide his obscure or hesitating or unpractised intelligence" (139). The lack he feels in the meantime makes him yearn for another form of solace, that of romantic love: "Ah! If she would but come forth from that shining lake like a beautiful Ondine! Ah, if she would but step out from the green shade of that secret grove like a dryad of sylvan Greece!" (139). Both desires will be fulfilled by the annex's encounter with Sidonia.

Driven indoors by a storm that seems to warn him of the terrors of sexual love ("The oak roared, the beech shrieked, the elm sent forth its deep and long-drawn groan; while ever and anon, amid a momentary pause, the passion of the ash was heard in moans of thrilling anguish" [140]), Coningsby meets not a dryad or an Ondine, but a man with an exceedingly beautiful horse. With these figures, in the seclusion of the narrative annex, he will recover the lost "gushing and secret tenderness" (139) of boyhood in an adult form. For not the least of the precepts imparted to Coningsby by Sidonia is the appreciation of female beauty, a lesson that converts school-boy desire into mature heterosexuality (by means of a horse). Tellingly, the Arabian mare makes a stronger first impression than the stranger himself: "The remarkable beauty of the animal so attracted Coningsby's attention, that it prevented him catching even a glimpse of the rider" (140). Later, Coningsby confesses:

"I long to see your mare again," said Coningsby. "She seemed to me so beautiful."

"She is not only of pure race," said the stranger, "but of the highest and rarest breed in Arabia . . . Come round to the stable and see her." . . .

"The Daughter of the Star" stood before Coningsby with her sinewy shape of matchless symmetry; her burnished skin, black mane, legs like those of an antelope, her little ears, dark speaking eye, and tail worthy of a Pacha. And who was her master, and whither was she about to take him? (146–7)

The narrative annex channels the erotic energy of the mentor relationship into Coningsby's desire to achieve in politics, using the bait of the mare to promise one of the rewards for excelling. (In fact marriage will be one of the pragmatic steps in Coningsby's alliance-forging career.) The Daughter of the Star provides Coningsby with his first impression of a sexual female creature, as opposed to the ethereal goddess of his imaginings. She also embodies the racial purity that her master advocates, a theory that Sidonia advances as if simultaneously to tweak English readers with his unconverted presence in Old England and to reassure them that any converts he wins will not engage in miscegenation. The eroticism that Poovey discovers in Coningsby's raptures about Manchester machinery begins here, with Sidonia's talk.

Because the inn is short on space, the landlord fortuitously asks if Coningsby and the dark stranger can share a room until the storm subsides. More than his notable beauty (140–1), the stranger's remarks impress Coningsby. Responding to the young man's interest in visiting Athens, the stranger takes the opportunity to establish his enthusiasm for modernized, industrial England: "'I have seen it,' said the stranger, slightly shrugging his shoulders; 'and more wonderful things. Phantoms and spectres! The Age of Ruins is past. Have you seen Manchester?'" (141). (Coningsby will arrive in that city primed to read in its industrial machinery the future of the human race.) Although the stranger enters the world of the novel through a violent storm and a self-consciously residual literary setting, he works efficiently to propel Coningsby to the emergent parts of the "real" world that will make him a more able politician. The stranger alludes to the significant location of their meeting: "'Well, according to Cervantes, [adventures] should begin in an inn'" (141). Yet he deliberately distances himself from Spanish models, teaching Coningsby pride in English customs and virtues, symbolized in this scene by a plate of bacon and eggs, which Coningsby deprecates as "simple fare."

"Nay, a national dish," said the stranger, glancing quickly at the table, "whose fame is a proverb. And what more should we expect under a simple roof! How much better than an omelette or a greasy olla, that they should give us in a posada! 'Tis a wonderful country, this England! What a napkin! How spotless! And so sweet; I declare 'tis a perfume. There is not a princess throughout the South of Europe served with the cleanliness that meets us in this cottage." (142)

Sidonia's nationalistic rapture about the cleanliness of English servants and simplicity of the fare (in contrast to those of the persecuting Spanish) sets the tone for the conversation that follows: no wonder that Harry Coningsby will lead the New Generation, if scrambled eggs and clean napkins can so inspiringly teach him the superiority of his nation.[22] The stranger flatters the young man by listening to his replies "with a serious and fixed attention" (143–4) and by alluding to his potential for greatness: "'The history of Heroes is the history of Youth'" (146). Before departing, he wins Coningsby's pledge of devotion (147).

Although he has completed his task of activating Coningsby's ambition, Sidonia remains a marvellous agent in the political novel. He nudges the action along in the direction Disraeli (the politician) would take it and his fantastic shimmer derives at least as much from Disraeli (the novelist)'s fascination with his imagined double as from Coningsby's impressions. The rich, handsome, brilliant, and exotic Sidonia (whose history is narrated analeptically in Book IV, chapter 10) manipulates the outcome of "Young England"'s plot more effectively from the margin, even as he wryly deprecates the romance fictionality of the annex that lets him into the "adventure." Despite Sidonia's impact on Coningsby as a man of the world, he is as much tall-dark-stranger as anything else. A foreign prince with an exotic horse, the stranger gallops out of a fairy tale into the political world of England in the 1830s. There he will bail out the Exchequer; appear at the most important dinner parties; have a hand in legislation from outside Parliament; remain coolly unaware of the women who are smitten with him; and continue to guide young Coningsby.

In terms of narrative structure, the annex controverts prescriptions for generic and spatial separation. Disraeli uses the safely insulated zone of the forest inn to frame the miraculous events and Sidonia's remarkable powers. This seems to promise that the social world will not be further ruptured. Sidonia, *persona* of the forest, enters homes and halls, like Disraeli himself. Sidonia stands for Disraeli, as he might be had he been rich, entirely Jewish, an alien, and safely distanced from Holywell Street or other urban communities of contemporary Jews. The heroic and cultured Sidonia is an unassimilated Jew. Disraeli was born a Jew and began his religious education before his father Isaac withdrew from his synagogue following a dispute. Although Disraeli's father never converted, he had his four children baptized into the Church of England. (Benjamin was thirteen, the age of Bar Mitzvah.) Because of this conversion, Disraeli was able to enter Parliament and eventually serve as Prime Minister. He believed that Christianity was the fulfillment of Judaism and attended church throughout his life.[23]

Sidonia's belief in the principle of race is inextricably tied up with the political fate of England and his aristocratic disciple, entering the political realm, fulfills two birthrights – his own and Sidonia's – simultaneously. The meeting in the annex provides a setting apart from the public, political world, where the Jew can teach the Englishman how best to serve England and himself, by believing in a national character and heroism whose best exemplar is the Jewish outsider. In George Eliot's *Daniel Deronda* (1876), the insider learns from the mentor to look outside England for his true realm of endeavor. Yet in *Daniel Deronda* the annex that contains the inspirational teacher takes over the novel, resulting in a lopsided but ultimately more interesting and open-ended narrative. What starts out seeming like an annex turns out to be a truer center than the dispersed and dissipated locations of the English social world. Sidonia's intervention, on the other hand, promotes a view of history which stems from Judaism, promising the fulfillment of English national destiny *within* Jewish destiny. Sidonia's asexuality represents a promise that this will not be accomplished through intermarriage, but the homosocial eroticism of Coningsby's conversion to manhood suggests that the English depend upon Jewish agency, if rites of initiation are to be efficacious.

In a deflating and openly anti-Semitic piece, *Punch* ridicules both Disraeli's theory of racial purity ("'Look at that old clothes-man,' said we to ourselves; 'who would think that the unmixed blood of Caucasus runs through the veins of that individual who has just offered us nine-pence for our penultimate hat'"[24]) and his ambition to reform British political institutions:

Mr. DISRAELI has written no less than three novels to further the great cause of Jewish ascendency, and to prove that the battle of the constitution is to be fought in Holywell Street . . . It is evident that Mr. DISRAELI has determined in his own mind, that until there is a Mosaic Parliament, sitting in Rag Fair, the object of his great mission will be unaccomplished. ("The Jewish Champion" 145)

The effort of Disraeli's critics to rewrite his sphere of influence as the Jewish commercial district and his ambition as purely financial is focused upon the figure of Sidonia, voice, exemplar, and agent of Disraeli's "great cause."

As I have suggested, Sidonia's presence within the political novel affronted reviewers who recognized Disraeli (and Rothschild) in the depiction of the exemplary Jew. Not surprisingly, the critics did not hesitate to express their views in an anti-Semitic fashion, nor to identify the fictional with the authorial figure. Later in Disraeli's career, the critic Richard Grant White writes of the Tory Premier's vulgarity:

Mr. Disraeli is by birth a British subject, and from earliest association and habit he speaks and writes the English language; but it is beyond the power of all accidents of nativity or acts of Parliament to make him an English man. His political critics have more than once complained that, as a politician, with all his subtlety and his craft, he is not able to understand Englishmen. The very good reason might be given for this that he is not English, but Jewish.[25]

Disraeli's Un-Englishness manifests itself, according to White, in his prose style, "glaring, bedizened, and vitiated by a vulgar splendour and cheap grandeur" ("Styles" 260). The bitter review of *Coningsby* in *Fraser's Magazine* mocks Sidonia's assertion that Jews and Mohammedans are particularly clean and promises, facetiously, to "refrain from an absurd custom to which we had addicted ourselves. We will not hold our noses any more when a Jew comes between the wind and our nobility, for Mr. Disraeli, who ought to know, assures us that to be at once filthy and a Jew is impossible" ("Coningsby" 76).[26] Even a positive assessment of the character Sidonia describes him as not belonging to the world of the novel. He

appears ever and anon, as a *deus ex machina*, like the sorcerer of the eastern story; since, without possessing any necessary connection, that we can perceive, with the plot of these volumes, he comes in and goes out as a sort of inspired interlocutor, very able, very eloquent, very learned, brimful of wisdom, a treble millionaire in fortune, a companion of princes in politics, and a genuine Jew in religion. His character is well conceived and powerfully painted, but might as easily be transferred into any other novel or story, just as well as the present. ("Coningsby," *Eclectic Review,* 56)

One of a few sympathetic contemporaries, Disraeli's colleague Richard Monckton Milnes, presents Sidonia's thesis in a positive light, still emphasizing the character's racial difference:

Himself of Hebrew race, he makes no demands on Christian sympathy, he raises no cry of sorrow and exile, but avows his belief in the permanent and prospective truth of the ancient tradition, that to that race and its influences Providence ever entrusts the chief agency in the destinies of mankind . . . there is something deeply interesting, in our cold sceptical days, in this bold avowal, by one of them, of his faith in their continuous greatness.[27]

For most of his critics, Sidonia's eloquence, his learning, his similarity to a sorcerer, or, to take the negative views, his "absurd" championing of the Jews, and his own Jewishness all mean that he cannot belong – that he cannot mix with English forms.

Disraeli deliberately embeds Sidonia in a narrative annex at the heart of Old England in order to underline both his own extraordinarily successful assimilation and to challenge readers with a purer, richer, and perhaps even more influential Jew than himself. He offers the reassurance of the residual form – only romance – to mitigate the potentially threatening and nakedly egotistical promise that the political conversion of England will be effected by an outsider who is already on the inside.

CRUSHED AND USED UP IN *HARD TIMES*

Engulfed and then cast out of the craw of Dickens' industrialized landscape in *Hard Times*, the worker Stephen Blackpool falls out of England into Old Hell Shaft, where he lies dying, his very absence driving the novel's accusatory plot along. The true criminal, Tom Gradgrind, has cast suspicion on the innocent worker, who has troubles enough with an alcoholic wife (from whom he cannot get divorced); friction at his workplace (where he disappoints his co-workers by refusing to join the union); and an impossible love affair (with a woman so good that she prevents Stephen's wife from poisoning herself, although that would remove the impediment). Retrieved, like Alton Locke before him, Stephen ends up all but used up. The annex crushes and finishes with the expendable body of the worker and invites readers to contemplate their complicity, as plot-consumers, in the displacement and disposal of characters. Yet the narrative annex also emphasizes Dickens' identification with his character Stephen Blackpool, the working man trapped in an impossible marriage, who recognizes injustice but resists combination, and refrains from blaming individuals for his plight. (When he finally gets a chance to clear his name, Stephen does not accuse Tom Gradgrind directly, but exercises gentlemanly forbearance even as he utters his last words.) Like the middle-class readers of *Household Words*, in which the serial version of *Hard Times* appeared,[28] Stephen Blackpool is no opponent of industry. Instead he departs the "muddle" of earthly existence in a saintly expiration.

When Dickens undertook the writing of a serial fiction to bolster the sales of his journal, he struggled with a mode of writing that had to be adapted to severe limitations in space. The result is a much more streamlined fiction than any of the other mature work, more closely resembling the fabular Christmas books, which Dickens had recently read aloud to a working-class audience in Birmingham.[29] Whether *Hard Times* is approached as a moral fable or an industrial novel, its brevity and relative paucity of places and plot-lines makes it possible to identify the particular episode employing the strategies of a narrative annex, in this case the climactic discovery and rescue of Stephen Blackpool from a disused mine shaft. The evocative language used by Dickens to describe the experience of writing *Hard Times* suggests the lengths (or rather depths) to which his spatial representation is to be driven. He wrote to Forster that "The difficulty of the space is CRUSHING. Nobody can have an idea of it who has not had an experience of patient fiction-writing with some elbow room always, and open places in perspective."[30]

Stephen Blackpool's story is one aspect of the novel with which Dickens felt particularly satisfied, writing "I have done what I hope is a good thing with Stephen, taking the story as a whole" and noting in his number plan the episode when Stephen is found and rescued from Old Hell Shaft: "the great effect."[31] Yet just before the narrative annex in chapter 6, "Starlight," of the third book, "Garnering," Dickens' narrator comments on Stephen Blackpool's continuing absence, which makes him vulnerable to Tom Gradgrind's blame-shifting:

The smoke-serpents were indifferent who was lost and found, who turned out good or bad; the melancholy mad elephants, like the Hard Fact men, abated nothing of their set routine, whatever happened. Day and night again, day and night again. The monotony was unbroken. Even Stephen Blackpool's disappearance was falling into the general way, and becoming as monotonous a wonder as any piece of machinery in Coketown. (*Hard Times* 275)

When Stephen's absence has become a part of the machine-driven, Hard Fact routine of Coketown, the plot's wonder must be rescued from the fictional world's prevailing monotony. Having converted a character who once shared in the work of lending his perspective on that world[32] into a mere "piece of machinery," Dickens uses the narrative annex to reconvert Stephen Blackpool from absent to present, vengeful to forgiving, alive to dead. By bringing the worker character into the fold of focalization, by giving him a consciousness and representing his thoughts, however awkwardly, Dickens creates the expectation that he will follow Stephen to the end. The residual form of the picaresque, with its jolts and bumps and drops underlies Stephen Blackpool's misadventure. The reader cannot follow Stephen Blackpool, since the narration vested in him becomes mute when he disappears. Here, in the least digressive of Dickens' novels, the annex reveals the hiding hole in a novel crushingly short on space.

Sissy and Rachael together make the excursion away from Coketown that marks the entrance of an alternative fictional realm.[33] In contrast to the opening scene of Elizabeth Gaskell's *Mary Barton*, in which workers walk in groups to Green Heys Fields outside Manchester (39–46), Sissy's and Rachael's flight from "the smoke" denies the possibility of really getting away from the industrial city. They begin with a train trip; and even a few miles out of town, they find and enter a landscape that is a hybrid of the natural and the industrial, a middle place:

Though the green lanscape was blotted here and there with heaps of coal, it was green elsewhere, and there were trees to see, and there were larks singing (though it was Sunday), and there were pleasant scents in the air, and all was overarched by a bright blue sky. In the distance one way, Coketown showed as a black mist; in another distance, hills began to rise; in a third, there was a faint change in the light of the horizon, where it shone upon the far-off sea. (283)

Sissy and Rachael enter into the exhausted landscape "under their feet" (283), "sometimes getting over a fragment of a fence so rotten that it dropped at a touch of the foot, sometimes passing near a wreck of bricks and beams overgrown with grass, marking the site of deserted works. They followed paths and tracks, however slight" (283). This entrance into the annex frames the scene with unreachable horizons – the hills, the sea – and circumscribes the characters' access, suggesting both their limitations and their (unacknowledged) search by directing attention to their feet.

When they come upon Stephen's hat in the grass, a sign of both his presence and his absence, Sissy and Rachael instigate a shift into a different generic mode, where Dickens shows the cooperative action of the rescue as a blend of imagination and technical know-how, where the emergency itself can effect near-miraculous changes. A man in a drunken slumber, for example, hearing of Stephen's misfortune, "started out to a pool of dirty water, put his head in it, and came back sober" (286). (In the earlier pages of the novel, a habit of drink has been harder to break!) A fictional world divided into antithetical realms of fact and fancy rallies to the rescue in a universalizing scene of suspense and pity. In this narrative annex we see Dickens the popular journalist working up out of melodrama an emergent form whose descendent episodes – baby Jessica in the well – still command an audience, and whose themes – the avoidance of fixing blame; the celebration of on-the-spot nameless heroes; the focus on the pitiable spectacle of the mangled victim – survive unaltered to this day.

The contrast with Dickens' journalistic campaign in *Household Words* to effect reform in the "factory accident question"[34] is striking. In the first installment, "Preventable Accidents," the author Henry Morley concludes that the people responsible, out of carelessness and negligence, for failing to take safety measures that could prevent accidents "must be punished for the wrong they do and the suffering they cause."[35] Having decided against depicting a strike or an industrial accident in his novel,[36] Dickens moves in the annex away from the industrial scene to an undermined green world in which the Condition of England question goes deeper than dangerous factories, unenforced regulations, and irresponsible owners. Although the disused mine shaft into which Stephen Blackpool falls is not an "unfenced shaft,"[37] a term specifically designating dangerous constructions *inside* factories (particularly in textile mills), it is the product of someone's making. For Old Hell Shaft is not a natural feature of the landscape, but a notorious man-made booby-trap that renders particularly green places – "mounds where the grass was rank and high, and where brambles, dock-weed, and such-like vegetation were confusedly heaped together" (283–4) – especially suspect. Unlike the mill-gears, wheels, drums, pulleys, and mechanical teeth that threaten workers, grass is the only sign of danger in this landscape: "Dismal stories were told in that country of the old pits hidden beneath such indications" (284). When Sissy follows the sign of the hat, she nearly falls in: "at their very feet, was the brink of a black ragged chasm, hidden by the thick grass" (284). Though the hole is all that remains of an abandoned mine, it signifies a devouring maw, as well as a used-up resource. Yet as the subject of "dismal stories," Old Hell Shaft prolifically stimulates fresh narratives of personal disasters.

George Orwell cries out in exasperation that Dickens' "radicalism is of the vaguest kind, and yet one always knows that it is there . . . He has no constructive suggestions, not even a clear grasp of the nature of the society he is attacking, only an emotional perception that something is wrong."[38] This might be a description of Stephen Blackpool's analysis of his situation. Something *is* wrong, for too many lives have been lost. The transaction of the narrative annex makes material the expendable body of the worker, a fact which Stephen himself points out in his dying speech:

"I ha' fell into th' pit, my dear, as have cost wi'in the knowledge o' old fok now livin, hundreds and hundreds o' men's lives – fathers, sons, brothers, dear to thousands an thousands, an keepin 'em fro' want and hunger. I ha' fell into a pit that ha' been wi' th' Fire-damp crueller than battle. I ha' read on't in the public petition, as onny one may read, fro' the men that works in pits, in which they ha' pray'n and pray'n the lawmakers for Christ's sake not let their work be murder to 'em, but to spare 'em for th' wives and children that they loves as well as gentlefok loves theirs. When it were in work, it killed wi'out need; when 'tis let alone, it kills wi'out need. See how we die an no need, one way an another – in a muddle – every day!" (289–90)

Stephen's awareness of his own expendability, and his frank account of the lost lives of the hundreds and hundreds who have already died, does not lead him to point an accusing finger. One of the men who has been lowered down the shaft relates Stephen's story to the expectant crowd, establishing that Stephen has in fact obeyed the summons he is suspected of evading:

He had come straight away from his work, on being written to, and had walked the whole journey; and was on his way to Mr. Bounderby's country-house after dark, when he fell. He was crossing that dangerous country at such a dangerous time, because he was innocent of what was laid to his charge, and couldn't rest from coming the nearest way to deliver himself up. The Old Hell Shaft, the pitman said, with a curse upon it, was worthy of its bad name to the last; for, though Stephen could speak now, he believed it would soon be found to have mangled the life out of him. (288)

When Stephen is brought out of the pit, he has been converted into an object, a spectacle "to make the head swim, and oppress the heart" (289).

The annex presents an object of pity whose mangled body replaces the countless victimized workers with a single "figure of a poor, crushed, human creature" (289). Veiled with a gauze of sentimentality, the tender death-scene directs the attention to a spiritual narrative that replaces the schemes and outrages that have brought Stephen to this pass: "And at that time the pale, worn, patient face was seen looking up at the sky, with the broken right hand lying bare on the outside of the covering garments, as if waiting to be taken by another hand" (289). Stephen and Rachael, who will never be united now, gaze at the star that has shone on Stephen while he lay in the shaft: "'In my pain an trouble, lookin up yonder, – wi' it shinin' on me – I ha' seen more clear, and ha' made it my dyin prayer that aw th' world may on'y coom toogether more, an get a better unnerstan'in o'one another, than when I were in't my own weak seln'" (291). With this feeble wish for cooperation and understanding, Dickens dispatches Stephen to his martyr's fate: "It was soon a funeral procession. The star had shown him where to find the God of the poor; and through humility, and sorrow, and forgiveness, he had gone to his Redeemer's rest" (292). Drained of significance as an actor in any story except the Christian plot of redemption, Stephen Blackpool becomes, as Ruskin notes, a "dramatic perfection instead of a characteristic example of an honest workman."[39] At the same time, he has been emptied out of personality. While down in the shaft, he advances Tom's criminal plot; drawn back out of it, he does not need to live to finish that story.

When Stephen speaks, he remarks on the history of the shaft, but his attention is already focused on the star that has taught him to forgive those who have victimized him:

"It ha' shined into my mind . . . If soom ha' been wantin' in unnerstan'in me better, I, too, ha' been wantin' in unnerstan'in them better. When I got thy letter, I easily believen that what the yoong ledy sen a done to me, an what her brother sen an done to me, was one, an that there were a wicked plot betwixt 'em. When I fell, I were in anger wi' her, an hurrying on t' be as onjust t' her as oothers was t' me. But in our judgements, like as in our doins, we mun bear and forbear." (290–1)

Old Hell Shaft converts Stephen Blackpool from a moral agent into a representative virtue, the victim who forgives as he expires. In the annex, the worker as character is transformed back into the worker as thing; having been used by his drunken wife, his employer, and even his fellow workers, Stephen Blackpool is at last used up by his maker.

This narrative annex attracts the attention of Dickens' contemporaries, who register a wide range of reactions to Stephen Blackpool and his fate. On the one hand, Dickens' ideal working man seems to have pleased some readers. The reviewer for the *Westminster Review* admires Stephen Blackpool's "rugged steadfastness, sturdy truth, upright bearing, and fine Northern English dialect,"[40] and even generally negative assessments of the novel single out Stephen for praise.[41] Yet later descriptions of Stephen as "little more than a diagrammatic figure" and an unconvincing working man[42] were anticipated by contemporaries. In 1856 E. H. Yates and R. B. Brough published a parody of *Hard Times* with a "refinished" ending that aims its satire directly at the events of the narrative annex:

It would seem that the striking want of poetical justice in the usually-received termination of this otherwise excellent story, wherein none of the good people were made happy, and the wicked were most inadequately punished, had caused the author to tremble for his popularity among the female portion of the community – who, it is well known, will stand no liberties of that description.[43]

The parody contrives to poison Stephen's wife, to marry Stephen and Louisa, to dispatch Bounderby in an industrial accident ("He was a self-made man, but he had not made himself of sufficiently strong materials to resist the influence of the melancholy-mad elephants" ["*Hard Times (refinished)*" 154]), and to consign Mr. Gradgrind to the Circus, where he works as a clown. It begins with the scene at Old Hell Shaft and parodies both Stephen's piety and his conversion into a martyr. How does he feel? " 'Hoomble and happy, lass. I be grateful and thankful. I be obliged to them as have brought charges o' robbery agin me . . . I do only look on my being pitched down that theer shaft, and having all my bones broke, as a mercy and a providence, and God bless ev'rybody!'" (143). In the refinished *Hard Times*, Stephen is revived with a drink of rum and water, to Mr. Bounderby's irritation: "'O here!' Mr. Bounderby blustered forward: 'I'm not going to stand this. If a man suspected of robbing Josiah Bounderby, of Coketown's Bank is to feel "much better," I should like to know what's the use of Old Hell Shafts'" (145). The *use* of Old Hell Shafts is evident to this parodist (R. B. Brough) as a device to dispense with – and canonize – Stephen Blackpool.

While Stephen's piety strikes Brough as ridiculous, under the circumstances, the critic in the *British Quarterly Review* is equally annoyed because Stephen's religious character springs out of a hostile environment: "Mr. Dickens has characters of great moral beauty, but care seems to be taken that this beauty of character shall come into existence, not only apart from any religious influences, but in circumstances most alien to such influences."[44] Margaret Oliphant puts the complaint most directly, suggesting that Dickens unfairly misleads his readers and misuses his best character:

Stephen Blackpool is only introduced to bring out the greater villainy of the wretched little rogue of the story, and to be made a forced example, in his domestic circumstances, of the unequal pressure of the law upon the rich and poor – and, in his death, of the carelessness and neglect to which so many lives are sacrificed . . . When we have said all this, we still leave undiminished our condemnation of the book, – a story made on the didactic principle, with all its events forced into proofs of an untenable theory, and with almost the only life among its personages, which thoroughly interests us, thrown away, forsooth, to show the evils of that carelessness, which, in great matters and little matters, from Balaklava to the Lancashire coal-pits, is undoubtedly becoming a rather remarkable feature of our national character.[45]

Aside from the novel's didacticism, which hinders its success by binding it within the limits of a preconceived idea, Oliphant objects most strenuously to Dickens' willful wasting of his character in "the petulant theory of a man in a world of his own making, where he has no fear of being contradicted, and is absolutely certain of having everything his own way" ("Dickens" 453). Oliphant's criticism is driven by an aversion to overt worldmaking, especially the sort of craft that does not scruple to create an auxiliary space that drops out of the surface of the confining fiction. This sort of structure is particularly well suited to the stark contrasts of melodrama. In W. H. C. Nation's *Under The Earth; Or, the Sons of Toil: A Romantic Drama, in Three Acts* (1867), an adaptation of the novel for the stage, the hole in the ground serves as the locus not only of Stephen's downfall, but of a heroic descent by Rachael, who hauls

Stephen back out of the pit. Here Old Hell Shaft is expanded from the narrative annex into one of the two main locations of the play, Sleary's circus having been eliminated from the drama entirely. (Bitzer plays Sissy Jupe's role in the search for Stephen.) In the melodrama, the alternative realm to the Hard Fact world of Coketown is rewritten as a zone of heartrending heroism, rather than as a locale of fancy.[46]

Since the fictional realms of *Hard Times* (town, households, institutions, and the circus) are only lightly tethered to the real social world Dickens criticizes, the annex he creates seems paradoxically more literal than the fictional world to which he connects it. Oliphant's yoking of the mines of Lancashire and the debacle of the Crimean conflict to a national character beset by carelessness suggests that Stephen's fall into Old Hell Shaft makes a fitting emblem for the Victorian predicament. Dickens' narrative annex undermines the reform he advocates, for even if schools were to take account of Fancy and families were reconstituted into properly nurturing forms, the extent of the Condition of England includes ancient fractures older and deeper than the schematized realms so easily praised and blamed. Charles Dickens kills Stephen Blackpool to make this point.

THE SPELL OF THE BLOOD-STAINED BLACK BODY

A first-person confessional narrative, what a contemporary critic aptly called a "picaresque novel of the soul,"[47] provides the vehicle for H. G. Wells' broadside of blame, *Tono-Bungay*. Wells uses a narrative annex to create a space in which his sinning protagonist can violate the one commandment he has not broken: thou shalt not kill. In this novel, the dark conversion of George Ponderevo predicts that the end product of England's commercial achievement will be the perfection of naval destroyers. A reviewer for the *Spectator* writes "Nothing could be more pessimistic. We are on the eve of tremendous discoveries in the direction of applied science; but, as a set-off, the race is degenerating, and the individuals who 'come through' – like the narrator – do so by virtue of vehement self-assertion, by stifling the voice of conscience, by a callous disregard of human life and family ties."[48]

Far away from England on a West African island, George Ponderevo's inexplicable and cowardly murder of a black man, in a narrative annex, emblematizes the many victims of the patent medicine, Tono-Bungay, and establishes a link between George's actions and his report of the cancerous decay of England. Since George causes the spectacle of morbidity and corruption, the events on Mordet Island mark the climax of his guilty confession. Despite George's protestations to the contrary, his act of murder in the narrative annex is not incidental. Although the so-called "quap episode" has attracted the attention of most critics of the novel, few of those who defend its presence in the novel on thematic grounds have attempted to integrate the dead black man's body back into the plot, or to understand what the murder might mean. Those who have commented on it see a symbolic resonance with the metaphors of death and decay, so that George's act merely amplifies the point that his narration already makes. When he slays the black man, George successfully struggles to kill his conscience, as well. The entire narration emanates from a character who has all but exonerated himself, but whose personal guilt permeates his entire depiction of the Condition of England. Wells uses the narrative annex to open up and then slam shut the redemptive narratives that provide an escape hatch from the pessimistic atmosphere of so many political novels.

Better known for his scientific romances and utopias, Wells wrote several "full-dress novels,"[49] but *Tono-Bungay* stands out among them for its imitation of the great Victorian forms of *Bildungsroman* and Condition of England novel.[50] Wells uses these forms to structure a confessional narrative whose protagonist narrates and demonstrates the moral decay of England. *Tono-Bungay* tells the story of the rise and fall of a purveyor of patent medicines, Uncle Teddy Ponderevo, through the eyes of his nephew George. By means of George's picaresque wanderings up from the servant class and through society, with a mobility that is facilitated by the inefficacious elixir that gives the novel its title and central metaphor, Wells' novel adds another opinion to the diagnosis of the Condition of England.[51] According to the author, it blends "a certain proportion of scientific fantasia with what he considered to be humorous observation; the 'quap' nonsense, for instance, in what was really a three-decker novel in *Tono-Bungay*."[52]

It is difficult to avoid falling under the spell of Wells' characteristic flippancy, evident in the voice of his narrator in this partially autobiographical fiction. The reviewer in the *Spectator* complains that "it is difficult to avoid identifying the views of the author with those of the narrator" ("Tono-Bungay" 346), and the writer in the *Times Literary Supplement* wonders how to extract a moral: "How far are the opinions of George Ponderevo, who tells this story, to be taken for those of Mr. H. G. Wells? How far does George Ponderevo stand, in Mr. Wells' eyes, for what the Moralities would call *Humanum Genus*?"[53] George's first-person narration self-consciously undermines its literariness even as Wells attempts a "social panorama in the vein of Balzac" (Wells, *Experiment,* II. 503). George Ponderevo warns his readers not to expect a streamlined, or Jamesian, narration:

I warn you this book is going to be something of an agglomeration. I want to trace my social trajectory (and my uncle's) as the main line of my story, but as this is my first novel, and almost certainly my last, I want to get in, too, all sorts of things that struck me, things that amused me and impressions I got – even though they don't minister directly to my narrative at all . . . My ideas of a novel all through are comprehensive rather than austere. (*Tono-Bungay* 5–6)

This manifesto not only declares Wells' adherence to the Victorian "loose baggy" form, but justifies the inclusion (late in his story, in the fourth chapter of the third book) of the quap episode – the narrative annex – as the great Tono-Bungay empire teeters on the edge of disaster.

When Uncle Teddy Ponderevo sends George to an island off the coast of Africa to steal the quap, a valuable radioactive substance (or crap?) needed to save his bankrupt uncle from ruin, George breaks from his normal problem-solving, relatively cool and uninvolved behavior, which has allowed him to stay distant from Uncle Teddy's criminal negligence. When in a gratuitous act of aggression George shoots an African in the back, the black man's body will not stay buried. Condensed into one corpse in the narrative annex, the black man's body calls up all the bodies that have been victimized by the entrepreneur's patent medicine. The annex serves not only to introduce an emblem of decay, however, but also to provide a ground for the rising Englishman, "the new type, cultured polytechnically,"[54] to act out his most destructive fantasies of power and aggression. Though the radioactive, hull-rotting, and cancerous quap is a good candidate for a globally threatening other, George meets a more conventional representative of otherness in the annex. The nightmarish aftermath of the murder unwrites the consequences of the act (there is no corpse left in the end, for it has been rescued for proper burial by the never-seen native islanders), allowing George to deny its significance and to embark on a new career as a maker of destroyers.

The circumstances of the voyage to the island arise in the novel as yet another adventure in a picaresque, but one that takes the protagonist far from the country houses that have anchored the meandering narration. Like the voyages in Wells' *The Island of Doctor Moreau* (1896) and Conrad's *Heart of Darkness* (1899–1902),[55] this adventure takes the narrator out to sea. Uncle Teddy Ponderevo, the inventor and purveyor of the totally useless (strychnine-laced) patent medicine, Tono-Bungay, convinces his nephew George to travel to an island off the coast of West Africa where heaps of quap lie waiting to be stolen. Yet it is not just the departure from England that marks the expedition as an annex; it is the way in which the "novelist" himself can barely explain why he must tell this part of his story: "That expedition to Mordet Island stands apart from all the rest of my life, detached, a piece by itself with an atmosphere of its own" (375). Because the narrator habitually comments on the way he crafts his life into a novel, he announces the peculiarly independent properties of the annex and hints at the difficulty of containing it: "It would, I suppose, make a book by itself – it has made a fairly voluminous official report – but so far as this novel of mine goes it is merely an episode, a contributory experience, and I mean to keep it at that" (375).

George's desire to contain the events that transpire in the annex within the bounds of his *Bildungsroman* should not obscure the fact that he *does* report them to his readers. To what extent George's novel matches the official report we do not know (although we recall the implied disparity between Kurtz' actions and his report to the Society for the Suppression of Savage Customs in *Heart of Darkness*) but the killing of the black man certainly goes unreported. George's confession is protected on all sides by a bigger story, as if the killing were an event that could only be surrounded, not explained.

The novel opens with two big bricks of paragraphs, detailing the great variety of people (in rank, profession, and type) that George Ponderevo has met in his "miscellaneous tasting of life" (3). Between these two brick-like paragraphs, Ponderevo smears a line of mortar, an insubstantial paragraph of its own: "And once (though it is the most incidental thing in my life) I murdered a man" (4). The guilty conscience of the narrating character creates the narrative annex, in which his obsessive interactions with his victim belie the annex's "incidental" contents. Until the killing in the annex, George has only aided in the packaging of Tono-Bungay, the poisonous patent medicine with which Teddy Ponderevo would dose the world. Clever with inventions, George steps in with a "whoosh" of imagination and streamlines the handling and packing of Tono-Bungay. If his hands are dirty, they are dirty because he finds better ways for the machinery of the assembly line to do what workers' hands would have done. His complicity can be measured in the distance he puts between himself and the consumption of Tono-Bungay by its millions of gullible purchasers.

Even in George's personal life, proximity endangers. His love affairs cannot work because he expertly avoids intimacy. He is an engaging narrator because his self-proclaimed distance from the events he narrates permits him to assume an ironic tone, covered with a flaking veneer of naïveté. The success of this voice has unduly influenced interpretations of the novel, as many critics have adopted George's assertions at face value, particularly his denials and hesitations about the place of the quap episode in his narration. David Lodge persuasively suggests that the "frame" of the novel (its descriptions of landscapes, townscapes, houses, shops, and domestic and commercial interiors) is in fact its real subject, as well as the means by which Wells gets at the Condition of England (*"Tono-Bungay"* 114). The first critic of *Tono-Bungay* to see the quap episode as an integral piece of symbolic action within the novel, Lodge instigates a host of interpretations seconding the motion. Earlier critics condemn the episode in George's terms, noting its detachment, its episodic quality, and its unmatching atmosphere. Lodge also adopts George's views, but he emphasizes theme rather than technique. Picking up and essentially repeating George's interpretation of the quap, Lodge regards the heap of radioactive stuff as emblematic of civilization's condition, for it can only decay and disintegrate (*"Tono-Bungay"* 135).

We should regard the narrator's self-interpreted emblems warily, for Wells shows us that George is a master at presenting emblems that he can mock from a distance. Having reprinted the front cover of "The Sacred Grove: A Weekly Magazine of Art, Philosophy, Science, and Belles Lettres," its contents ("A Hitherto Unpublished Letter from Walter Pater; Charlotte Brontë's Maternal Great Aunt; The Genius of Shakespeare") flanked by puffs for Tono-Bungay ("Have you a Nasty Taste in your Mouth? It is Liver . . . The Best Pill in the World for an Irregular Liver"), George comments, "As a matter of fact, nothing could be more entirely natural and representative of the relations of learning, thought and the economic situation in the world . . . the quiet conservatism of the one element embedded in the aggressive brilliance of the other; the contrasted notes of bold physiological experiment and extreme mental immobility" (268–9). George peppers his narration with ads for Tono-Bungay, always mildly satirizing them, as intelligent readers of advertisements like to think they do as a matter of course. George, however, falls for one aspect of the myth he markets. He believes that Tono-Bungay has become a universal medium, not unlike money, in which everything else is embedded. Thus the poisonous dose that diffuses through the social world becomes a metaphoric cancer, afflicting everything, and handily diminishing the significance of his own culpability.

Wells depicts the voyage to Africa not as an escape, but as an engulfment. Though he sails away from England, George is swallowed up by a world that will not be kept at a distance:

> But so it was I made my voyage to Africa, and came at last into a world of steamy fogs and a hot smell of vegetable decay, and into sound and sight of surf and distant intermittent glimpses of the coast. I lived a strange concentrated life through all that time, such a life as a creature must do that has fallen in a well. (381)

Unlike Stephen Blackpool, however, George's fall into the well does not convert revenge into forgiveness, nor anger into pious anticipation of the next world. Instead, Wells uses the narrative annex to demonstrate the hazards to George Ponderevo's soul.

In 1908, Wells published an account of his personal theology, *First & Last Things: A Confession of Faith and Rule of Life*.[56] Culminating in an endorsement of socialism, this volume sheds light on what Wells accomplishes through the negative example of George Ponderevo's narrative. Wells expresses belief in the common humanity of others: "Each human being I see as essentially a circle of thought between an internal and an external world" (*Confession* 55); and deplores the division that keeps the "real solidarity of mankind" from achieving "the stupendous possibilities of deliberate self-development" (69). Hate separates humans from one another, although it may motivate their banding together, and love, which multiplies rather than eliminating its objects, "is a thing more comprehensive and enduring" (108–9). These principles lead to Wells' condemnation of wrong ways of living:

> it is manifest we condemn living in idleness or on non-productive sport, on the income derived from private property, and all sorts of ways of earning a living that cannot be shown to conduce to the constructive process. We condemn trading that is merely speculative, and in fact all trading and manufacture that is not a positive social service; we condemn living by gambling or playing games for either stakes or pay. Much more do we condemn dishonest or fraudulent trading and every act of advertisement that is not punctiliously truthful. (118)

George's *Bildungsroman*, and his observations of Uncle Teddy's career, demonstrate, in sequence, each of the wrong ways of living. His action on Mordet Island combines theft with a worse crime, a murder that is a pure act of hatred, for here George becomes so detached that he cannot imagine the humanity of his victim. The life of a creature that has fallen into a well is entirely isolated, selfish, and ultimately lethal. The anonymous reviewer in the *Nation* (London) takes this point of view, writing "George Ponderevo breaks during his life every one of the commandments. He is guilty of murder, adultery, and thieving on a grand scale . . . And so this adventure – as the whole human adventure – takes upon itself, at best, an aspect of failure: of so many things done with ill purpose, of so many with no purpose at all."[57] Read in this light, *Tono-Bungay* becomes the *Bildungsroman* of a sociopath.

The narrative annex frames the endangered body within an artificially depopulated story of financial success. George describes the quest for the quap, the cure for Tono-Bungay, as a disease: "The malaria of the quap was already in my blood" (385). Yet not just the unethical prospecting infects, but the radioactive quap itself, which makes the sailors sick as they quarry it. Far away from England in the Conradian jungle, George connects the radioactivity of the quap with the Condition of England:

But there is something – the only word that comes near it is cancerous – and that is not very near, about the whole of quap, something that creeps and lives as a disease lives by destroying; an elemental stirring and disarrangement, incalculably maleficent and strange . . . It is in matter exactly what the decay of our old culture is in society, a loss of traditions and distinctions and assured reactions. When I think of these inexplicable dissolvent centres . . . I am haunted by a grotesque fancy of the ultimate eating away and dry-rotting and dispersal of all our world. (386–7)

Strongly reminiscent not only of Conrad's modern vision, this quasi-allegorical reading of the quap on Mordet Island connects the episode to dystopic islands such as the Ireland of Book v of *The Faerie Queene*. We are reminded of C. S. Lewis' remarks on the corrupting effect of the Irish experience on Spenser's imagination. Wells depicts a similar process, in which soul-death and the decay of the modern world exhibit mutual contamination. When the men sicken, George turns into a virtual slave driver in order to get the quap into the hold. "I hated all humanity during the time that the quap was near me" (389). This is an excuse, a denial of the vengeful hatred that motivates the murder. After all, the quap does not appear to harm the black residents of Mordet Island; George is the lethal agent who penetrates their world. These scenes of a cruel and murderous George, supervising his wilting crew and burying

his victim, paradoxically reinscribe the human body within an insistent-
ly dehumanizing frame.

The annex marks the beginning of the end of the possibilities of the
Bildungsroman. The killing of the black man marks the real first step in the
soul-death of a man who will go on to design a destroyer, which sails
down the Thames in the last chapter of the novel. Not surprisingly, the
hero of that putative story of development cannot explain the significance of his actions:

It was the most unmeaning and purposeless murder imaginable. Even as I write
down its well-remembered particulars there comes again the sense of its
strangeness, its pointlessness, its incompatibility with any of the neat and
definite theories people hold about life and the meaning of the world. I did this
thing and I want to tell of my doing it, but why I did it and particularly why I
should be held responsible for it I cannot explain. (391)

It seems that no one, not even the most exasperated critic, holds George
responsible.[58] Because the killing is contained by the annex, the
radiocative glow of the quap outshines the murder. Wells devises the
murder in the narrative annex in order to drive George's narration. He
makes the point that no safe distance exists from which to criticize a
corrupt society, that the story itself relies on a corrupt and corrupting
power source. Contaminated by his own action, George describes a
diseased and decaying world. The vividness of this rendering of late
Victorian and early twentieth-century England should not distract the
reader from George's own part in destroying the world.

The murder scene in the narrative annex shows that the nameless
victim has a physical specificity that hovers between stereotype and the
imaginative description of a Wellsian monster:

He wasn't by any means a pretty figure. He was very black and naked except
for a dirty loin-cloth, his legs were ill-shaped and his toes spread wide and the
upper edge of his cloth and a girdle of string cut his clumsy abdomen into folds.
His forehead was low, his nose very flat and his lower lip swollen and purplish-
red. His hair was short and fuzzy, and about his neck was a string and a little
purse of skin. He carried a musket, and a powder flask was stuck in his girdle.
(391)

"It was a curious confrontation," George comments coolly. The black
man runs away, frightened by the even more horrifying apparition of
the invading thief or slave-driver on his island. When the reader's gaze
falls back on George, it is to witness the murder: "And with that
instantly I brought both feet together, raised my gun, aimed quite

coolly, drew the trigger carefully and shot him neatly in the back" (392). George drags the "frightfully smashed" corpse to a muddy place and half buries him. In the night, the uncanny force of the murdered man asserts itself: "The black body which I saw now damaged and partly buried, but which, nevertheless, I no longer felt was dead but acutely alive and perceiving, I mixed up with the ocherous slash under my uncle's face" (393). In George's dream, the image of Teddy Ponderevo's cut throat overwrites guilt with blame, as if to justify the murder by identifying the true object of George's hatred. The corpse infects and enchants the island: "The next day was utterly black with my sense of that ugly creature's body. I am the least superstitious of men, but it drew me. It drew me back into those thickets to the very place where I had hidden him" (394). The corpse ("it") possesses a power greater than the killed man ("him"). An animal disinters the corpse, and George buries the "swollen and mangled carcass" once more. The next day, as the logic of horror demands, George finds an empty grave: "there were human footmarks and ugly stains round the muddy hole from which he had been dragged" (394). The annex releases decay into the fictional world by transferring it from metaphor into a metonymy, the human corpse who represents all the victimized. George can leave the body behind, but not the corruption, for it emanates from him.

One would think that George would never forget his encounter with the black man, but the flight from the island with the quap wipes away his consciousness of guilt. He claims, "I was released from the spell of that bloodstained black body all mixed up with grey-black mud. I was going back to baths and decent food and aeronautics and Beatrice" (395). All that remains for the novel is the loss of the quap (it sinks the ship by rotting its very fabric), the bankruptcy and death of Teddy Ponderevo, and George's escape into a lucrative business building destroyers. George asserts that his failure in love haunts his story: "It haunts this book, I see, that is what haunts this book, from end to end" (449), but what really permeates the novel is a point of view emanating from a murderer.

George describes England as a sterile world, populated by childless women, useless schemers, and above all wasters: "It is all one spectacle of forces running to waste, of people who use and do not replace, the story of a country hectic with a wasting aimless fever of trade and money-making and pleasure-seeking!" (450). This England is the logical outcome of the utilitarian England of *Hard Times*, for using up things –

and people – is its unmistakable method.[59] With no space left on the globe for founding new worlds, the island to which the novel unexpectedly veers serves only as the site of some valuable material which can be hauled away for profit. On his destroyer, George muses on the boats he passes: "They stand out, bound on strange missions of life and death, to the killing of men in unfamiliar lands" (457). The ultimate failure of humanity in Wells' vision occurs when its mission becomes the conversion of the living into the dead.

More natural, more ancient, more remote, the narrative annexes in the three novels discussed in this chapter channel the desires or guilty fantasies of fictions that grapple with the Condition of England. The boundary crossings are elaborated from a walk in the woods, to an excursion through a perilously undermined landscape, to a sea-voyage. Yet the annexes do not depict uninhabited margins, or places in which the Condition of England can be forgotten. Already filled up, already in use, they frame representative, simplistic, often stereotypical stand-ins for the welter of otherness that the surrounding fictional worlds cannot admit.

Because H. G. Wells' *Tono-Bungay* was published in 1908–9,[60] it is not usually discussed with Victorian political novels. Indeed, although Wells describes his effort to write a "real full-length novel . . . on Dickens–Thackeray lines" (*Experiment*, II. 639), the action of *Tono-Bungay* ends in the Edwardian period, with the protagonist sailing a destroyer out of the Thames.[61] Critics have recognized emergent modern form in *Tono-Bungay*, particularly in the episode – the stealing of the quap – that I treat above as a narrative annex.[62] Structurally, this narrative annex is no different from those we have seen in mid nineteenth-century novels, but the turn into the twentieth century and the transition to a new period alters the reception of certain narrative techniques. In the review in the *Nation*, for instance, we can see how ideas about modernity come around to justify and celebrate aspects of narrative form that earlier critics would have deplored as episodic, incidental, and improbable. *Tono-Bungay* depicts

the astonishing life of the twentieth century . . . comes to the heart of modern life; and goes far to interpret through the medium of fiction, the meaning of all its multitudinous energies and aims . . . It is a confusion, because modern life is a confusion. It passes as a series of episodes, random and disconnected, because all experience which is not numbed by custom or hedged in to irrevocable routine must necessarily be random and disconnected in such a tumultuous, fragmentary world.[63]

Remarkably, the critic recuperates episodic confusion itself to emergent modernity. When Wells' narrator declares his intention to flout James' proscription of loose baggy monsters, he deliberately employs Victorian techniques, including digressions, interpolated essays, and a narrative annex. The New York *Nation* notes the novel's "recurrence to the Victorian manner, although the substance of the story is of today,"[64] but Francis Hackett proclaims "Because it suggests the three-ring Thackerayan plot, and is crammed with philosophy, it has been set down as a mid-Victorian effusion. It is no more mid-Victorian than the Flatiron."[65] As these reactions suggest, *Tono-Bungay* presents an especially vivid example of the novel's capacity to contain residual and emergent forms simultaneously within a (still) dominant genre. The form Wells adopts is Victorian, including the narrative annex within it, but here the presence of an emergent form coincides with the reviewer's consciousness of modernity. A technique that has been present throughout Victorian fiction becomes associated with modern form, and the process of reinventing the image of the Victorian novel begins.

CHAPTER 6

Victorian annexes and modern form

If you were not born in Arcadia, you linger in fancy on its margin; your thoughts are busy with the flutes of antiquity, with daffodils, and the classic poplar, and the footsteps of the nymphs, and the elegant and moving aridity of ancient art. Why dedicate to you a tale of a caste so modern; – full of details of our barbaric manners and unstable morals; – full of the need and the lust of money, so that there is scarce a page in which dollars do not jingle; – full of the unrest and movement of our century, so that the reader is hurried from place to place and sea to sea, and the book is less a romance than a panorama; – in the end, as blood-bespattered as an epic? . . . The tone of the age, its movement, the mingling of races and classes in the dollar hunt, the fiery and not quite unromantic struggle for existence with its changing trades and scenery, and two types in particular, that of the American handy-man of business and that of the Yankee merchant sailor – we agreed to dwell upon at some length . . . After we had invented at some expense of time this method of approaching and fortifying our police novel, it occurred to us it had been invented previously by someone else, and was in fact – however painfully different the results may seem – the method of Charles Dickens.

Robert Louis Stevenson and Lloyd Osbourne "Epilogue,"
The Wrecker (1891)

Throughout this study I have argued that metaphors of place, zone, and realm appear to be indispensable to the Victorians as they define and redefine the job of the novel. Equally important are metaphors of boundaries, although the critics' repeatedly drawn lines in the sand get scuffed by risqué French fiction, didactic social-problem novels, sensation fiction, "vulgar" realism, flagrantly episodic narratives, and, notoriously, novels attempting to deal with sexuality frankly, such as the naturalistic work of George Moore. The lively contest between novelists and cultural watchdogs (often novelists themselves, serving as readers for publishers, or as anonymous reviewers) results not in homogeneity, though the vast majority of the 60,000 plus works of Victorian fiction must have pleased their readers by comfortably reproducing the standard three-volume product.[1] Instead, at the level of the most noteworthy novels of the period – for nearly all of the tiny canon of works that make up our "Victorian novel" received the attention of contemporary critics – we find many traces of a seventy-year-long negotiation of the boundaries of representation. Generic mixture (particularly in the case of social fiction), the inclusion of politically sensitive topics, the depiction of scurrilous characters without clear reprobation of vice, and representation of any action or character that might bring a blush to the cheek of the young person earn condemnation[2] for crossing a line whose existence everyone acknowledged, if not applauded.[3]

In the twentieth century we have been more attentive to the cases involving the limits on representation of sexuality, though, as I have attempted to show, in narrative annexes novelists often blend rather daring allusions to sexuality with other unpopular, risky, or discomforting subjects. For instance, as John Sutherland notes, the publisher Smith rejected a novel by Harriet Martineau for its favorable depiction of Catholicism.[4] In 1851 "Papal Aggression" made Catholic-bashing a safer strategy, as Charlotte Brontë may have realized as she created the overtly anti-Catholic outer world, and the carefully bounded narrative annexes, of *Villette*. Though Geraldine Jewsbury, reading for the publisher Bentley, rejected manuscripts on the basis of immorality (she had Mudie's standards in mind), she also reacted negatively to fiction in foreign settings (particularly when the characters were not English), to novels focusing on money and business, to books about the laboring class that lacked higher-class characters to attract the sympathies of middle-class readers, and to fiction that retold or imagined the life of Christ.[5] Potentially blasphemous stories (or those that invited a blasphemous response); distastefully attentive representation of laborers or the poor; sordid, depressing, or too-technical approaches to the world of work (humor helped); or off-putting otherness unleavened by Englishness – all might doom a manuscript passing through Jewsbury's hands (*Mudie's* 126–9). While common sense demands that we refrain from celebrating a lost alternative tradition of the Victorian novel, made up of daring, experimental, socially responsible, and *unpublished* manuscripts, it is important to note that some of what the Victorians wrote did not get into print because of these broadly applied strictures.

The fact that some Victorian novelists succeeded in representing unpopular characters, subjects, settings, and plot-lines shows not only that different publishers took different risks (for insanity and bigamy, to name only two of the ingredients of sensation fiction, were too popular *not* to publish and circulate), but also that some novelists could earn exemptions from the rules. As John Sutherland observes, the practice of awarding advance contracts to successful authors allowed these privileged few to achieve "artistic autonomy" (*Victorian Novelists* 78), resulting in historical novels (by Eliot, Charles Reade, and Thackeray), social problem novels (Charlotte Brontë), political novels (Trollope), and intricate multiplot fiction (Dickens). Not only subjects, but ways of constructing fiction could be limited by the critical consensus, for, as Sutherland notes, in Dickens' case, "complexity was a luxury earlier success had entitled him to" (80). Indeed, as I have suggested throughout the preceding chapters, narrative technique and the subjects of fiction must be considered together, since reviewers' censure of formal matters often encodes disapproval of the contents of novels, and novelists' formal choices often reveal their struggles with the demands and constraints on representation.

Though some novelists succeeded in ignoring the critics (G. H. Lewes screened Eliot's reviews), none could afford to defy *all* of the strictures that composed a negative theory of the novel, for the material conditions of publishing (in periodicals, parts, and triple-deckers) affected every one of them. In narrative annexes we can see the Victorians' positive engagement with a constraining novel theory, with the demand for length created by prevailing modes of publication, and with the social and cultural assumptions of probability and permissibility. Recognizing the centrality to the Victorian novel's project of these seemingly marginal, brief, and peculiar episodes enables us to see more vividly how narrative annexes call attention to the ongoing contest about representation, to the diversity of Victorian fictional worldmaking, and to the continuity of narrative technique that runs from sixteenth- and seventeenth-century narrative (Sidney, Spenser, Cervantes) through the eighteenth- and nineteenth-century novel to the modern period.

The residual forms often employed in narrative annexes to Victorian novels bespeak novelists' familiarity with fiction before the novel. While I have taken care throughout this study to treat romance as a mode of fiction co-present and intermingled with the nineteenth-century novel, I have also suggested that Victorians often employ strategies redolent of earlier literature at moments when they work to negotiate limits on representation. In the hope that I could complicate the conventional opposition of novel and romance, I have endeavored to treat the generic shifting of narrative annexes with specificity and attention to their differences, naming (for instance) a dream vision, a fairy tale, a world transformed by storm, a tumble off the road of plot into a picaresque pitfall, and a turn to the mode of prophecy. Treating each of these unique generic shifts as a narrative annex draws attention to the diversity of what Rosalie Colie, writing about the mixed forms of the Renaissance, calls the "resources of kind."[6] By not tracing a single or several strands of this generic mixture (enumerating dreams in novels, or storm scenes, or fairy tales), I have eschewed taxonomy and exhaustiveness in favor of a different sort of breadth. The variety of genres called up temporarily in annexes, within a wide range of novelistic kinds, suggests to me the flexible worldmaking and world-altering powers of the Victorian novelists. These powers seem to me to betoken a growing confidence on the part of nineteenth-century novelists (rooted in the success and rise in status of fiction from the 1840s onwards), a confidence that encourages the employment of a blend of old and new techniques, and inspires more ambitious and more diverse representation.

Though many novelists of mid-century and later may have unwittingly imbibed their Spenser in deep draughts of Walter Scott, they also read *The Faerie Queene*, *The Arcadia*, *Don Quixote*, *Gargantua* and *Pantagruel*, the Arabian Nights, and perhaps most importantly, the plays of Shakespeare. In all these works, Victorian novelists discovered, among other things, what Harry Berger describes as the "second worlds" and "green worlds" of Renaissance fiction.[7] A formal technique of framing worlds within worlds, this strategy (in narrative) enables some of early modern fiction's most interesting inclusions to occur, but their form and not their content concerns me here. While the Arabian Nights, *The Decameron*, and *The Canterbury Tales* use frames to hold series of embedded tales, the progress of characters into second worlds and green worlds endows fiction with some of the advantages of representational diversity, changed conventions, and alternate settings, without implying a narrative structure that could be stretched out infinitely by further embedding. As I elaborate below, the bounded, finite limits proposed by the second world or green world not only make this strategy the closest analogue to narrative annexes, but also suggest the formal devices that best address the needs of Victorian novelists without compromising the overall impression of their verisimilar novelistic worldmaking. Berger's analysis of the power of second worlds and green worlds suggests what novelists had to gain by creating temporary, alternative fictional workspaces within their novels. Regarding texts as alternative worlds (M. H.

Abrams' *heterocosm*), Berger sees a fruitful interaction with the imaginative worlds of the texts' creation, and influentially argues that fictional, philosophical, and scientific "worlds" enable early modern thinkers to accomplish imaginative work. As a "technique of mind," the second world "separate[s] itself from the casual and confused region of everyday existence," and "promises a clarified image of the world it replaces" ("Second World and Green World"46). Reading Cervantes, for instance, Victorian novelists see the progress of Don Quixote and Sancho Panza through generically and spatially differentiated realms, and also see that it is accomplished without hindering the overall effect of a unified theme.[8] While eighteenth-century novelists (and early Victorians, such as the Dickens of *The Pickwick Papers*) often adopt the Cervantine strategy of embedding tales, Victorian novelists hoping to achieve "unity of theme" recognized a flexible tool in the continuous and yet altered imaginative spaces of the second world or green world.

Relying on simultaneously shifted setting and genre, narrative annexes also closely resemble the houses within Spenser's Faerie Land, the woods of Shakespeare, and the ubiquitous islands of Renaissance fiction. Traces of old associations with these worlds within worlds remain in the Victorian annexes they inspire. Disraeli combines the Shakespearian green world with the Cervantine inn; Dickens' American swamp metamorphoses into a Spenserian monster's terrain. Meredith calls up a Prospero's isle for his "Ferdinand" and "Miranda," but spares them parental stage-managing. Brontë blends fairy tale, Bunyan, and the desert wastes of the Hebrew Bible; Kingsley fleshes out the antiquarian dream and progress of the soul with an evolutionary vision. Wells' Mordet Island owes its lineaments not only to Conrad, but to the Ireland of Book v of *The Faerie Queene*, and to the space-bound situations of countless *picaros* and English rogues. As in Spenser's houses, annexes often contain scenes of reading or instruction, in which secondary narrators relate tales, but the physical connection of annex to surrounding world allows events more active than reading or listening to transpire, with significant consequences for plots. The contiguity of primary and secondary worlds differs strikingly from the tale placed inside another narrative level, as it binds the narrative to consecution and character established in the primary realm of the text. In annexes characters reappear after long absences; enter worlds that might exclude them; meet priests, Jews, and black men; plot, eavesdrop, starve, and commit murder. The boundary between the primary world (like Faerie Land) and the "second world" of the annex (like the House of

Holiness, Alma's House, or the Bower of Bliss) possesses a physical status as part of setting, emphasized by the characters' crossing. Like Don Quixote, Red Cross Knight, or Raphael Hythlodaeus, characters traverse the territory separating worlds, enter the annex, and depart again.[9] Unlike the reader's relation to the primary world of a novel (you can't get there from here), characters entering annexes are connected to points of departure in the primary world and to arrival in an alternative world, analogous to the secondary world of Victorian fantasy. Yet Victorian novelists send their characters across borders into representational realms that deepen and complicate the terrain of nineteenth-century fiction, without relinquishing the effect of reality.

Narrative annexes enable them to do so without abandoning verisimilar fictional worlds, or the socially and psychologically mimetic realms of realistic fiction. Indeed, even as narrative annexes use the resources of residual kinds in Victorian fiction, they often approach subjects more "realistically," representing bodily sensations such as sexual desire and hunger, reporting in a journalistic fashion scenes that affront comfortable blinkered domesticity, or going places that a respectable middle-class (female) protagonist or reader would not go. Seeing the realistic novel as romance's opposite has disabling consequences when we try to think about genre and space, so strongly associated in criticism of romance.[10] Pamela Schirmeister, for instance, sees representations of places as figuring the writing of romance, and asserts that the perennial linkage of romance and place contrasts with place in realistic fiction, even in regional literature depending upon evocation of a specific location (*Consolations* 3–4). In fact, the senses of place as location, generic convention, and prior literary utterance that Schirmeister reads in romance also function in regional and realistic fiction, and not only when novelists employ narrative annexes. The briefly evoked alternative places and genres of narrative annexes call attention not only to the commingling of realism and romance, but also to the normative representations of social and domestic places in the Victorian novel. No less than in romance, settings in the realistic novel evoke place, genre, and tradition. In his thinly veiled portrait of Caroline Norton, *Diana of the Crossways* (1885), George Meredith thematizes the spatial and generic relationship of the possible and the probable by calling attention to a character who traverses physical space and arrives at evocative settings. When, in chapter 8, Thomas Redworth rides all night hoping to deliver Lady Dunstane's letter to Diana, he passes though a shadowy churchyard. If anything, Meredith's nod to gothic heightens the realistic country-house setting of the following scenes. Though the figures Redworth thinks he sees vanish, Meredith conjures up this setting to undermine its creepy associations, for as his character reflects, "A ride down to Sussex to see ghosts would be an odd experience; but an undigested dinner of tea is the very grandmother of ghosts."[11] Rather, Meredith characterizes realistic and wish-fulfilling ways of thinking in a fairy-tale trope that illustrates the imperative to go beyond the normative and the likely: "The long ride and nightfall, with nothing in view, had obscured his mind to the possible behind the probable; again the possible waved its marshlight" (*Diana* 71). In the tradition of Charlotte Brontë, the settings of realism include states of mind figured as spaces. Just on the other side of the hedge, or at the end of the winding path, the alternative places of narrative annexes can be read as figures of possibility, in fiction hemmed-in by requirements of probability.

Critical accounts of novelists' challenges to prevailing norms of form and content often celebrate the resourcefulness, inventiveness, and courage of their heroines and heroes, and I hope that I have sufficiently conveyed my admiration for the Victorians. Yet despite their use of emergent forms, and their efforts to create alternative spaces for representation, I do not mean to praise them for a freedom they do not exercise, or for attitudes they do not possess. By using the terminology of Raymond Williams' "residual," "dominant," and "emergent" forms as neutrally as possible, I avoid suggesting a progressive model that moves towards modernity as towards improvement and greater liberation. Rather than telling a story about the origins of modern fictional techniques, I draw attention to how novelists' productive encounters with the subjects they represent stimulate the use in narrative annexes of old kinds of stories and places, or new modes and settings (or a mixture of both) without abandoning the advantageous package of the conventional Victorian novel. Because I focus on a formal strategy used to alter the dominant form of the novel, it is vital to underline three generalizations about narrative annexes. First, narrative annexes do not represent a coherent politics of story. They contest the limitations of the fictional worlds in which they occur in a variety of different ways. Second, the "residual" and "emergent" generic contrasts that accompany annexes' shifted settings do not necessarily coincide with retrograde or progressive impulses on the novelists' part. Though I have focused on the intertwined representation of sexuality, class, and conscience in narrative annexes, I believe that a careful reading of Victorian novels of faith and doubt, for instance, would reveal many uses of narrative annexes to approach the representation of the sacred. In other words (my third generalization), narrative annexes undoubtedly do more in the Victorian novel than this study reveals.

In the remainder of this brief conclusion, I consider the pragmatic and aesthetic concerns that contribute to the use of the altered settings and kinds of narrative annexes. Recounting the reasons for Victorian novelists' interest in creating alternate fictional workspaces – marked by borders that characters cross boldly, blindly, inadvertently, or deliriously – leads to one of the oddest junctures in the history of the novel. Early descriptions of the innovations of modern fiction, following Henry James' strictures, often characterize the Victorian novel as undisciplined, meandering, cluttered, and formless. In order to celebrate the formal rigor of the dramatic novel beloved of Percy Lubbock, the unity of modern fiction necessarily contrasts with the disorder and superfluities of the novels of earlier generations. Working without the benefit of a "theory of fiction," the story goes, Victorian novelists made a mess of the form by aiming for length, using copious incidents, multiple plots, and unrelated episodes. Certainly, many Victorian novels suffer from these infelicities of form, though even the writer of the baggiest sequences of baggy monsters (Anthony Trollope) could turn out tight, unified, dramatic novels such as *Cousin Henry* (1879), or *An Eye for an Eye* (1879). Henry James' famous repudiation of Trollope's technique not only sets the new standard for fiction, characterizes the huge multiplot novel as the quintessential Victorian form, and condemns the intrusive, omnipotent, and distracting narrator, but elides many continuities between Victorian and modern form. I intend neither to locate the modern in the Victorian, nor vice versa, but to end by suggesting the relationship between narrative annexes and modern form.

The effort to write a truly modern book using techniques suitable to the "tone of the age," as the "Epilogue" to *The Wrecker* by Robert Louis Stevenson and Lloyd Osbourne shows, may lead to the reinvention of the method of earlier novelists. In the other direction, the critical reaction to the form and content of Wells' *Tono-Bungay* illuminates the way in which Victorian narrative strategies can suddenly appear to be the very stuff of modernity. Few novelists acknowledge so frankly as Stevenson a debt to Victorian technique, nor risk declaring so openly as Wells the desire to imitate the out-moded triple-decker. The division of fiction in the 1880s into serious novels and popular romances may account for the difference, since Wells, Stevenson, Haggard, Conan Doyle, and the other late-Victorian romancers claimed not to invent a new form of novel, but to return fiction to its delightful origins, recapturing the pleasures of childhood reading, and innovating only in telling stranger stories, and more exciting adventures. In a dichotomy still reflected in the late twentieth-century's distinction between serious and popular "genre" fiction, the serious modern novel assimilates form, craft, and technique as if it were their original possessor, and creates a new image of the Victorian novel.

According to the generation that followed them, the Victorian novelists were hampered both by a lack of theory, and by too many prescriptions on representation. They leave too much out, and they put too much in. Early twentieth-century critics, theorists, and reviewers (I exempt Leslie Stephen, an eminent Victorian even in this century) separate these two complaints, and begin to obscure the ways in which Victorians used fictional form to include the very materials they were supposed to have omitted. As the enormous – and relatively rare – multiplot novel comes to stand for the Victorian novel as a whole, the criticism of its form as too large, too capacious, and too disrespectfully rending the veil of illusion occludes the presence of a more unified dramatic novel throughout the nineteenth century. Brownell's 1901 defense of Thackeray's "technic" suggests the degree to which James' novel theory had taken over many of the positions articulated by Lewes and other Victorian critics. Brownell writes of the long Victorian novel:

Its form is particularly, uniquely elastic, and it possesses epic advantages which it would fruitlessly forgo in conforming to purely dramatic canons. Its art is the handmaid of its purpose . . . Its sole artistic standard is fitness; its measure, the adaptedness of means to end . . . To force the note of "art" in the novel is to circumscribe its area of interest and limit its range of expression. It is a sacrifice to formalism that is at once needless and useless.[12]

This atypical protest alerts us to a dichotomy less obvious than the distinction, reinvented in the 1880s, between novel and romance. The short and artful modern novel comes into focus in contrast to the long and artless Victorian fiction. In Wilbur Cross's 1899 account, the shorter, dramatic form of fiction attaches itself to newness, modernity, and things to come. "What is to happen in the first quarter of the twentieth century," he writes, "it would be most hazardous to prophesy."[13] Cross risks little in asserting what had become the conventional wisdom about the twentieth-century novel, that "besides tearing down and building anew the internal structure of the novel, the contemporary novelists would seem also to have modified permanently its outer form" (*English*

Novel 293). Hence technique itself, in the analysis of twentieth-century critics of the novel, belongs to modernity. As late as 1955 we find Walter Allen arguing that the "great Victorians, for the most part, used the novel in order to render a broad panoramic view of society. Variety of scene, prodigality of character creation, was what they were after . . . This is why, as against the Victorians, James and Conrad insisted so strongly on the necessity of an adequate technique in a novelist."[14] If the Victorians possess technique at all, in Allen's view it becomes an inadequate technique once the goals of variety and abundance are discredited.

Proponents of modern form were eager to suggest that Victorian novelists lacked control of their craft. The three-volume form made an easy target. Yet the tyranny of the triple-decker novel, enforced until 1894 by the policies of the circulating libraries, and ended by the same institutions, also occasioned much complaint by Victorian novelists and critics. The flaw most often noticed by Victorians was the filler employed by writers to pad stories falling short of the required length. Extraneous dialogue, interpolated stories, authorial or narratorial digressions, and descriptive set pieces received the criticism of reviewers, especially when these tell-tale strategies appeared in the second volume. In novels published serially, critics noticed these same flaws, as well as overly eventful, episodic plotting.[15] Writing at mid-century, an anonymous critic in *Fraser's Magazine* conveys both the ways in which novels may fail to please, and the standard of unity to which critics held novelists:

One of the great achievements – perhaps the greatest – in the art of the novelist is unity. If we cannot get that, the next best thing is progress. Let us, at all events, feel that we are moving. But this matter of progress must not be confounded with a mere facility in the invention of incidents. A novel may be crammed with incidents, yet stand still all the time. Incidents that do not contribute to the onward movement of the plot, go for nothing beyond the creation of an episodical interest, which is always doubtful in effect. Isolated circumstances no more constitute progress than bustle constitutes action.[16]

Though the rise of the one-volume novel towards the end of the century heightened critics' awareness of what was wrong with many tripledeckers, Victorian reviewers had real standards by which they evaluated formal success and failure.

Less than ten years later, for example, G. H. Lewes holds novels to the formal standards of drama, opining: "The object of construction is to free the story from all superfluity. Whatever is superfluous – whatever lies *outside* the real feeling and purpose of the work, either in incident, dialogue, description, or character – whatever may be omitted without in any degree lessening the effect – is a defect in construction."[17] Lewes' remarks, representing the ideals of his generation, illuminate novelists' use of narrative annexes. Though they challenge the dominant precept of unity, by altering setting and genre, narrative annexes do not go so far as to make the novels in which they occur collections of loosely related episodes. Because the events taking place in narrative annexes contribute substantively to plot, they cannot be omitted without altering the story in a debilitating way. Yet narrative annexes, the second worlds or green worlds of novelistic dramatic form, manifestly lie "outside" the primary realm of the fiction, as their surrounding borders emphasize. The generic and spatial differentiation of the annex participates in the contest between dramatic and epic form, for the competing analogy (novel as epic) permits not only length, episodes, and inflated numbers of characters, but also what William Crary Brownell, writing at the turn of the century, identifies as "subordinate spaces."[18]

Though not representing a capitulation to one theory of the novel or the other, narrative annexes plainly announce that their divergence from normative fictional worlds cannot be dismissed as superfluous. Because episodes, dialogue, description, digressions, and interpolations signal the use of filler, novelists differentiate narrative annexes from these strategies. Though an annex may indeed fill out a volume of a triple-decker, or provide the incident necessary to enliven a weekly installment, it cannot be dismissed as padding. Indeed, no novelist hoping to get away with a little unnoticeable stretching of a two-volume story to fit the three-volume form would import such strange and striking contents into a novel. The emphatic deployment of spatial and generic difference announces an intentional departure that meditates on formal and ideological limitations.

Perhaps because modern fiction contests most vigorously these very limitations, a curious amnesia about the narrative technique of the Victorians develops. Yet the realm of contrasting place and genre, entered by crossing a boundary between worlds, retains its power as an imaginative construction in twentieth-century fiction. Because the change in norms of representation inevitably alters the contents of modern narrative annexes, they cannot be identified by the themes I have stressed in this study. Even as they experiment with discontinuity, anachrony, and fragmentation, twentieth-century novelists did not fail to notice the advantages of this peculiarly Victorian technique, a figure for alternative possibilities that preserves norms of contiguity, consecution, and character. Sometimes, as in D. H. Lawrence's *Women in Love* (1921), the movement to an island space reminiscent of Meredith's narrative annex evokes romance only to repudiate it; in other cases, the technology of twentieth-century travel makes the car-trip or airplane journey a particularly modern way of achieving a romance transition. In Joyce's *Ulysses* (1922) and Virginia Woolf's *Orlando* (1928) simultaneous shifts in setting and genre become the very substance of modernist experiment. As in the Victorian annexes, emergent and residual forms can be conjured up in annexes. Woolf evokes the Victorian most self-consciously in her Strachey-esque biography of Elizabeth Barrett Browning's cocker spaniel, *Flush* (1933). When Flush is stolen and cast into a cellar by dog thieves, brave Miss Barrett determines to ransom him:

Henry Barrett met her and told her that in his opinion she might well be robbed and murdered if she did what she threatened. She told Wilson to call a cab. All trembling but submissive, Wilson obeyed. The cab came. Miss Barrett told Wilson to get in. Wilson, though convinced that death awaited her, got in. Miss Barrett told the cabman to drive to Manning Street, Shoreditch. Miss Barrett got in herself and off they drove. Soon they were beyond plate-glass windows, the mahogany doors and the area railings. They were in a world that Miss Barrett had never seen, had never guessed at. They were in a world where cows are herded under the bedroom floor, where whole families sleep in rooms with broken windows; in a world where vice and poverty breed vice and poverty. They had come to a region unknown to respectable cab drivers.[19]

To Woolf, the Victorian discovery of worlds within the Victorian world is quaintly and humorously commemorated in a narrative annex.

Notes

1 NARRATIVE ANNEXES: ALTERED SPACES, ALTERED MODES

1 "The Death of the Lion," *The Novels and Tales of Henry James*, New York Edn., vol. xv, *The Lesson of the Master, The Death of the Lion, The Next Time, and Other Tales* (New York: Charles Scribner's Sons, 1909) 115.

2 Thomas Hardy, *The Mayor of Casterbridge*, ed. Martin Seymour-Smith (Harmondsworth: Penguin Books, 1978) 258. Subsequent references to this edition appear within the text.

3 Seymour Chatman, *Story and Discourse: Narrative Structure in Fiction and Film* (Ithaca: Cornell University Press, 1978) 53–6.

4 George Eliot, *Adam Bede*, ed. Stephen Gill (Harmondsworth: Penguin Books, 1980) 426. Subsequent references to this edition appear within the text.

5 Charles Dickens, *The Life and Adventures of Martin Chuzzlewit.* ed. P. N. Furbank (Harmondsworth: Penguin Books, 1986) 442.

6 William Makepeace Thackeray, *Vanity Fair: A Novel Without a Hero* (1847–8) ed. Geoffrey and Kathleen Tillotson, Riverside Editions (Boston: Houghton Mifflin, 1963) 265.

7 Bram Stoker, *Dracula* (New York: Grosset and Dunlap, 1897) 2.

8 In narratological terms, sub-diegetic levels nested within the diegesis. See Gerard Genette, *Narrative Discourse, An Essay in Method*, trans. Jane E. Lewin (Ithaca: Cornell University Press, 1980).

9 The phrase is Hilary Schor's. See *Scheherazade in the Marketplace: Elizabeth Gaskell and the Victorian Novel* (Oxford University Press, 1992) 26.

10 Elizabeth Gaskell, *Mary Barton. A Tale of Manchester Life* (1848), ed. Stephen Gill (Harmondsworth: Penguin Books, 1970).

11 Walter Scott's influential formulation distinguishes between romance, which is "marvellous," and the novel, in which "events [are] accommodated to the ordinary train of human events and the modern state of society" ("Essays on Romance," *Miscellaneous Prose Works* vol. vi [Edinburgh: Adam & Charles Black, 1852] 127).

12 George Meredith, *The Ordeal of Richard Feverel: A History of a Father and a Son* (1859), ed. John Halperin, The World's Classics (Oxford University Press, 1984). Subsequent references to this edition appear within the text.

13 George Levine, *The Realistic Imagination: English Fiction from Frankenstein to Lady Chatterley* (University of Chicago Press, 1981) 204. Subsequent references appear within the text.

14 See Alastair Fowler, *Kinds of Literature: An Introduction to the Theory of Genres and Modes* (Cambridge, MA: Harvard University Press, 1982).

15 For a starting point, see Wolfgang Iser, *Prospecting: From Reader Response to Literary Anthropology* (Baltimore: The Johns Hopkins University Press, 1989) 272. Subsequent references appear within the text.

16 Thomas Hardy, "The Profitable Reading of Fiction," *Forum* (March 1888) 57.

17 I am indebted to John Hollander for pointing out that a significant literary use of the term "annex" in English draws upon this sense of supplementing. Walt Whitman appends supplementary, separately paginated "annexes" of poems to his *Leaves of Grass*. See Walt Whitman, *Leaves of Grass: A Textual Variorum of the Printed Poems*, 3 vols., ed. Sculley Bradley, Harold W. Blodgett, Arthur Golden, William White (New York University Press, 1980) I. xvii.

18 See George Levine, *The Realistic Imagination*; Leo Bersani, *A Future for Astyanax: Character and Desire in Literature* (New York: Columbia University Press, 1984); and Edwin M. Eigner, *The Metaphysical Novel in England and America: Dickens, Bulwer, Melville, and Hawthorne* (Berkeley: University of California Press, 1978). Subsequent references to these studies appear within the text.

19 *Figures of Conversion: "The Jewish Question" & English National Identity* (Durham: Duke University Press, 1995) 93.

20 *Desire and Domestic Fiction: A Political History of the Novel* (Oxford University Press, 1987) 253. The nineteenth-century novel is represented here only by *Jane Eyre* and *Wuthering Heights*, about which Armstrong concludes that, in their achievement of order, nineteenth-century novels "subordinate" all other forms of difference, including class distinctions, to gender difference (4).

21 See for example Gillian Beer, *Darwin's Plots: Evolutionary Narrative in Darwin, George Eliot and Nineteenth-Century Fiction* (London: Routledge & Kegan Paul; Boston Ark Paperbacks, 1983); Catherine Gallagher, *The Industrial Reformation of English Fiction: Social Discourse and Narrative Form 1832–1867* (University of Chicago Press, 1985); Humphrey House, *The Dickens World*, 2nd edn. (Oxford University Press, 1961); George Levine, *Darwin and the Novelists: Patterns of Science in Victorian Fiction* (University of Chicago Press, 1988); Mary Poovey, *Uneven Developments: The Ideological Work of Gender in Mid-Victorian England* (University of Chicago Press, 1988).

22 For a portion of this story, see John Speirs, *Poetry Towards Novel* (London: Faber and Faber, 1971).

23 I allude here to Rosalie L. Colie, *The Resources of Kind: Genre-Theory in the Renaissance*, ed. Barbara K. Lewalski (Berkeley: University of California Press, 1973). See also Fowler, *Kinds of Literature*; Barbara Keifer Lewalski,

Paradise Lost *and the Rhetoric of Form* (Princeton University Press, 1985); Claudio Guillen, *Literature as System* (Princeton University Press, 1971); Gary Saul Morson, *The Boundaries of Genre* (Austin: University of Texas Press, 1981); and Sergei Eisenstein, "Lectures on Literature," *The Psychology of Composition*, ed. and trans. Alan Upchurch (Calcutta: Seagull Books, 1987) 88.

24 Raymond Williams, *Marxism and Literature* (Oxford University Press, 1977). Subsequent references to this edition appear within the text.

25 See Ross Murfin, "Novel Representations: Politics and Victorian Fiction," *Victorian Connections*, ed. Jerome McGann, Virginia Victorian Studies (Charlottesville: University Press of Virginia, 1989) 31–59.

26 See the influential article by Harry Berger, Jr., "The Renaissance Imagination: Second World and Green World," *Centennial Review of Arts and Sciences* 9 (1965) 36–78 (rpt. with notes in *Second World and Green World: Studies in Renaissance Fiction-Making*, selected and arranged by John Patrick Lynch [Berkeley: University of California Press, 1988] 3–40).

27 See Robyn R. Warhol, *Gendered Interventions: Narrative Discourse in the Victorian Novel* (New Brunswick: Rutgers University Press, 1989).

28 For a sample of narrative theorists on fictional worlds, see Alexander Gelley, *Narrative Crossings: Theory and Pragmatics of Prose Fiction* (Baltimore: The Johns Hopkins University Press, 1987); Felix Martinez-Bonati, *Fictive Discourse and the Structures of Literature*, trans. Philip W. Silver (Ithaca: Cornell University Press, 1981); and his "Toward a Formal Ontology of Fictional Worlds," *Philosophy and Literature* 7 (1983) 182–95; Ruth Ronen, "Space in Fiction," *Poetics Today* 7:3 (1986) 421–38. Wolfgang Iser's books and essays from *The Act of Reading: A Theory of Aesthetic Response* (Baltimore: The Johns Hopkins University Press, 1978) through *The Fictive and the Imaginary: Charting Literary Anthropology* (Baltimore: The Johns Hopkins University Press, 1993) represent a career-long interest in readers and fictional worlds. On the philosophy of possible worlds, see Nelson Goodman, *Ways of Worldmaking* (Indianapolis: Hackett, 1978); Thomas Pavel, *Fictional Worlds* (Cambridge, MA: Harvard University Press, 1986); and Marie-Laure Ryan, *Possible Worlds, Artificial Intelligence, and Narrative Theory* (Bloomington and Indianapolis: Indiana University Press, 1991).

29 D. A. Miller, *Narrative and Its Discontents: Problems of Closure in the Traditional Novel* (Princeton University Press, 1981) 141–2. Subsequent references appear within the text.

30 See E. M. Forster, *Aspects of the Novel* (New York: Harcourt, Brace and World, 1927) 67–78; Roland Barthes, *S/Z*, trans. Richard Miller (New York: Hill and Wang, 1974); Boris Tomashevsky, "Thematics," in Lee T. Lemon and Marion J. Reis, trans., *Russian Formalist Criticism: Four Essays* (Lincoln: University of Nebraska Press, 1965) 61–95.

31 Joseph Frank, "Spatial Form in Modern Literature," *Sewanee Review* 53 (1945) 221–46, 433–56; for subsequent considerations of the concept, see the essays in Jeffrey R. Smitten and Ann Daghistany, eds., *Spatial Form in*

Narrative (Ithaca: Cornell University Press, 1981), and Frank's response to his critics in Joseph Frank, *The Idea of Spatial Form* (New Brunswick: Rutgers University Press, 1991), especially 67–132.

32 Victor Shklovsky, "Sterne's *Tristram Shandy:* Stylistic Commentary," in Lemon and Reis, *Russian Formalist Criticism* 25–57; Gerard Genette, *Narrative Discourse* 33–85.

33 Michel de Certeau, "Spatial Stories," *The Practice of Everyday Life,* trans. Steven F. Rendall (Berkeley: University of California Press, 1984) 115.

34 Goodman, *Ways of Worldmaking* 7–16. Subsequent references appear within the text.

35 Pavel, *Fictional Worlds* 10. Subsequent references appear within the text.

36 The gender distinction is unavoidable: H. Rider Haggard's *King Solomon's Mines* (1885), for instance, opens with a dedication "to all the big and little boys who read it" (Harmondsworth: Penguin Books, 1987).

37 See Gillian Beer, *The Romance*, Critical Idiom (London: Methuen, 1970) 5.

38 See Richard Chase, *The American Novel and its Tradition* (Garden City: Doubleday, 1957); Joel Porte, *The Romance in America: Studies in Cooper, Poe, Hawthorne, Melville, and James* (Middletown, CT: Wesleyan University Press, 1969); Lionel Trilling, *The Liberal Imagination: Essays on Literature and Society* (London: Secker and Warburg, 1964) 205–22; and the cogent critique of this tradition in Nicolaus Mills, *American and English Fiction in the Nineteenth Century: An Antigenre Critique and Comparison* (Bloomington: Indiana University Press, 1973).

39 Mikhail Bakhtin, *The Dialogic Imagination: Four Essays by M. M. Bakhtin,* ed. Michael Holquist, trans. Caryl Emerson and Michael Holquist (Austin: University of Texas Press, 1981).

40 See Robert Alter, *Partial Magic: The Novel as a Self-Conscious Genre* (Berkeley: University of California Press, 1975); Rosemarie Bodenheimer, *The Politics of Story in Victorian Social Fiction* (Ithaca: Cornell University Press, 1988); Ian Duncan, *Modern Romance and Transformations of the Novel: The Gothic, Scott, Dickens* (Cambridge University Press, 1992); Gallagher, *The Industrial Reformation of English Fiction;* and Schor, *Scheherezade in the Marketplace.*

41 Richard Brodhead, *Hawthorne, Melville, and the Novel* (University of Chicago Press, 1976) 13.

42 John Forster, *The Life of Charles Dickens,* ed. J. W. T. Ley (London: Cecil Palmer, 1928) 626. Dickens refers to Miss Wade's story in *Little Dorrit.*

43 See Roman Jakobson's comments on contiguity in realism in "Two Aspects of Language and Two Types of Aphasic Disturbances," in Roman Jakobson and Morris Hale, *Fundamentals of Language* (The Hague: Mouton, 1956) 53–82.

44 For a brief survey, see Joseph Kestner, *The Spatiality of the Novel* (Detroit: Wayne State University Press, 1978).

45 For an exemplary pairing of setting and genre in criticism of American fiction, see Philip Fisher, *Hard Facts: Setting and Form in the American Novel* (New York: Oxford University Press, 1987) esp. 9–14. See also Steven

Hutchinson's excellent *Cervantine Journeys* (Madison: University of Wisconsin Press, 1992) for an illuminating study of tropes of motion and journeying.

46 See Leonard Lutwack, *The Role of Place in Literature* (Syracuse University Press, 1984); Gillian Tindall, *Countries of the Mind: The Meaning of Place to Writers* (London: Hogarth Press, 1991); Philippa Tristram's interdisciplinary *Living Space in Fact and Fiction* (London: Routledge, 1989); and cf. Bronislawa Balutowa's monograph on setting, *Spatial Complex: A Study of Spatial Problems in Fiction Illustrated with Examples from Representative Works of English Short Fiction 1900–1925* (Warsaw: n.p., 1979).

47 Raymond Williams, *The Country and the City* (New York: Oxford University Press, 1973); Richard Gill, *Happy Rural Seat: The English Country House and the Literary Imagination* (New Haven: Yale University Press, 1972); Marilyn R. Chandler, *Dwelling in the Text: Houses in American Fiction* (Berkeley: University of California Press, 1991).

48 See Tom Henighan, *Natural Space in Literature: Imagination and Environment in Nineteenth and Twentieth Century Fiction and Poetry* (Ottawa: Golden Dog Press, 1982) 105–44; Arnold Kettle's influential "Introduction to *Tess of the d'Urbervilles*" (1966) in Albert J. LaValley, ed., *Twentieth-Century Interpretations of* Tess of the d'Urbervilles (Englewood Cliffs, NJ: Prentice-Hall, 1969); Arthur Pollard, "Hardy and Rural England," *Thomas Hardy Annual Number 1*, ed. Norman Page (Atlantic Highlands, NJ: Humanities Press, 1982) 33–43; Raymond Williams, *The Country and the City*; Denys Kay Robinson, *The Landscape of Thomas Hardy*, with photographs by Simon McBride (Exeter: Webb and Bower, 1984). On the Brontës, see Arthur Pollard, *The Landscape of the Brontës*, with photographs by Simon McBride (New York: E. P. Dutton, 1988).

49 See Philippa Tristram, *Living Space in Fact and Fiction*; Rhoda Flaxman, *Victorian Word Painting: Toward the Blending of Genres* (Ann Arbor: UMI Research Press, 1987); Robert Harbison, *Eccentric Spaces: A Voyage Through Real and Imagined Worlds* (New York: Alfred A. Knopf, 1977).

50 See Roland Barthes, "Introduction to the Structural Analysis of Literature," rpt. in *Image–Music–Text*, trans. Stephen Heath (New York: Hill and Wang, 1977) 77–124; Seymour Chatman, *Coming to Terms: The Rhetoric of Narrative in Fiction and Film* (Ithaca: Cornell University Press, 1990) 22–37; Philippe Hamon, "The Rhetorical Status of the Descriptive," *Yale French Studies* 61 (1981) 1–26; Wallace Martin, *Recent Theories of Narrative* (Ithaca: Cornell University Press, 1986) 122–3; 229–30.

51 Chatman, *Story and Discourse*; Genette, *Narrative Discourse*; Shlomith Rimmon-Kenan, *Narrative Fiction: Contemporary Poetics* (London: Methuen, 1983); and Mieke Bal, *Narratology: Introduction to the Theory of Narrative*, trans. Christine van Boheemen (University of Toronto Press, 1985). Rimmon-Kenan provides the most useful redaction and analysis of Genette's terms and typologies.

52 See Chatman, *Story and Discourse* 101–7; Bal, *Narratology* 43–54, 93–9.

53 See Bal, *Narratology* 96–7; Lutwack, *The Role of Place* 34, 62. For an insightful

discussion of place as a *figure* for literary convention, see Jay MacPherson, *The Spirit of Solitude: Conventions and Continuities in Late Romance* (New Haven: Yale University Press, 1982).

54 For a critical summary of work on embedding, see William Nelles, "Stories within Stories: Narrative Levels and Embedded Narrative," *Studies in the Literary Imagination* 25:1 (1992) 79–96. See also Robert Alter, *Partial Magic: The Novel as a Self-Conscious Genre*; John Barth, "Tales within Tales within Tales," *Antaeus* 43 (1981) 45–63 (Genette derives from Barth a typology of embedded tales as explanatory, predictive, thematic, persuasive, distractive, and obstructive, in *Narrative Discourse* 227–37); Viveca Furedy, "A Structural Model of Phenomena with Embedding in Literature and Other Arts," *Poetics Today* 10:4 (1989) 745–69; Jurij Lotman, *The Structure of the Artistic Text* (1971), trans. Gail Lenhoff and Ronald Vroon, Michigan Slavic Contributions 7 (Ann Arbor: University of Michigan Press, 1977) 209–31. Following Genette, see Bal, *Narratology* 134–48, and Susan S. Lanser, *The Narrative Act* (Princeton University Press, 1981) 133–4. On *mise en abyme*, see Lucien Dällenbach, *The Mirror in the Text* (University of Chicago Press, 1989), and Moshe Ron, "The Restricted Abyss: Nine Problems in the Theory of *Mise en Abyme*," *Poetics Today* 8 (1987) 417–38. On analeptic narrative episodes, see Francis Berry, *The Shakespeare Inset: Word and Picture* (New York: Theatre Arts Books, 1965).

55 D. A. Miller, *The Novel and the Police* (Berkeley: University of California Press, 1988) 3.

56 See Yi-Fu Tuan, *Space and Place: The Perspective of Experience* (Minneapolis: University of Minnesota Press, 1977): "Enclosed and humanized space is place. Compared to space, place is a calm center of established values" (54). This clarification of terms is clearly not accepted across disciplinary boundaries, as Michel de Certeau arrives at exactly the same formulation and the opposite assignment of terms, writing "Space is a practiced place," in *The Practice of Everyday Life* 117. See also Trevor J. Barnes and James S. Duncan, eds., *Writing Worlds: Discourse, Text & Metaphor in the Representation of Landscape* (London: Routledge, 1992); Derek Gregory, *Ideology, Science, and Human Geography* (London: Hutchinson University Library, 1978); and William E. Mallory and Paul Simpson-Housely, eds., *Geography and Literature: A Meeting of the Disciplines* (Syracuse University Press, 1987).

57 See Iser, *The Fictive and the Imaginary*; Christopher Herbert, *Culture and Anomie: Ethnographic Imagination in the Nineteenth Century* (University of Chicago Press, 1991). There is widespread diffusion in literary study of Van Gennap's, Turner's, and Geertz' theories. See for instance Sarah Gilead, "Liminality, Anti-liminality, and the Victorian Novel," *ELH* 53:1 (1986) 183–97; for the reverse influence of literary theory on anthropology, see Edward M. Bruner, "Ethnography as Narrative," in Turner and Bruner, *The Anthropology of Experience* 139–55.

58 See Victor W. Turner, *Dramas, Fields, and Metaphors: Symbolic Action in Human Society* (Ithaca: Cornell University Press, 1974). Subsequent references to this edition appear within the text.

59 Mikhail Bakhtin, *Rabelais and his World* (1968), trans. Helene Iswolsky (Bloomington: Indiana University Press, 1984).

60 *Walter Benjamin: Towards a Revolutionary Criticism* (London: Verso, 1981) 148.

61 For a persuasive (Foucauldian) application of this idea to the novel, see Terry Castle's *Masquerade and Civilization: The Carnivalesque in Eighteenth-Century Culture and Fiction* (Stanford University Press, 1986).

62 Particularly realism of the body, or "gross naturalism" (*Rabelais* 31).

63 Peter Stallybrass and Allon White, *The Politics and Poetics of Transgression* (Ithaca: Cornell University Press, 1986) 4, 13.

64 Mary Poovey, *Making a Social Body: British Cultural Formation 1830–1864* (University of Chicago Press, 1995) 1–2. Subsequent references appear within the text.

65 Jerome Buckley, ed., *The Worlds of Victorian Fiction*, Harvard English Studies 6 (Cambridge, MA: Harvard University Press, 1975) v. Subsequent references to this edition appear within the text.

66 See Mary Louisa Molesworth's *The Tapestry Room*, illus. by Walter Crane (London: Macmillan and Co., 1879); Charles Kingsley's *Water Babies* (London and Cambridge: Macmillan and Co., 1862–3); George MacDonald's *At the Back of the North Wind* (1871), illus. by Jessie Wilcox Smith (Philadelphia: D. McKay, 1919); *The Princess and the Goblin* (1872), illus. by Jessie Wilcox Smith (Philadelphia: D. McKay, 1920); and *The Princess and Curdie* (1882) (Philadelphia: J. B. Lippincott, 1883); and Lewis Carroll's Alice books (*Alice in Wonderland* and *Through the Looking-glass* [1865, 1871], ed. Roger Lancelyn Green [Oxford University Press, 1971]).

67 See Stephen Prickett, *Victorian Fantasy* (Sussex: Harvester Press, 1979) xiii.

68 George MacDonald's fairy tales often include a fantastic transition. See for instance "The Wise Woman, or The Lost Princess: A Double Story" (1874), in George MacDonald, *The Wise Woman and Other Fantasy Stories* (Grand Rapids: Wm. B. Eerdmans Publishing Co., 1980) 1–108.

69 See C. N. Manlove, *Modern Fantasy: Five Studies* (Cambridge University Press, 1975); Eric S. Rabkin, *The Fantastic in Literature* (Princeton University Press, 1976) 41; Ann Swinfen, *In Defense of Fantasy: A Study of the Genre in English and American Literature since 1945* (London: Routledge and Kegan Paul, 1984) 3; and, though idiosyncratic, see Tzvetan Todorov, *The Fantastic: A Structural Approach to a Literary Genre* (1970), trans. Richard Howard (Ithaca: Cornell University Press, 1975) 25.

70 J. R. R. Tolkien, "On Fairy-Stories," *Tree and Leaf* (Boston: Houghton Mifflin, 1965) 3–84. Rpt. in *The Tolkien Reader* (New York: Ballantine Books, 1966) 3–84; subsequent references in the text refer to this edition.

71 George MacDonald, "The Fantastic Imagination," rpt. in *Fantasists on Fantasy: A Collection of Critical Reflections By Eighteen Masters of the Art*, ed. Robert H. Boyer and Kenneth J. Zahorski (New York: Avon Books, 1984) 14–21. Subsequent references to this edition appear within the text.

72 Philip Sidney, *An Apology for Poetry* (c. 1579), ed. Forrest G. Robinson (New York: Macmillan/Library of Liberal Arts, 1970) 14.

73 T. E. Apter, *Fantasy Literature: An Approach to Reality* (Bloomington: Indiana University Press, 1982) 111. See also Rosemary Jackson, *Fantasy: The Literature of Subversion* (London: Methuen, 1981).

74 George MacDonald, *Phantastes* (1858), in *Phantastes and Lilith: Two Novels by George MacDonald*, introduction by C. S. Lewis (Grand Rapids: William B. Eerdmans, 1964). Subsequent references to this edition are made in the text.

75 See the distinction between low and high fantasy in Kenneth J. Zahorski and Robert H. Boyer, "The Secondary Worlds of High Fantasy," in Schlobin, *The Aesthetics of Fantasy Literature and Art* 56–81; in the same volume, see George P. Landow, "And the World Became Strange: Realms of Literary Fantasy" 105–42.

76 H. Rider Haggard, *She* (1887), ed. Daniel Karlin, The World's Classics (Oxford University Press, 1991) 48.

77 For theoretical treatments of this opposite tendency, see Sanford Budick and Wolfgang Iser, eds., *Languages of the Unsayable: The Play of Negativity in Literature and Literary Theory* (New York: Columbia University Press, 1989); Wolfgang Iser, "Interaction Between Text and Reader," *Prospecting* 31–41; Gerald Prince, "The Disnarrated," *Style* 22:1 (1988) 1–8; and for a practical example, see James R. Kincaid, "Hardy's Absences," *Critical Approaches to the Fiction of Thomas Hardy*, ed. Dale Kramer (London: Macmillan, 1979) 202–14.

78 See E. R. Curtius, *European Literature and the Latin Middle Ages*, trans. Willard Trask, Bollingen Series 36 (Princeton University Press, 1953) 59; Timothy Hampton, *Writing from History: the Rhetoric of Exemplarity in Renaissance Literature* (Ithaca: Cornell University Press, 1990); John D. Lyons, *Exemplum: The Rhetoric of Example in Early Modern France and Italy* (Princeton University Press, 1989).

79 In Genettian schemes of narrative duration, ellipsis denotes the relation of zero discourse time to some units of lapsed story time. See Genette, *Narrative Discourse* 86–112; Rimmon-Kenan, *Narrative Fiction* 51–6. Annexes fill out the spot of a potential ellipsis with scene, summary, dilation, and dialogue.

80 Gerald Prince, *A Dictionary of Narratology* (Lincoln: University of Nebraska Press, 1987) 52. Subsequent references appear within the text.

81 In this way, what Edward Said calls the "authority" of the beginning "maintains the continuity of its course." See *Beginnings: Intention and Method* (1975) (New York: Columbia University Press, 1985) 83.

2 VICTORIAN CRITICS, NARRATIVE ANNEXES, AND PRESCRIPTIONS FOR THE NOVEL

1 "J. A.," "Framley Parsonage," *Sharpe's London Magazine* n.s. 19 (July 1860) 103.

2 I borrow Walter M. Kendrick's epithet. *The Novel Machine: The Theory and Fiction of Anthony Trollope* (Baltimore: The Johns Hopkins University Press, 1980).

3 Henry James, *Partial Portraits* (1888), new introduction by Leon Edel (Ann Arbor: University of Michigan Press, 1970) 116.

4 See the collection of notices of Trollope's novels in Donald Smalley, ed., *Trollope: The Critical Heritage* (London: Routledge and Kegan Paul; New York: Barnes and Noble, 1969). Trollope's reviewers frequently remarked his faithful reproduction of society, his representation of characters from "all" classes, and his fidelity to ordinary life.

5 Exceptions would include *Lady Anna* (London: Chapman and Hall, 1873–4) and *The Fixed Period* (London: Blackwood, 1881–2), although within the genres governing these fictions, improbability is virtually irrelevant.

6 Anthony Trollope, *An Autobiography* (1883), The Oxford Trollope, Crown Edition, general eds. Michael Sadleir and Frederick Page (Oxford University Press, 1950) 192. Subsequent references to this edition appear within the text.

7 *Castle Richmond* (1860) (New York: Dover Publications, 1984) 309. Subsequent references to this edition, a photostatic reprint of the first edition, appear within the text.

8 The government responded to the famine by instituting a public works program, and by setting up soup kitchens, workhouses, and, ultimately, outdoor relief. Of the government's failures, Arthur Pollard writes that it "refused to subsidise private estate work such as land reclamation and drainage; it refused to stop the export of grain from Ireland; at first it insisted that the food that it had prudently imported should be sold at market prices; it refused to ratify the Lord Lieutenant's firm measures for dealing with disorder" (*Anthony Trollope* [London, Henley, and Boston: Routledge and Kegan Paul, 1978] 10).

9 [J. R. Beard?], "Factory Life – Mary Barton," *British Quarterly Review* 9:17 (February 1849) 121.

10 Helen Garlinghouse King, ed., "Trollope's Letters to the *Examiner*," *The Princeton University Library Chronicle* 26:2 (1965) 71–110. Subsequent references to this reprint of the letters appear within the text.

11 Ruth apRoberts notes the lack of descriptive set-pieces in Trollope's novels. See *Trollope: Artist and Moralist* (London: Chatto and Windus, 1971) 17–18.

12 *The Macdermots of Ballycloran* (1847), 3 vols., intro. Robert Lee Wolff (New York: Garland Publishing, 1979) I. 202–3.

13 See Owen Dudley Edwards, "Anthony Trollope, the Irish Writer," *Nineteenth-Century Fiction* 38:1 (1983) 7.

14 Michael Sadleir, *Anthony Trollope: A Commentary* (Boston: Houghton Mifflin, 1927) 385–6. More recent critics have deplored instead Trollope's use of the scenes of famine in "a conventional Trollopian romance." See R. C. Terry, *Anthony Trollope: The Artist in Hiding* (London: Macmillan, 1977) 190–2.

15 See Janet Egleson Dunleavy, "Trollope and Ireland," *Trollope Centenary Essays*, ed. John Halperin (New York: St. Martin's Press, 1982) 53–69.

16 See the illustration reproduced in Victoria Glendinning's *Anthony Trollope* (New York: Alfred A. Knopf) 104ff.; and R. C. Terry's account of the "tableaux of suffering," in *Anthony Trollope* 191.

17 "Castle Richmond," *Spectator* (19 May 1860) 477.

18 See also [Geraldine Jewsbury], "New Novels," *Athenaeum* 1699 (19 May 1860) 681. She writes, "The remarks on the Irish famine are, on the whole, true and judicious, and the description of things, during that terrible time, very true and real."

19 "Belles Lettres," *Westminster Review* 74 (October 1860) 588.

20 "Castle Richmond," *Saturday Review* (19 May 1860) 643.

21 "Castle Richmond," *Saturday Review* 643.

22 Ross Murfin, "Novel Representations: Politics and Victorian Fiction" 49.

23 See Kendrick, *The Novel Machine*.

24 The plots are often derived from earlier sources, particularly from the early English drama that Trollope collected and annotated. See Geoffrey Harvey, *The Art of Anthony Trollope* (London: Weidenfeld and Nicolson, 1980); Christopher Herbert, *Trollope and Comic Pleasure* (University of Chicago Press, 1987); and Elizabeth R. Epperly, *Anthony Trollope's Notes on the Old Drama* (University of Victoria, 1988).

25 Terry Eagleton, *Criticism and Ideology: A Study in Marxist Literary Theory* (London: New Left Books; New York: Schocken Books, 1976) 181.

26 The novels to which Trollope refers are *Nina Balatka* (1866–7) and *Linda Tressel* (1867–8).

27 Robert Tracy, "'The Unnatural Ruin': Trollope and Nineteenth-Century Irish Fiction," *Nineteenth-Century Fiction* 37:3 (1982) 360.

28 L. J. Swingle, *Romanticism and Anthony Trollope: A Study in the Continuities of Nineteenth-Century Literary Thought* (Ann Arbor: University of Michigan Press, 1990) 41, 38–58.

29 David Skilton, *Anthony Trollope and His Contemporaries: A Study in the Theories and Conventions of Mid-Victorian Fiction* (London: Longmans, 1972) 146. Subsequent references appear within the text.

30 See P. D. Edwards, *Anthony Trollope, his Art and Scope* (University of Queensland Press, 1977).

31 See Jane Nardin, "The Social Critic in Anthony Trollope's Novels," *SEL* 30 (1990) 679–96.

32 So, for instance, Lady Glencora Palliser appears briefly in *Miss Mackenzie* (1865), a novel otherwise unrelated to the Palliser series. Characters such as the Old Duke of Omnium show up in more than half-a-dozen novels, and functionaries such as the attorney Chaffanbrass and the Disraelian figure Sidonia surface here and there in social and political scenes. Some novels, such as *The Last Chronicle of Barset*, offer an almost panoramic view of characters introduced in earlier books.

33 John Kucich, "Transgression in Trollope: Dishonesty and the Antibourgeois Elite," *ELH* 56:3 (1989) 598, 616, 604.

34 Henry James, "Preface to The Tragic Muse," *The Art of the Novel*. Ed. R. P. Blackmur (New York: Scribners, 1934) 84.

35 Peter K. Garrett, *The Victorian Multiplot Novel: Studies in Dialogical Form* (New Haven: Yale University Press, 1980) 2. Subsequent references to this work appear within the text.

36 *Poetics*, trans. Leon Golden (Englewood Cliffs, NJ: Prentice-Hall, 1968) 22.
37 Charles Dickens, *Oliver Twist* (1837), ed. Peter Fairclough and intro. Angus Wilson, Penguin Classics (Harmondsworth: Penguin Books, 1985) chapter 17, 168–9. Subsequent references to this edition appear within the text.
38 George Eliot, *Middlemarch: A Study of Provincial Life* (1871–2), ed. W.J. Harvey, Penguin Classics (Harmondsworth: Penguin Books, 1985) 297.
39 Edwin Muir, *The Structure of the Novel* (1928) (London: The Hogarth Press, 1957) 59. Subsequent references to this edition appear within the text.
40 See W. J. T. Mitchell, "Space, Ideology, and Literary Representation," *Poetics Today* 10 (1989) 91.
41 Jerome Thale, "The Problem of Structure in Trollope," *Nineteenth-Century Fiction* 15 (1960) 149.
42 For an outstanding account of the Victorian novel as a mixed form, see James R. Kincaid, *The Novels of Anthony Trollope* (Oxford: Clarendon Press, 1977).
43 Walter Allen, *The English Novel: A Short Critical History* (New York: E. P. Dutton, 1954) 310.

3 NORMS AND NARROW SPACES: THE GENDERING OF LIMITS ON REPRESENTATION

1 Nathaniel Hawthorne, *The House of the Seven Gables* (1851), ed. Milton R. Stern (Harmondsworth: Penguin Books, 1981) 1–2. Subsequent references to this edition appear within the text.
2 The middle-class is a notoriously tricky category. Although Victorian novels obviously include aristocrats and working people, they more amply represent the gentry, the professional classes, and employers and their families. I use the term "middle-class" to suggest those people with the means and advantages necessary to attempt to attain, or maintain, respectability. See G. Kitson Clark, *The Making of Victorian England* (Cambridge, MA: Harvard University Press, 1962) 118–35, 253–74.
3 Graham Greene, *The Honorary Consul* (New York: Viking, 1973) 10.
4 On morality and the novel, see Richard Stang, *The Theory of the Novel in England, 1850–1870* (New York: Columbia University Press; London: Routledge and Kegan Paul, 1959) 191–224. Subsequent references appear within the text.
5 [David Masson], "Literature and the Labour Question" 208.
6 [Richard Holt Hutton], "The Author of Heartsease and the Modern Schools of Fiction," *Prospective Review* 10:40 (1854) 460–82. Subsequent references to this review appear within the text.
7 [George Henry Lewes], "Currer Bell's 'Shirley,'" *Edinburgh Review* 91 (January 1850) 166. Lewes may draw here on Walter Scott's figure of the reader as cab-passenger in his postscript to *Waverley* (1814). Subsequent references to this review appear within the text.
8 [F. W. Pollock], "British Novelists – Richardson, Miss Austen and Scott," *Fraser's Magazine* 61 (January 1860) 31.

9 "The Progress of Fiction as an Art," *Westminster Review* 60 (October 1853) 343–4. Gordon Haight attributes this essay to George Eliot ("Dickens and Lewes," *PMLA* 71 [1956] 166–79) but the editors of *The Wellesley Index to Victorian Periodicals* regard its authorship as anonymous.

10 See also Lewes' "The Lady Novelists," *Westminster Review* 58 (July 1852) 129–41.

11 *The Collected Works of Walter Bagehot: The Literary Essays (in two volumes)* ed. Norman St. John-Stevas (Cambridge, MA: Harvard University Press, 1965). This collection contains most of Bagehot's literary essays from the *National Review* and the *Saturday Review*. Subsequent references to essays included in this edition ("The Waverley Novels," *National Review* [April 1858] 44–75; "Charles Dickens," *National Review* [October 1858] 76–107; "Lost and Won," *Saturday Review* [April 1859] 150–6; "La Griffe Rose," *Saturday Review* [September 1862] 263–8; "Sterne and Thackeray," *National Review* [April 1864] 279–312; and "John Milton," *National Review* [July 1859] 108–49) appear within the text.

12 Had Bagehot read Charlotte Brontë's novels? Although Bagehot did not write a full essay on Brontë, he contrasts her with Eliot in his essay, "The Novels of George Eliot," *National Review* 11 (April 1860) 191–219. Bagehot remarks in 1858 on the "atrocious species of plain heroines" that Brontë's *Jane Eyre* spawned and complains that "possibly none of the frauds which are now so much the topic of common remark are so irritating as that to which the purchaser of a novel is a victim on finding that he has only to peruse a narrative on the conduct and sentiments of an ugly lady" (*Collected Works* 220).

13 For an early feminist reading of this problem, see Carol T. Christ, "Imaginative Constraint, Feminine Duty, and the Form of Charlotte Brontë's Fiction," *Women's Studies* 6 (1979) 287–96.

14 See Nancy K. Miller's influential essay, "Emphasis Added: Plots and Plausibilities in Women's Fiction," *PMLA* 96:1 (1981) 36–48.

15 See Ruth Bernard Yeazell's excellent article, "The Boundaries of *Mansfield Park*," *Representations* 7 (1984) 133–52.

16 See, canonically, Sandra M. Gilbert and Susan Gubar, *The Madwoman in the Attic: The Woman Writer and the Nineteenth-Century Literary Imagination* (New Haven: Yale University Press, 1979).

17 In this I am indebted to the example of Susan Stanford Friedman's work. See "Lyric Subversion of Narrative in Women's Writing: Virginia Woolf and the Tyranny of Plot," *Reading Narrative: Form, Ethics, Ideology*, ed. James Phelan (Columbus: Ohio State University Press, 1989) 162–85.

18 Such as those who wrote in to the *London Review* to complain about one of Trollope's stories. See Glendinning, *Anthony Trollope* 288n.

19 On the influence of the libraries, see Guinevere L. Griest, *Mudie's Circulating Library and the Victorian Novel* (Bloomington: Indiana University Press, 1970), and John A. Sutherland, *Victorian Novelists and Publishers* (University of Chicago Press, 1976).

20 Bagehot's appreciation of Eliot could not take account of *Middlemarch* (1871–2) or *Daniel Deronda* (1876).

21 In "Waverley Novels" he makes the distinction between the "ubiquitous" and the "romantic." In "Charles Dickens," Bagehot divides novels into three kinds, the "ubiquitous," the "miscellaneous," and the "sentimental." Dickens he sees as delineating "nearly all that part of our national life which can be delineated – at least, within the limits social morality prescribes to social art" ("Charles Dickens" 83).

22 See Stang, *The Theory of the Novel*, 139–49.

23 On Eve and Satan, see Bagehot's July 1859 essay from the *National Review*, "John Milton," in *The Collected Works* 134–5; 144–5.

24 *Sharpe's London Magazine* n. s. 6 (June 1855) 339–40.

25 See Ruth Bernard Yeazell, "More True than Real: *Jane Eyre*'s 'Mysterious Summons,'" *Nineteenth-Century Fiction* 29 (1974) 127–43.

26 For a discussion of this impulse in another context, see John Kucich's excellent chapter on Charlotte Brontë in *Repression in Victorian Fiction: Charlotte Brontë, George Eliot, Charles Dickens* (Berkeley: University of California Press, 1987) 34–113.

27 See [Elizabeth Rigby], *"Vanity Fair –* and *Jane Eyre" Quarterly Review* 84 (December 1848) 153–85, 174–5.

28 Charlotte Brontë, "Author's Preface" to the second edition of *Jane Eyre*. All references to the novel come from *Jane Eyre* (1847), ed. Margaret Smith (Harmondsworth: Penguin Books, 1981).

29 See *"Vanity Fair –* and *Jane Eyre,"* in which Elizabeth Rigby remarks on the novel's "coarseness of language and laxity of tone" (163) and decides that "altogether the autobiography of Jane Eyre is preeminently an anti-Christian composition" (173). Subsequent references to this review appear within the text. See also the *Spectator* 20 (6 November 1847) 1074–5. Brontë's preface fanned the flames; see the *Christian Remembrancer* 15 (April 1848) 396–409, which wishes that the author would "be a little more trustful of the reality of human goodness, and a little less anxious to detect its alloy of evil" (409). For excerpts from these and other notices of Brontë's work, see Miriam Allott, ed., *The Brontës: The Critical Heritage* (London and Boston: Routledge & Kegan Paul, 1974).

30 Bodenheimer, *The Politics of Story* 163. See also Jerome Beaty, *"Jane Eyre* and Genre," *Genre* 10 (1977) 619–54.

31 See Sandra Gilbert, "Plain Jane's Progress," *Signs* 2 (1977) 779–804; Jane Millgate, "Jane Eyre's Progress," *English Studies Anglo-American Supplement* 50 (1969) xxi–xxix.

32 See Peter Allan Dale, "Charlotte Brontë's 'tale half-told': The Disruption of Narrative Structure in *Jane Eyre," Modern Language Quarterly* 47:2 (1986) 108–29; John Maynard, *Charlotte Brontë and Sexuality* (Cambridge University Press, 1984) 131–2; Melodie Monahan, "Heading Out is Not Going Home: Jane Eyre," *SEL* 28 (1988) 589–608.

33 See Karen E. Rowe, "'Fairy-born and human-bred': Jane Eyre's Education

in Romance," *The Voyage In: Fictions of Female Development*, ed. Elizabeth Abel, Marianne Hirsch, and Elizabeth Langland (Hanover: University Press of New England, 1983) 69–89.

34 On the "equivocal and often erratic nature of Brontë's radicalism," see Roy Parama, "Unaccommodated Woman and the Poetics of Property in *Jane Eyre*," *SEL* 29:4 (1989) 713–27. On Charlotte Brontë and social class, see Terry Eagleton, *Myths of Power* (London: Macmillan, 1975); Susan L. Meyer's excellent "Colonialism and the Figurative Strategy of *Jane Eyre*," *Victorian Studies* 33:2 (1990) 247–68; Jina Politi, "*Jane Eyre* Class-ified," *Literature and History* 8:1 (1982) 56–66; and Igor Webb, *From Custom to Capital: The English Novel and the Industrial Revolution* (Ithaca: Cornell University Press, 1981) 70–86.

35 [John Eagles], "A Few Words about Novels," *Blackwood's Magazine* 64 (October 1848) 459–74. Signed "Aquilius."

36 See the reviews of [H. F. Chorley], *Athenauem* (23 October 1847) 1100–1; [A. W. Fonblanque], *Examiner* (27 November 1847) 756–7; and the reviews of anonymous writers in the *Critic* (30 October 1847) 277–8, in *Era* (14 November 1847) 9, and in *People's Journal* (November 1847) 9.

37 [Edwin Percy Whipple], "Novels of the Season," *North American Review* 67 (October 1848) 357. Subsequent references to this review appear within the text.

38 For Charlotte Brontë's amused response to this review, see her 22 November 1848 letter to W. S. Williams, in Muriel Spark, ed., *The Letters of the Brontës: A Selection* (Norman: University of Oklahoma Press, 1954) 153–5. One volume of an authoritative edition of Brontë's correspondence has recently appeared: *1829–1847* vol.1 of *The Letters of Charlotte Brontë with a Selection of Letters by Family and Friends*, ed. Margaret Smith (Oxford: Clarendon Press, 1995). For Brontë letters written after 1847, I use Spark if possible, and, if not, T. Wise and A. Symington, eds., *The Brontës: Their Lives, Friendship and Correspondence*, 4 vols. (Oxford: Shakespeare Head Press, 1932).

39 G. H. Lewes, "Recent Novels: French and English," *Fraser's Magazine* 36 (December 1847) 693. Subsequent references to this review appear within the text. For a useful account of Charlotte Brontë's response to Lewes' criticism, see Bette London, "The Pleasures of Submission: *Jane Eyre* and the Production of the Text," *ELH* 58:1 (1991) 195–213.

40 See Griest, *Mudie's Circulating Library*, 138–42.

41 Brontë responds to a letter from Lewes containing the substance of the review, which appeared shortly afterward in *Fraser's*.

42 Letter from "C. Bell" to G. H. Lewes, 6 November 1847, in Smith, *Letters of Charlotte Brontë* i. 559–61. Subsequent references to the letter in Smith's edition appear within the text.

43 Brontë's infamous reaction to Lewes' recommendation of *Pride and Prejudice* underscores her rejection of a hemmed-in art: "a carefully fenced, highly cultivated garden, with neat borders and delicate flowers; but . . . no open country, no fresh air, no blue hill, no bonny beck. I should hardly like to live

with her ladies and gentlemen, in their elegant but confined houses" (Letter to G. H. Lewes, 12 January 1848, [in Spark, *Letters* 143].

44 [Margaret Oliphant], "Modern Novelists – Great and Small," *Blackwood's Edinburgh Magazine* 77 (May 1855) 557, my emphasis. Subsequent references to this review appear within the text.

45 Charlotte Brontë to W. S. Williams, 12 May 1848. (in Wise and Symington, *The Brontës* ii. 215–16).

46 Letter to G. H. Lewes, 12 January 1848 (in Spark, *Letters* 142).

47 Charlotte Brontë, *Shirley* (1849), ed. Andrew and Judith Hook (Harmondsworth: Penguin Books, 1987). Subsequent citations refer to this edition.

48 On the distinction between narrative annexes and interpolated or embedded texts, see my earlier discussion on pages 7–8, 31–2, and 39.

49 Cf. my earlier view of the novel's interpolations: Suzanne Keen, "Narrative Annexes in Charlotte Brontë's *Shirley*," *Journal of Narrative Technique* 20:2 (1990) 107–19.

50 Lewes was later to revise his views about women novelists, but at the time of this review he had not yet begun to know Marian Evans. See Allott, *The Critical Heritage* 160.

51 The shift in focus and interest from Caroline to Shirley was noted by early critics. See the excerpts of reviews of *Shirley* in Allott, *The Critical Heritage* 117–70.

52 Joseph Allen Boone, *Tradition Counter Tradition: Love and the Form of Fiction* (University of Chicago Press, 1987) 14–15.

53 Letter to George Smith on 30 October 1852 (in Spark, *Letters* 188).

54 Charlotte Brontë, *Villette* (1853), ed. Mark Lilly, introduction by Tony Tanner (Harmondsworth: Penguin Books, 1987). Subsequent references to this edition appear within the text.

55 Ruth Bernard Yeazell, *Fictions of Modesty: Women and Courtship in the English Novel* (University of Chicago Press, 1991) 176–7.

56 See Charles Burkhart, "The Nuns of Villette," *Victorian Newsletter* 44 (1973) 8–13; Christina Crosby, "Charlotte Brontë's Haunted Text," *SEL* 24:4 (1984) 701–15; Gilbert and Gubar, *The Madwoman in the Attic*, 406–76; Robert B. Heilman's 1958 essay, "Charlotte Brontë's 'New Gothic,'" rpt. in Gregor, *The Brontës* 96–109; Mary Jacobus, "The Buried Letter: Feminism and Romanticism in *Villette*," *Women Writing and Writing About Women*, ed. Mary Jacobus (London: Croom Helm, 1979) 42–60; E. D. H. Johnson, "'Daring the Dread Glance': Charlotte Brontë's Treatment of the Supernatural in *Villette*," *Nineteenth-Century Fiction* 20 (1966) 325–36; Eve Kosofsky Sedgwick, *The Coherence of Gothic Conventions* (New York: Arno Press, 1980) 138–45; Tony Tanner, "Introduction," *Villette* 7–54; and Maria M. Tatar, "The Houses of Fiction: Toward a Definition of the Uncanny," *Comparative Literature* 33 (1981) 167–82.

57 See Paul Wotipka, "Ocularity and Irony: Pictorialism in *Villette*," *Word and Image* 8:2 (1992) 100–8.

58 See Andrew D. Hook, "Charlotte Brontë, the Imagination and *Villette*," in Gregor, *The Brontës* 137–56.

59 See Rosemary Clark-Beattie, "Fables of Rebellion: Anti-Catholicism and the Structure of *Villette*," *ELH* 53:4 (1986) 821–47. The historical background for Brontë's anti-Catholicism, according to Clark-Beattie, is the increase of defections to Rome as a result of Puseyism, but, more importantly, the reestablishment of the Roman Catholic hierarchy in England in 1850, under Cardinal Wiseman.

60 Karen Lawrence, "The Cypher: Disclosure and Reticence in *Villette*," *Tradition and the Talents of Women*, ed. Florence Howe (Urbana: University of Illinois Press, 1991) 87–101.

61 For accounts in a psychoanalytic vein, see Sally Shuttleworth, "'The Surveillance of a Sleepless Eye': The Constitution of Neurosis in *Villette*," in Levine and Rauch, *One Culture: Essays in Science and Literature* 313–35; Athena Vrettos, "From Neurosis to Narrative: The Private Life of the Nerves in *Villette* and *Daniel Deronda*," *Victorian Studies* 33:4 (1990) 551–79.

62 On Lucy's unreliability, see Janice Carlisle, "The Face in the Mirror: *Villette* and the Conventions of Autobiography," *ELH* 46 (1979) 263–89; Gilbert and Gubar, *The Madwoman in the Attic* 419; Mary Jacobus, "The Buried Letter" 43; Earl Kneiss, *The Art of Charlotte Brontë* (Athens: Ohio University Press, 1969); John Kucich, *Repression in Victorian Fiction* 38; Helene Moglen, *Charlotte Brontë: The Self Conceived* (New York: Norton, 1976); Nancy Sorkin Rabinowitz, "'Faithful Narrator' or 'Partial Eulogist': First-Person Narration in Brontë's *Villette*," *Journal of Narrative Technique* 15:3 (1985) 244–55. Alone among the critics, Brenda R. Silver defends Lucy's reliability in "The Reflecting Reader in *Villette*," in Abel, Hirsch, and Langland, *The Voyage In* 90–111.

63 On the prevailing anti-Catholicism of the novel, see Rosemary Clark-Beattie's detailed analysis in "Fables of Rebellion"; Robert Newsom, "*Villette* and *Bleak House*: Authorizing Women," *Nineteenth-Century Literature* 46:1 (1991) 54–81, 61–4.

64 See Joseph Allen Boone's treatment of the sexualized cityscape of Lucy's night excursion in "Depolicing *Villette*: Surveillance, Invisibility, and the Female Erotics of 'Heretic Narrative,'" *Novel: A Forum on Fiction* 52:2 (Fall 1992) 20–42.

65 Alethea Hayter reports that Charlotte Brontë never took opium, although Elizabeth Gaskell, who had taken it as a medicine, felt that Brontë's imaginative recreation of a drugged trance was true to life. *Opium and the Romantic Imagination* (Berkeley: University of California Press, 1968) 296–7.

66 "Villette," *Athenaeum* (12 February 1853) 186–8. Subsequent references to this review appear within the text. For a concurring twentieth-century view, see Ann Ronald, "Terror-Gothic: Nightmare and Dream in Ann Radcliffe and Charlotte Brontë," *The Female Gothic*, ed. Juliann E. Fleenor (Montreal: Eden Press, 1983) 176–86.

67 Letter to George Smith on 30 October 1852, in Spark, *Letters* 188.

68 G. H. Lewes, "Ruth and Villette," *Westminster Review* 69 (April 1853) 476, 485. Of the opium-induced trip into the night streets of Villette, which he

quotes, he writes "This is not the writing of fiction: it is prose poetry of the very highest order" (489).

69 ["A Farewell to Angria"] *c.* 1839. Undated and untitled manuscript, printed in "The Early Manuscripts of Charlotte Brontë: A Bibliography," compiled by C. W. Hatfield. *The Brontë Society Publications: Transactions* 37 (1924) 230–1. Subsequent references to this manuscript appear within the text.

70 Thackeray, for instance, writes in a letter, "That's a plaguey book that *Villette*. How clever it is – and how I don't like the heroine" (Allott, *The Critical Heritage* 198).

4 NARRATIVE ANNEXES, SOCIAL MOBILITY, AND CLASS ANXIETY

1 "Observations on the Effects of Novel-Reading, and on the Advantages of Openness and Confidence," *Lady's Magazine: or Mirror of the Belles Lettres, Fashions, Fine Arts, Music, Drama, &c.* 5 (June 1824) 318.

2 "English Novels," *Fraser's Magazine* 44 (October 1851) 375.

3 [Richard Holt Hutton], "George Sand," *National Review* 6 (January 1858) 37.

4 "Sir E. B. Lytton and Mrs. Grundy," *Fraser's Magazine* 41 (January 1850) 98. Subsequent references to this review appear within the text.

5 Kathleen Tillotson, *Novels of the Eighteen-Forties* (Oxford: Clarendon Press, 1954) 79, 79n.

6 Louis Cazamian defines the subgenre in *The Social Novel in England, 1830– 1850*, trans. Martin Fido (London: Routledge and Kegan Paul, 1973). See also Raymond Williams, "The Industrial Novels," *Culture and Society 1780– 1950* (New York: Columbia University Press, 1983) 87–109. Recent studies include Rosemarie Bodenheimer, *The Politics of Story*; Catherine Gallagher's influential *The Industrial Reformation of English Fiction*; and Joseph Kestner, *Protest and Reform: The British Social Narrative by Women, 1827–1867* (Madison: University of Wisconsin Press, 1985).

7 On Godwin and Carlyle, see Arnold Kettle, "The Early Victorian Social-Problem Novel," *From Dickens to Hardy*, vol. vi of *The Pelican Guide to English Literature* (Harmondsworth: Penguin Books, 1958) 169–87.

8 Although *Yeast* was not published in single-volume form until 1851, it was serialized in *Fraser's Magazine* from July through December 1848, the crucial year for Christian Socialists engaged with Chartism.

9 Martin Amis' *London Fields* (1989), Margaret Drabble's *The Gates of Ivory* (1991), and Iris Murdoch's *A Message to the Planet* (1989) are only a few of the recent Condition of England novels, while David Lodge revives the indus-trial novel in *Nice Work* (1988).

10 Raymond Williams, *Culture and Society* 109.

11 [W. E. Aytoun], "Alton Locke, Tailor and Poet: An Autobiography," *Blackwood's Edinburgh Magazine* 68 (November 1850) 608–10. On Gaskell, see [Beard?], "Factory Life – Mary Barton."

12 [Tom Taylor], "The Novels and Poems of the Rev. Charles Kingsley," *National Review* 1 (July 1855) 149.

13 "A Triad of Novels," *Fraser's Magazine* 42 (November 1850) 575.

14 See John Maynard, *Victorian Discourses on Sexuality and Religion* (Cambridge University Press, 1993) 85–140, including sixteen pages of illustrations from Kingsley's papers.

15 E. M. Forster's *Howards' End* (1910) (New York: St. Martin's Press, 1996) can be regarded as the overdetermined reiteration of this fate, befalling fiction's "rising men" when class boundaries are violated.

16 See Ross Murfin, "Novel Representations: Politics and Victorian Fiction," for a treatment of some major Victorian novelists' attitudes towards the extension of the franchise and the sometimes contradictory evidence of their novels' style of representation.

17 Hardy's essay "The Dorsetshire Labourer" appeared in *Longman's Magazine* 2 (July 1883) 252–69. Subsequent references appear within the text.

18 See Hardy's preface to the Wessex Edition of *The Mayor of Casterbridge* (London: Macmillan, 1912) vii.

19 Charles Kingsley, *Alton Locke, Tailor and Poet. An Autobiography*, (1850), ed. Elizabeth A. Cripps, The World's Classics (Oxford University Press, 1983). The text, which is based in the first edition (1850), retains the Cambridge passages, which Kingsley excised in the 1862 edition. Subsequent references to the 1983 edition appear within the text.

20 For the fullest analysis of the dream's functions, see R. D. Haynes' "The Multiple Functions of Alton Locke's 'Dreamland,'" *Cahiers Victoriens & Edouardiens* 25 (1987) 29–37.

21 See [David Masson], "Literature and the Labour Question," which reviews both *Alton Locke* and Mayhew's *London Labour and the London Poor*, in the *North British Review* 27 (February 1851) 207–27.

22 Kingsley adopted this pseudonym for his articles in *Politics for The People* (London, 1848) but was identifiable, along with Frederick Maurice. See [J. W. Croker], "Revolutionary Literature," *Quarterly Review* 178 (September, 1851) 524ff.

23 The generic mixture of the novel, especially the inclusion of didactic passages, was condemned by critics. See "A Triad of Novels," in *Fraser's Magazine* 575, and [W. E. Aytoun], "Alton Locke, Tailor and Poet: An Autobiography" 608–10. Subsequent references to Aytoun's review appear within the text.

24 Kingsley may have been thinking of John Donne's poem, "The Progress of the Soul," and of Lovel's dream in Walter Scott's novel *The Antiquary* (1816) (New York: Columbia University Press, 1995). I am indebted to Ian Duncan for directing my attention to *The Antiquary*.

25 1848 was the year of a cholera epidemic that killed 14,600 in London alone; cited in Charles Dickens, *Bleak House* (1853), ed. George Ford and Sylvere Monod, Norton Critical Edition (New York: W. W. Norton, 1977) 901. Subsequent references to this edition are noted in the text.

26 See Alan Rauch, "The Tailor Transformed: Kingsley's *Alton Locke* and the Notion of Change," *Studies in the Novel* 25:2 (1993) 196–213.
27 Cf. Gallagher, *The Industrial Reformation of English Fiction* 96–9.
28 Susan Chitty's biography *The Beast and the Monk: A Life of Charles Kingsley* (London: Hodder and Staughton, 1994) notes the eroticism of the dream sequence and connects it to Kingsley's guilt and frustration in marriage, 136–7. R. D. Haynes analyzes the sexual content of the dream as it relates to character development in "Multiple Functions," 30–3. Allen John Hartley sees Alton's "perversion" as part of the pattern imposed on his lapsing protagonist by Kingsley, in *The Novels of Charles Kingsley: A Cristian Socialist Interpretation* (Folkestone: Hour-Glass Press, 1997) 67.
29 Cf. Leo J. Henkin, *Darwinism in the English Novel: 1860–1910* (New York: Corporate Press, 1940) 42. Although *Alton Locke* appeared before *The Origin of Species* (1859), Kingsley corresponded with Darwin and other eminent scientists. See Cripps' introduction to *Alton Locke*, xviii–xix, and Gillian Beer, *Darwin's Plots: Evolutionary Narrative in Darwin, George Eliot and Nineteenth-Century Fiction* (Boston: Ark Paperbacks, 1983).
30 In 1845, Thomas Cooper, the Chartist poet, published *The Purgatory of Suicides: A Prison-rhyme in Ten Books* (London: J. How), a book that went through several editions in the years of the Chartist agitation. Aside from writing poetry and journalism for a Chartist paper, Alton Locke's "life" does not closely resemble Cooper's autobiography, which was, in any case, published long after Kingsley's novel. Cf. *The Life of Thomas Cooper* (London: n. p., 1872).
31 "A Triad of Novels" 576.
32 The reviewer's allusion to Spenserian stanzas suggests that he has perused the real Chartist poet's verses.
33 "The Rev. Charles Kingsley," *Blackwood's Edinburgh Magazine* 67 (June 1855) 627.
34 Margaret Farrand Thorp suggests that an autobiographical impulse impelled Kingsley, who had suffered a nervous breakdown at age sixteen, to include the dream sequence (*Charles Kingsley: 1819–1875* [Princeton University Press, 1937] 11).
35 Quoted in Thomas Hughes' "Prefatory Memoir" to *Alton Locke, Tailor and Poet: An Autobiography*, vol. VII of *The Life and Works of Charles Kingsley in Nineteen Volumes* (London: Macmillan and Co, 1902) 20.
36 *The Mayor of Casterbridge* was the first novel Hardy wrote after relocating to Max Gate in Dorset. Michael Millgate, *Thomas Hardy: A Biography* (New York: Random House, 1982) 234. Subsequent references to this biography appear within the text.
37 Richard Little Purdy and Michael Millgate, eds., *The Collected Letters of Thomas Hardy*, 5 vols. (Oxford: Clarendon Press, 1978) V. 210. Subsequent references appear within the text.
38 Lennart A. Björk, ed, *The Literary Notebooks of Thomas Hardy*, 2 vols. (New York University Press, 1985) I. 55, 123.

39 The reviewer for the *Westminster Review* ("Belles Lettres," July and October 1886), bewildered by the description of *Crime and Punishment* as realistic (298), finds *The Mayor of Casterbridge* an uncomplicated example of realistic representation (300). William Dean Howells, better informed about Continental fiction, praises Hardy's "very frank and simple way of dealing with every kind of life, and of approaching men and women as directly as if they have never been written about before." This accomplishment places Hardy "abreast of Tolstoi and the greatest of the Continental realists" ("Editor's Study," *Harper's New Monthly Magazine* [November 1886] 961–2). Similarly, William Morton Payne, in "Recent Fiction," *Dial* (July 1886), finds Hardy one of the best English novelists practicing "uncompromising" realism (67). Although judgments about plausibility and improbability recur in reviews of Hardy's novels, it was not until 1949 that a critic stressed Hardy's anti-realism. See Albert J. Guerard, *Thomas Hardy: The Novels and Stories* (Oxford University Press, 1949).

40 The 12 June 1886 review of the novel in the *Dial* compliments "the cleverly hit-off country folk" ("Minor Fiction," 198), as does almost every review. See for example the *Saturday Review* (29 May 1886) 757; and for a negative review of Hardy's "bumpkins," *Critic* (17 July 1886) 30–1.

41 On the revisions Hardy made for publication of the novel in book form, see James Gibson, "Hardy and his Readers," *Thomas Hardy: The Writer and his Background*, ed. Norman Page (London: Bell and Hyman, 1980) 201–2.

42 F. E. Hardy, *The Life of Thomas Hardy 1840–1928* (London: Macmillan, 1962) 179.

43 Contemporary reviewers were, for the most part, untroubled by the novel's complexity of incident. See "Novels of the Week," *Athenaeum* (29 May 1886) 711; and "Recent Fiction," *Critic* (3 July 1889) 5. William Morton Payne objected to the plot's unexpected revelations, writing in *Dial* ("Recent Fiction") that "Such a plot as he delights in reminds one of nothing so much as of a fox engaged in escaping its pursuers. In this case the readers are the pursuers, and the fox that turns and doubles and tries to throw them off the scent is the secret of the plot" (68).

44 21–22 November 1885, after completing *The Mayor of Casterbridge* (*The Life of Thomas Hardy*, 176).

45 See Elaine Showalter, "The Unmanning of *The Mayor of Casterbridge*," *Critical Approaches to the Fiction of Thomas Hardy*, ed. Dale Kramer (London: Macmillan, 1979) 99–115.

46 See Leonora Epstein, "Sale and Sacrament: The Wife Auction in *The Mayor of Casterbridge*," *English Language Notes* 24:4 (1987) 54.

47 I am indebted to Rosemarie Morgan for pointing out that a pub of this name still exists in Dorchester, and that tradition holds that Peter's Finger "wags" at heavy drinkers.

48 See, canonically, D. A. Dike, "A Modern Oedipus: *The Mayor of Casterbridge*," *Essays in Criticism* 2 (April 1952) 167–79; John Paterson, "*The Mayor of Casterbridge* as Tragedy," *Hardy: A Collection of Critical Essays*, ed. A. J.

Guerard (Englewood Cliffs, NJ: Prentice-Hall, 1963) 91–112; and Robert C. Schweik, "Character and Fate in *The Mayor of Casterbridge*," in Draper, *Hardy: The Tragic Novels* 133–47.

49 On Hardy's derivation of the wife-sale from his reading of 1820s editions of the local newspaper, and his transcription of items into his commonplace book, "Facts: From Newspapers, Histories, Biographies, and Other Chronicles – (Mainly Local)," see Christine Winfield, "Factual Sources of Two Episodes in *The Mayor of Casterbridge*," *Nineteenth-Century Fiction* 25:2 (1970) 224–31. On other influences, see Michael Taft, "Hardy's Manipulation of Folklore and Literary Imagination: The Case of the Wife-Sale in *The Mayor of Casterbridge*," *Studies in the Novel* 13:4 (1981) 399–407. For the most thorough interpretation of wife sales, see E. P. Thompson, "The Sale of Wives," *Customs in Common* (London: The Merlin Press, 1991) 404–66.

50 Gayle Rubin, "The Traffic in Women: Notes on the 'Political Economy' of Sex," *Toward an Anthropology of Women*, ed. Rayna R. Reiter (New York: Monthly Review Press, 1975) 174.

51 Thomas Hardy, *The Mayor of Casterbridge* (1886) ed. Martin Seymour-Smith (Harmondsworth: Penguin Books, 1978) 138. Subsequent references in the text to *The Mayor of Casterbridge* refer to this edition.

52 Claude Lévi-Strauss, *The Elementary Structures of Kinship*, trans. James Bell *et al.* (Boston: Beacon Press, 1969) 65. For a contemporary source, see Edward Westermarck, *The History of Human Marriage* (1881) (New York: Macmillan and Co., n. d.) 399–400, cited in Epstein, "Sale and Sacrament," 52, 52n.

53 Showalter points out that the child with Susan Newson is also sold and purchased in the furmity woman's tent ("The Unmanning of *The Mayor of Casterbridge*," 103).

54 See Martin Seymour Smith's "Introduction" to the Penguin Edition of *The Mayor of Casterbridge* (52).

55 Charles Dickens, *Dombey and Son* (1848), ed. Peter Fairclough with an introduction by Raymond Williams (Harmondsworth: Penguin Books, 1984) 738.

56 See Robert Keily, "Vision and Viewpoint in *The Mayor of Casterbridge*," *Nineteenth-Century Fiction* 23:2 (1968) 189–200.

57 See Lawrence Dessner's discussion of overhearing in "Space, Time, and Coincidence in Hardy," *Studies in the Novel* 24:2 (1992) 162. Cf. Ross Murfin, *Swinburne, Hardy, Lawrence and the Burden of Belief* (University of Chicago Press, 1978) 132.

58 John Paterson, in "*The Mayor of Casterbridge* as Tragedy" sees these as signs of Casterbridge's demoralization by its unsavory past, but attributes to the criminality no more than a symbolic function (104, 104n).

59 *Fire From Heaven: Life in an English Town in the Seventeenth Century* (New Haven: Yale University Press, 1992) 264.

60 For a fascinating and thorough treatment of written texts within the novel, see Earl Ingersoll, "Writing and Memory in *The Mayor of Casterbridge*," *English Literature in Transition (1880–1920)* 33:3 (1990) 299–309. Ian Gregor, in

The Great Web: The Form of Hardy's Major Fiction (London: Faber and Faber, 1974) 116–17, sees the letters as symptoms of the author's troubled plotting, along with other incidents Hardy attributes to the exigencies of serial publication.

61 On Dorchester skimmingtons, see David Underdown, *Fire From Heaven*, 264–5.

62 Ruth A. Firor, *Folkways in Thomas Hardy* (New York: Russell & Russell, 1931) 241.

63 "Miasma," *Household Words* 8 (1854) 348.

64 Merryn Williams, *A Preface to Hardy*, 2nd edn. (London: Longman, 1993) 109.

65 See Daniel R. Schwarz, "Beginnings and Endings in Hardy's Major Fiction" in Kramer, *Critical Approaches*, 17–35.

66 See John Kucich, "Moral Authority in the Late Novels: The Gendering of Art," *The Sense of Sex: Feminist Perspectives on Hardy*, ed. Margaret R. Higonnet (Urbana: University of Illinois Press, 1993) 221.

67 *Thomas Hardy*, ed. Sue Roe, Feminist Readings (Atlantic Highlands, NJ: Humanities Press International, 1990) 41.

68 Laurence Lerner sees envy as the main motivation for the skimmington ride and notes that the inhabitants of Mixen Lane are both criminals and poorer, though still respectable, citizens. *Thomas Hardy's* The Mayor of Casterbridge: *Tragedy or Social History* (London: Sussex University Press, 1975), 79. Michael Millgate interprets the same events as rooted in class hostility, in *Thomas Hardy: His Career as a Novelist* (New York: Random House, 1971) 224.

69 All male agricultural laborers did not become enfranchised until 1918.

5 OLDER, DEEPER, FURTHER: NARRATIVE ANNEXES AND THE EXTENT OF THE CONDITION OF ENGLAND

1 Cf. Henry Mayhew's 1849–50 *Morning Chronicle* articles, collected as *London Labour and the London Poor* (1861–2), 4 vols. (New York: Dover, 1968).

2 Disraeli introduces this phrase in the second novel of the Young England trilogy: *Sybil, or The Two Nations.*

3 See Kettle, *From Dickens to Hardy* 186.

4 See Ruth Yeazell, "Why Political Novels Have Heroines: *Sybil, Mary Barton,* and *Felix Holt,*" *Novel: A Forum on Fiction* 18:2 (1985) 126–44.

5 Benjamin Disraeli, *Coningsby: Or the New Generation* (1844), ed. Thom Braun (Harmondsworth: Penguin Books, 1983); Charles Dickens, *Hard Times for These Times* (1854), ed. and intro. David Craig (Harmondsworth: Penguin Books, 1969. Rpt. 1987); H. G. Wells, *Tono-Bungay* (1909) (New York: The Modern Library, 1935). Subsequent references to these editions appear within the text.

6 As Daniel Bivona argues, Disraeli's Young England Trilogy traces this trajectory. See "Disraeli's Political Trilogy and the Antinomic Structure of

Imperial Desire," *Novel: A Forum on Fiction* 22:3 (1989) 305–25. Subsequent references to this article appear within the text.

7 I do not mean to suggest that Jews, workers, or dead bodies are represented in the novel for the first time in these instances, or even that they are mainly absent from nineteenth-century novels. See Richard Faber, *Proper Stations: Class in Victorian Fiction* (London: Faber and Faber, 1971); Harold Fisch, *The Dual Image: The Figure of the Jew in English and American Literature* (London: World Jewish Library, 1971), especially the bibliography; U. C. Knoepflmacher, "The Counterworld of Victorian Fiction and *The Woman in White*," in Buckley, *The Worlds of Victorian Fiction* 351–70; Anne Aresty Naman, *The Jew in the Victorian Novel: Some Relationships Between Prejudice and Art* (New York: AMS Press, 1980); and Bruce Robbins' excellent *The Servant's Hand: English Fiction From Below* (New York: Columbia University Press, 1986).

8 Michael Ragussis, *Figures of Conversion: "The Jewish Question" & English National Identity* (Durham, NC: Duke University Press, 1995) 13.

9 Mary Poovey, *Social Body* 139. Subsequent references appear within the text.

10 Thom Braun, *Disraeli the Novelist* (London and Boston: Allen & Unwin, 1981) 13. Subsequent references to this study appear within the text.

11 "Coningsby; Or, the New Generation," *Fraser's Magazine* 30 (July 1844) 72. Subsequent references appear within the text. Not every reviewer objected. See A. Hayward, "*Coningsby*," *Edinburgh Review* 80 (October 1844) 517–25.

12 "Coningsby," *Eclectic Review* 4th series 16 (July 1844) 51.

13 See *New Monthly Magazine* 71 (June 1844) 206–15.

14 The preponderance of critics agree that the novel represents this reconciliation through Coningsby's marriage and political career. Cf. Nils Claussen, "Disraeli and Carlyle's 'Aristocracy of Talent': The Role of Millbank in *Coningsby* Reconsidered," *Victorian Newsletter* 70 (1986) 1–5.

15 John Holloway, *The Victorian Sage: Studies in Argument* (London: Macmillan, 1953) 103.

16 For the most thorough treatment of Sidonia's literary antecedents and his function in the novel, see A. H. Frietzsche, "Action is Not For Me; Disraeli's Sidonia and the Dream of Power," *Utah Academy Proceedings* 37 (1960) 45–9. See also Montagu Frank Modder, *The Jew in the Literature of England to the End of the Century* (Philadelphia: The Jewish Publication Society of America, 1939) 192–210.

17 [William Thackeray], *Morning Chronicle* (13 May 1845).

18 [William Thackeray], *Morning Chronicle* (13 May 1844).

19 G. H. Lewes, "Disraeli," *British Quarterly Review* 10 (August 1849) 127.

20 Eugene Forcade, "De la Jeune Angleterre," *Revue des Deux Mondes*, 5th series 7 (1 August 1844) 385–417. Reprinted in translation in R. W. Stewart, ed., *Disraeli's Novels Reviewed, 1826–1968* (Metuchen, NJ: The Scarecrow Press, 1975) 188. See also Robert O'Kell, "Disraeli's 'Coningsby': Political Manifesto or Psychological Romance?" *Victorian Studies* 23:1 (1979) 57–78; and

Daniel R. Schwarz, *Disraeli's Fiction* (London and Guildford: Macmillan, 1979) 93.

21 See for instance, "Coningsby," *Eclectic Review* 50–71. Subsequent references appear within the text.

22 For an account of the significance of the persecution of the Jews in forming English national identity in the Victorian period, see Ragussis, *Figures of Conversion* 126.

23 For brief treatments of Disraeli's life, see Richard A. Levine, *Benjamin Disraeli* (New York: Twayne, 1968); Schwarz, *Disraeli's Fiction*; John Vincent, *Disraeli* (Oxford University Press, 1990). For a full-length biography, see Stanley Weintraub, *Disraeli: A Biography* (New York: Dutton, 1993).

24 "The Jewish Champion," *Punch* 12 (1847) 145.

25 Richard Grant White, "The Styles of Disraeli and Dickens," *Galaxy* (NY) 10 (August 1870) 260. Subsequent references appear within the text.

26 Thackeray takes up this theme in his satiric "Codlingsby," credited to B. de Shrewsbury, Esq., in *Punch* (January–June 1847) 166, 198–9, 213–14, 223.

27 [Richard Monckton Milnes, signed "Real England"], "A Few Remarks on Coningsby," *Hood's Magazine* 1 (June 1844) 603–4.

28 From 1 April through 12 August 1854. The serial publication of the novel doubled and then quadrupled sales of *Household Words*. (See "A Note on the Text," *Hard Times* 37.) These figures suggest a contemporary popularity that is not reflected in the reviews of the novel in book form, nor in *Hard Times'* subsequent critical history, despite its intermittent championing by such notables as Ruskin, Shaw, and Leavis. See George Harry Ford and Lauriat Lane, Jr., eds., *The Dickens Critics* (Ithaca: Cornell University Press, 1961).

29 See *The Examiner* (7 January 1854) 5, for a contemporary account.

30 John Forster, *The Life of Charles Dickens* 1. 565. For an account of the composition of the novel, see John Butt and Kathleen Tillotson, *Dickens at Work* (London: Methuen, 1957) 201–21.

31 Cited in Butt and Tillotson, *Dickens at Work* 218n.

32 Dickens uses Stephen as the focalizer of some of the early episodes of the novel. See chapters 10–13.

33 On the fictional world of *Hard Times*, see Patricia E. Johnson, "*Hard Times* and the Structure of Industrialism: The Novel as Factory," *Studies in the Novel* 21:2 (1989) 128–37.

34 The series, mainly attributed to staff writer Henry Morley, overlapped with the publication of *Hard Times*, running from March 1854 to January 1856. See Peter W. J. Bartrip, "*Household Words* and the Factory Accident Controversy," *Dickensian* 75:1 (1979) 17–29.

35 [Henry Morley], "Preventible Accidents," *Household Words* 9 (18 March 1854) 106.

36 See Butt and Tillotson, *Dickens at Work* 209–10; Sylvere Monod, "Dickens at Work on the Text of *Hard Times*," *Dickensian* 64 (1968) 97–9.

37 As Nicholas Coles claims in "The Politics of *Hard Times*: Dickens the Novelist versus Dickens the Reformer," *Dickens Studies Annual* 15 (1986) 148,

174n; and cf. Joseph Butwin, "*Hard Times*; The News and the Novel," *Nineteenth-Century Fiction* 32 (1977) 166–87, to whom Coles incorrectly attributes this observation.

38 George Orwell, "Charles Dickens," cited in Ford and Lane, *The Dickens Critics* 168.

39 John Ruskin, "A Note on Hard Times," cited in Ford and Lane, *The Dickens Critics* 47.

40 [Jane Sinnett], "Belles Lettres," *Westminster Review* n. s. 6 (October 1854) 606. Sinnett attributes Dickens' success with characters from "humble life" and his failure with members of the cultivated classes to the complicated interiority of "more cultivated persons." Members of the poorer orders – Stephen notwithstanding – can be represented convincingly "from without" (606).

41 See [Margaret Oliphant], "Charles Dickens," *Blackwood's Edinburgh Magazine* 77 (April 1855) 451–66. "Stephen Blackpool and his womanly purehearted Rachael are beautifully sketched" (545).

42 Raymond Williams, *Culture and Society* 93. See also Philip Hobsbaum's hilarious critique of Stephen's martyrdom as a personal, not political, matter, in *A Reader's Guide to Charles Dickens* (London: Thames and Hudson, 1972) 182–3.

43 "*Hard Times (refinished)* by Charles Diggins," E. H. Yates and R. B. Brough, eds., *Our Miscellany* (London: Routledge and Co., 1856) 142n. Subsequent references appear within the text.

44 "Our Epilogue on Books," *British Quarterly Review* 20 (July 1854) 581–2.

45 [Margaret Oliphant], "Dickens" 454. Subsequent references appear within the text.

46 W. H. C. Nation, *Under The Earth; Or, the Sons of Toil: A Romantic Drama, in Three Acts* (1867), Dick's British Drama 59, in *English and American Drama of the Nineteenth Century*. (New York: Readex Microprint, 1970).

47 "Sorting the Seeds: A Survey of Recent Fiction," *Atlantic Monthly* 103 (May 1909) 706.

48 "Tono-Bungay," *Spectator* (27 February 1909) 346. Subsequent references appear within the text.

49 H. G. Wells, *Experiment in Autobiography: Discoveries and Conclusions of a Very Ordinary Brain (since 1866)*, 2 vols. (London: Victor Gollancz and the Cresset Press, 1934) II. 503. Subsequent references to this edition appear within the text.

50 See David Lodge, "*Tono-Bungay* and the Condition of England," in Bergonzi, *H. G. Wells: A Collection of Critical Essays* 110–39. Originally published in Lodge's *Language of Fiction* (London: Routledge and Kegan Paul, 1966) 214–42. Subsequent references to the reprint of this essay appear within the text.

51 This did not escape Wells' contemporaries. H. L. Mencken notes in his review, "The Novels that Bloom in the Spring, Tra-la!" *Smart Set* (April 1909): "But more important than the story itself is the criticism of British

civilization that Mr. Wells formulates in telling it . . . the principal character in this book is not Ponderevo, nor even that marvelous nephew of his who tells the story, but John Bull himself" (155).

52 H. G. Wells, writing in the third person of his own career, in "A Complete Exposé of this Notorious Literary Humbug," (1945) in Hammond, *H. G. Wells: Interviews and Recollections* 115.

53 "Tono-Bungay," *Times Literary Supplement* (11 February 1909) 52. For a judicious treatment of the correspondence between Wells' life and George's narration, see the following by J. R. Hammond: *An H. G. Wells Companion: A Guide to the Novels, Romances and Short Stories* (London: Macmillan, 1979) 149–50; "The Scenic Background of *Tono-Bungay*," *Wellsian* n. s. 1 (1976) 3–5; "The Narrative Voice in *Tono-Bungay*," *Wellsian* 12 (1989) 16–21. See also Jeffrey Sommers, "Wells' *Tono-Bungay*: the novel within the novel," *Studies in the Novel* 17:1 (1985) 69–79.

54 Francis Hackett, *Horizons: A Book of Criticism* (New York: B. W. Huebsche, 1919) 102.

55 The question of influence is complicated. Although Wells obviously has Conrad's *Heart of Darkness* in mind, Conrad himself may have drawn on Well's earlier fiction. See Patrick A. McCarthy, "*Heart of Darkness* and the Early Novels of H. G. Wells: Evolution, Anarchy, Entropy," *Journal of Modern Literature* 13:1 (1986) 37–60. Also, Wells caricatures Conrad in the captain of the Maud Mary. See Bernard Bergonzi, *The Turn of a Century: Essays on Victorian and Modern English Literature* (London: Macmillan, 1973) 98.

56 H. G. Wells, *First & Last Things: A Confession of Faith and Rule of Life* (London: Archibald Constable and Co., 1908). Subsequent references to this edition appear in the text.

57 "The Town of Vanity," *Nation* (13 February 1909) 760–2. Jerome Buckley comments, in *Season of Youth: The Bildungsroman from Dickens to Golding* (Cambridge, MA: Harvard University Press, 1974) on the disparity between the presentation of George the killer and George the protagonist (196–7).

58 Very few critics even *mention* the murder. Exceptionally, see J. R. Hammond, *H. G. Wells and the Modern Novel* 92–4.

59 See the discussion of *Tono-Bungay* in Thomas Richards, *The Imperial Archive: Knowledge and the Fantasy of Empire* (London: Verso, 1993) 88–104.

60 Serialized in the *English Review*, December 1908 – March 1909.

61 As J. R. Hammond shows, the events of the novel extend from mid-century to 1905 ("The Timescale of *Tono-Bungay*: A Problem in Literary Detection," *Wellsian* 14 (1991) 34–6).

62 See Hammond, *H. G. Wells and the Modern Novel* 85–102.

63 "The Town of Vanity." "He is plunging, in disconnected adventure, into a piratical raid into West Africa after 'quap,' a poisonous radio-active product of enormous value" (760). Of course, some contemporary critics use Victorian standards to judge the novel and condemn what the reviewer in the *Nation* admires. See for instance the review in the *Spectator*, 346.

64 "Current Fiction," *Nation*, New York, 88 (18 February 1909) 170.
65 Francis Hackett, *Horizons* 101. Originally published in the *Chicago Evening Post* (26 March 1909).

6 VICTORIAN ANNEXES AND MODERN FORM

1 Of course, I am only guessing. Not even John Sutherland claims to have read them all. For figures, see Sutherland's excellent *Stanford Companion to Victorian Fiction* (Stanford University Press, 1989) 1–3.
2 When they were condemned. As George Moore's *Literature at Nurse or Circulating Morals* (London: Vizetelly and Co., 1885), demonstrates, many evidently immoral passages appeared in novels (junk fiction) approved by Mudie's.
3 See Moore's pamphlet, *Literature at Nurse*.
4 John Sutherland, *Victorian Novelists* 107. Subsequent references appear within the text.
5 See Griest, *Mudie's* 126–9. Subsequent references appear within the text.
6 Colie, *The Resources of Kind*.
7 Berger, Jr., "Second World and Green World," 36. Subsequent references appear within the text.
8 See [Edward George Earle Bulwer-Lytton], "Caxtoniana; a Series of Essays on Life, Literature, and Manners" *Blackwood's Edinburgh Magazine* 93 (May 1863) 558.
9 See Pavel, *Fictional Worlds* 73–113.
10 See Pamela Schirmeister, *The Consolations of Space: The Place of Romance in Hawthorne, Melville, and James* (Stanford University Press, 1990). Subsequent references appear within the text.
11 George Meredith, *Diana of the Crossways* (1885) (New York: Modern Library, n.d.) 71. Subsequent references to this edition appear within the text.
12 William Crary Brownell, *Victorian Prose Masters: Thackeray, Carlyle, George Eliot, Matthew Arnold, Ruskin, George Meredith* (New York: Charles Scribner's Sons, 1901) 5–6. Subsequent references appear within the text.
13 Wilbur L. Cross, *The Development of the English Novel* (1899), seventh (corrected) edition (New York: Macmillan, 1930) 293. Subsequent references to this edition appear within the text.
14 Walter Allen, *Six Great Novelists: Defoe, Fielding, Scott, Dickens, Stevenson, Conrad* (London: Hamish Hamilton, 1955) 154–5.
15 See the discussion in Stang, *Theory of the Novel*, 91–134.
16 "English Novels," *Fraser's Magazine* 382.
17 [G. H. Lewes], "A Word about *Tom Jones*," *Blackwood's Edinburgh Magazine* 87 (March 1860) 333–4. Cited in Stang, *Theory of the Novel* 120.
18 Brownell, *Victorian Prose Masters* 8.
19 Virginia Woolf, *Flush* (1933) (New York: Harcourt Brace Jovanovich, 1961) 104–5.

Bibliography

ANONYMOUS NOTICES AND WORKS IN PERIODICALS

(For reviews of known authorship, see the author's name: e.g., Pollock, W. F. Attributions are derived from *The Wellesley Index to Victorian Periodicals* unless otherwise noted.)

"Belles Lettres." *Westminster Review* 70 (July 1886): 298–300.

"Belles Lettres." *Westminster Review* 74 (October 1886): 588–9.

"Castle Richmond." *Saturday Review* (19 May 1860): 643–4.

"Castle Richmond." *Spectator* (19 May 1860): 477.

"Coningsby." *Eclectic Review* 4th series 16 (July 1844): 50–71.

"Coningsby; Or, the New Generation." *Fraser's Magazine* 30 (July 1844): 71–84.

"Coningsby. Or, the New Generation." *New Monthly Magazine* 71 (June 1844): 206–15.

"Current Fiction." *Nation*, New York, 88 (18 February 1909): 170–1.

"English Novels." *Fraser's Magazine* 44 (October 1851): 375–91.

The Examiner (7 January 1854): 5.

"J. A." "Framley Parsonage." *Sharpe's London Magazine* n.s. 19 (July 1860): 103–5. Signed "J. A."

"Jane Eyre." *Christian Remembrancer* 15 (April 1848): 396–409.

"Jane Eyre." *Critic* (30 October 1847): 277–8.

"Jane Eyre." *Era* (14 November 1847): 9.

"Jane Eyre." *People's Journal* (November 1847): 9.

"Jane Eyre." *Sharpe's London Magazine* n.s. 6 (June 1855): 339–40.

"Jane Eyre." *Spectator* 20 (6 November 1847): 1074–5.

"The Jewish Champion." *Punch* 12 (1847): 145.

"A Letter from London." *Literary World* (24 July 1886): 249.

"The Mayor of Casterbridge." *Critic* (17 July 1886): 30–1.

"The Mayor of Casterbridge." *Saturday Review* (29 May 1886): 757.

"Miasma." *Household Words* 8 (1854): 348.

"Minor Fiction." *Dial* (12 June 1886): 198.

"Novels of the Week." *Athenaeum* (29 May 1886): 711.

"Observations on the Effects of Novel-Reading, and on the Advantages of Openness and Confidence." *Lady's Magazine: Or Mirror of the Belles Lettres, Fashions, Fine Arts, Music, Drama, &c.* 5 (June 1824): 318–20.

"Our Epilogue on Books." *British Quarterly Review* 20 (July 1854): 581–2.
"Our Library Table." *Athenaeum* (12 August 1854): 992.
"Recent Fiction." *Critic* (3 July 1889): 5.
"Sir E. B. Lytton and Mrs. Grundy." *Fraser's Magazine* 41 (January 1850): 98–111.
"Sorting the Seeds: A Survey of Recent Fiction." *Atlantic Monthly* 103 (May 1909): 705–6.
"Tono-Bungay." *Spectator* (27 February 1909): 346.
"Tono-Bungay." *Times Literary Supplement* (11 February 1909): 52–3.
"The Town of Vanity." *Nation*, London (13 February 1909): 758–62.
"A Triad of Novels." *Fraser's Magazine* 42 (November 1850): 574–90.
"Villette." *Athenaeum* (12 February 1853) 186–8.

PRIMARY AND SECONDARY SOURCES

Abel, Elizabeth, Marianne Hirsch, and Elizabeth Langland, eds. *The Voyage In: Fictions of Female Development*. Hanover: University Press of New England, 1983.
Allen, Walter. *The English Novel: A Short Critical History*. New York: E. P. Dutton, 1954.
    Six Great Novelists: Defoe, Fielding, Scott, Dickens, Stevenson, Conrad. London: Hamish Hamilton, 1955.
Allott, Miriam, ed. *The Brontës: The Critical Heritage*. London and Boston: Routledge & Kegan Paul, 1974.
Alter, Robert. *Partial Magic: The Novel as a Self-Conscious Genre*. Berkeley: University of California Press, 1975.
apRoberts, Ruth. *Trollope: Artist and Moralist*. London: Chatto & Windus, 1971.
Apter, T. E. *Fantasy Literature: An Approach to Reality*. Bloomington: Indiana University Press, 1982.
Aristotle. *Poetics*. Trans. Leon Golden. Englewood Cliffs NJ: Prentice-Hall, 1968.
Armstrong, Nancy. *Desire and Domestic Fiction: A Political History of the Novel*. Oxford University Press, 1987.
Austen, Jane. *Mansfield Park* (1814). Ed. James Kinsley. Oxford University Press, 1990.
[Aytoun, W. E.]. "Alton Locke, Tailor and Poet: An Autobiography." *Blackwood's Edinburgh Magazine* 68 (November 1850): 592–610.
    "The Rev. Charles Kingsley." *Blackwood's Edinburgh Magazine* 77 (June 1855): 621–43.
Bagehot, Walter. *The Collected Works of Walter Bagehot: The Literary Essays (in two volumes)*. Ed. Norman St. John-Stevas. Cambridge, MA: Harvard University Press, 1965.
    "The Novels of George Eliot." *National Review* 11 (April 1860): 191–219.
Bakhtin, Mikhail. *The Dialogic Imagination: Four Essays by M. M. Bakhtin*. Ed. Michael Holquist. Trans. Caryl Emerson and Michael Holquist. Austin:

University of Texas Press, 1981.

Rabelais and his World (1968). Trans. Helene Iswolsky. Bloomington: Indiana University Press, 1984.

Bal, Mieke. *Narratology: Introduction to the Theory of Narrative*. Trans. Christine van Boheemen. University of Toronto Press, 1985.

Balutowa, Bronislawa. *Spatial Complex: A Study of Spatial Problems in Fiction Illustrated with Examples from Representative Works of English Short Fiction 1900–1925*. Warsaw: n.p., 1979.

Barnes, Trevor J., and James S. Duncan, eds. *Writing Worlds: Discourse, Text & Metaphor in the Representation of Landscape*. London: Routledge, 1992.

Barth, John. "Tales within Tales within Tales." *Antaeus* 43 (1981): 45–63.

Barthes, Roland. "Introduction to the Structural Analysis of Literature" (1966). *Image–Music–Text*. Trans. Stephen Heath. New York: Hill and Wang, 1977. 77–124.

S/Z. (1970). Trans. Richard Miller. New York: Hill and Wang, 1974.

Bartrip, Peter W. J. "*Household Words* and the Factory Accident Controversy." *Dickensian* 75:1 (1979): 17–29.

[Beard, J. R.?]. "Factory Life – Mary Barton." *British Quarterly Review* 9:17 (February 1849): 117–36.

Beaty, Jerome. "*Jane Eyre* and Genre." *Genre* 10 (1977): 619–54.

Beer, Gillian. "'Coming Wonders': Uses of Theatre in the Victorian Novel." *English Drama: Forms and Development: Essays in Honor of Muriel Clara Bradbrook*. Ed. Marie Axton and Raymond Williams. Cambridge University Press, 1977. 164–85.

Darwin's Plots: Evolutionary Narrative in Darwin, George Eliot and Nineteenth-Century Fiction. London: Routledge & Kegan Paul; Boston: Ark Paperbacks, 1983.

The Romance. Critical Idiom. London: Methuen, 1970.

Berger, Harry Jr. "The Renaissance Imagination: Second World and Green World," *Centennial Review of Arts and Sciences* 9 (1965): 36–78. Rpt. in an expanded form, in *Second World and Green World: Studies in Renaissance Fiction-Making*. Selected and arranged by John Patrick Lynch. Berkeley: University of California Press, 1988. 3–40.

Bergonzi, Bernard. *The Turn of a Century: Essays on Victorian and Modern English Literature*. London: Macmillan, 1973.

Bergonzi, Bernard, ed. *H. G. Wells: A Collection of Critical Essays*. Englewood Cliffs, NJ: Prentice-Hall, 1976.

Ed. *Tono-Bungay*. Riverside Edition. Boston: Houghton-Mifflin, 1966.

Berry, Francis. *The Shakespeare Inset: Word and Picture*. New York: Theatre Arts Books, 1965.

Bersani, Leo. *A Future for Astyanax: Character and Desire in Literature*. New York: Columbia University Press, 1984.

Bivona, Daniel. "Disraeli's Political Trilogy and the Antinomic Structure of Imperial Desire." *Novel: A Forum on Fiction* 22:3 (1989): 305–25.

Björk, Lennart A., ed. *The Literary Notebooks of Thomas Hardy*. 2 vols. New York University Press, 1985.

Blake, Robert. *Disraeli*. London: Eyre and Spottiswode, 1966.

Blake, William. *Selected Poetry and Prose of William Blake*. Ed. Northrop Frye. New York: Modern Library, 1953.

Bloom, Harold, ed. *Charles Dickens's* Hard Times. New York: Chelsea House Publishers, 1987.

Bodenheimer, Rosemarie. *The Politics of Story in Victorian Social Fiction*. Ithaca: Cornell University Press, 1988.

Boone, Joseph Allen. "Depolicing *Villette*: Surveillance, Invisibility, and the Female erotics of 'Heretic Narrative.'" *Novel: A Forum on Fiction* 52:2 (Fall 1992): 20–42.

Tradition Counter Tradition: Love and the Form of Fiction. University of Chicago Press, 1987.

Boumelha, Penny. *Charlotte Brontë*. Key Women Writers. Ed. Sue Roe. New York: Harvester Wheatsheaf, 1990.

Braun, Thom. *Disraeli the Novelist*. London and Boston: Allen & Unwin, 1981.

Brodhead, Richard. *Hawthorne, Melville, and the Novel*. University of Chicago Press, 1976.

Brontë, Charlotte. ["A Farewell to Angria"] Undated, untitled Angrian manuscript. "The Early Manuscripts of Charlotte Brontë: A Bibliography." Compiled by C. W. Hatfield. *The Brontë Society Publications: Transactions* 37 (1924): 220–35.

Jane Eyre (1847). Ed. Margaret Smith. Harmondsworth: Penguin Books, 1981.

Vol. 1 of *The Letters of Charlotte Brontë with a Selection of Letters by Family and Friends. 1829–1847*. Ed. Margaret Smith. Oxford: Clarendon Press, 1995.

Shirley (1849). Ed. Andrew and Judith Hook. Harmondsworth: Penguin Books, 1987.

Villette (1853). Ed. Mark Lilly. Harmondsworth: Penguin Books, 1987.

Brooks, Peter. *Reading for the Plot: Design and Intention in Narrative*. New York: Random House, 1984.

Brownell, William Crary. *Victorian Prose Masters: Thackeray, Carlyle, George Eliot, Matthew Arnold, Ruskin, George Meredith*. New York: Charles Scribner's Sons, 1901.

Bruner, Edward M. "Ethnography as Narrative," in Turner and Bruner, *The Anthropology of Experience* 139–55.

Buckley, Jerome. *Season of Youth: The Bildungsroman from Dickens to Golding*. Cambridge, MA: Harvard University Press, 1974.

Buckley, Jerome, ed. *The Worlds of Victorian Fiction*. Harvard English Studies 6. Cambridge, MA: Harvard University Press, 1975.

Budick, Sanford, and Wolfgang Iser, eds. *Languages of the Unsayable: The Play of Negativity in Literature and Literary Theory*. New York: Columbia University Press, 1989.

[Bulwer-Lytton, Edward George Earle]. "Caxtoniana; a Series of Essays on Life, Literature, and Manners." *Blackwood's Edinburgh Magazine* 93 (May 1863): 545–60.

Burkhart, Charles. "The Nuns of Villette." *Victorian Newsletter* 44 (1973): 8–13.

Butt, John, and Kathleen Tillotson. *Dickens at Work*. London: Methuen, 1957.

Butwin, Joseph. "*Hard Times*; The News and the Novel." *Nineteenth-Century Fiction* 32 (1977): 166–87.

Carlisle, Janice. "The Face in the Mirror: *Villette* and the Conventions of Autobiography." *ELH* 46 (1979): 263–89.

Carlyle, Thomas. *Chartism*. London: J. Fraser, 1840.

Carroll, Lewis. *Alice in Wonderland* and *Through the Looking-glass* (1865, 1871). Ed. Roger Lancelyn Green. Oxford University Press, 1971.

Castle, Terry. *Masquerade and Civilization: The Carnivalesque in Eighteenth-Century Culture and Fiction*. Stanford University Press, 1986.

Cazamian, Louis. *The Social Novel in England, 1830–1850* (1903). Trans. Martin Fido. London: Routledge & Kegan Paul, 1973.

Certeau, Michel de. *The Practice of Everyday Life*. Trans. Steven F. Rendall. Berkeley: University of California Press, 1984.

Cervantes Saavedra, Miguel de. *The Adventures of Don Quixote*. (1605, 1615). 2 vols. Trans. J. M. Cohen. Harmondsworth: Penguin Books, 1987.

Chandler, Marilyn R. *Dwelling in the Text: Houses in American Fiction*. Berkeley: University of California Press, 1991.

Chase, Karen. *Eros and Psyche: The Representation of Personality in Charlotte Brontë, Charles Dickens, and George Eliot*. New York: Methuen, 1984.

Chase, Richard. *The American Novel and its Tradition*. Garden City, NY: Doubleday, 1957.

Chatman, Seymour. *Coming to Terms: The Rhetoric of Narrative in Fiction and Film*. Ithaca: Cornell University Press, 1990.

Story and Discourse: Narrative Structure in Fiction and Film. Ithaca: Cornell University Press, 1978.

Chitty, Susan. *The Beast and the Monk: A Life of Charles Kingsley*. London: Hodder and Stoughton, 1974.

[Chorley, H. F.]. "Jane Eyre." *Athenaeum* (23 October 1847): 1100–1.

Christ, Carol T. "Imaginative Constraint, Feminine Duty, and the Form of Charlotte Brontë's Fiction." *Women's Studies* 6 (1979): 287–96.

Clark, G. Kitson. *The Making of Victorian England*. Cambridge, MA: Harvard University Press, 1962.

Clark-Beattie, Rosemary. "Fables of Rebellion: Anti-Catholicism and the Structure of *Villette*." *ELH* 53:4 (1986): 821–47.

Claussen, Nils. "Disraeli and Carlyle's 'Aristocracy of Talent': The Role of Millbank in *Coningsby* Reconsidered," *Victorian Newsletter* 70 (1986): 1–5.

Cohn, Dorrit. *Transparent Minds: The Representation of Fictional Consciousness*. Princeton University Press, 1978.

Coles, Nicholas. "The Politics of *Hard Times*: Dickens the Novelist versus Dickens the Reformer." *Dickens Studies Annual* 15 (1986) 145–79.

Colie, Rosalie L. *The Resources of Kind: Genre-Theory in the Renaissance*. Ed. Barbara K. Lewalski. Berkeley: University of California Press, 1973.

Conrad, Joseph. *Heart of Darkness*. London and Edinburgh: W. Blackwood & Sons, 1899–1902.

Cooper, Thomas. *The Life of Thomas Cooper.* London: n.p., 1872.

The Purgatory of Suicides: A Prison-rhyme in Ten Books. London: J. How, 1845.

Costa, Richard Hauer. "H. G. Wells' *Tono-Bungay*: Review of New Studies." *English Literature in Transition* 10 (1967): 89–96.

[Croker, J. W.]. "Revolutionary Literature." *Quarterly Review* 178 (September 1851): 491–535.

Crosby, Christina. "Charlotte Brontë's Haunted Text." *SEL* 24:4 (1984): 701–15.

Cross, Wilbur L. *The Development of the English Novel* (1899). Seventh (corrected) edition. New York: Macmillan, 1930.

Curtius, E. R. *European Literature and the Latin Middle Ages.* Trans. Willard Trask. Bollingen Series 36. Princeton University Press, 1953.

Dale, Peter Allan. "Charlotte Brontë's 'tale half-told': The Disruption of Narrative Structure in *Jane Eyre.*" *Modern Language Quarterly* 47:2 (1986): 108–29.

Dällenbach, Lucien. *The Mirror in the Text.* University of Chicago Press, 1989.

Dessner, Lawrence Jay. "Space, Time, and Coincidence in Hardy." *Studies in the Novel* 24:2 (1992): 154–72.

Dickens, Charles. *Bleak House* (1853–3). Ed. George Ford and Sylvere Monod. Norton Critical Edition. New York: W. W. Norton, 1977.

Dombey and Son (1848). Ed. Peter Fairclough. Intro. Raymond Williams. Harmondsworth: Penguin Books, 1984.

Hard Times for These Times (1854). Ed. and intro. David Craig. Harmondsworth: Penguin Books, 1987.

The Life and Adventures of Martin Chuzzlewit (1843–4). Ed. P. N. Furbank. Harmondsworth: Penguin Books, 1986.

Little Dorrit (1857). Ed. John Holloway. Harmondsworth: Penguin Books, 1985.

Oliver Twist (1837). Ed. Peter Fairclough. Intro. Angus Wilson. Penguin Classics. Harmondsworth: Penguin Books, 1985.

Dike, D. A. "A Modern Oedipus: *The Mayor of Casterbridge.*" *Essays in Criticism* 2 (April 1952): 169–79.

Disraeli, Benjamin. *Coningsby: Or the New Generation* (1844). Ed. Thom Braun. Harmondsworth: Penguin Books, 1983.

Sybil, or The Two Nations (1845). Ed. Thom Braun. Intro. R. A. Butler. Harmondsworth: Penguin Books, 1985.

Tancred, or The New Crusade. London: Henry Colburn, 1847.

Donne, John. *The Complete English Poems.* Ed. A. J. Smith. Harmondsworth: Penguin Books, 1986.

Draper, R. P. "The Mayor of Casterbridge." *Critical Quarterly* 25:1 (1983): 57–70.

Draper, R. P., ed. *Hardy: The Tragic Novels.* London: Macmillan, 1975.

Duncan, Ian. *Modern Romance and Transformations of the Novel: The Gothic, Scott, Dickens.* Cambridge University Press, 1992.

Dunleavy, Janet Egleson. "Trollope and Ireland," in Halperin, *Trollope Centenary Essays.* 53–69.

[Eagles, John]. "A Few Words about Novels." *Blackwood's Edinburgh Magazine* 64 (October 1848): 459–74. Signed "Aquilius."

Eagleton, Terry. *Criticism and Ideology: A Study in Marxist Literary Theory*. London: New Left Books; New York: Schocken Books, 1976.

Myths of Power. London: Macmillan, 1975.

Walter Benjamin: Towards a Revolutionary Criticism. London: Verso, 1981.

Edwards, Owen Dudley. "Anthony Trollope, the Irish Writer." *Nineteenth-Century Fiction* 38:1 (1983): 1–42.

Edwards, P. D. *Anthony Trollope, his Art and Scope*. University of Queensland Press, 1977.

Eigner, Edwin M. *The Metaphysical Novel in England and America: Dickens, Bulwer, Melville, and Hawthorne*. Berkeley: University of California Press, 1978.

Eisenstein, Sergei. *The Psychology of Composition*. Ed. and trans. Alan Upchurch. Calcutta: Seagull Books, 1987.

Eliot, George. *Adam Bede* (1859). Ed. and intro. Stephen Gill. Penguin Classics. Harmondsworth: Penguin Books, 1980.

Daniel Deronda (1876). Ed. and intro. Barbara Hardy. Penguin Classics. Harmondsworth: Penguin Books, 1986.

Middlemarch: A Study of Provincial Life (1871–2). Ed. W. J. Harvey. Penguin Classics. Harmondsworth: Penguin Books, 1985.

The Mill on the Floss (1860). Oxford Pocket Classics. London: Avenel Books, 1986.

"The Progress of Fiction as an Art." *Westminster Review* 60 (October 1853): 343–4.

Ellmann, Richard, ed. *Edwardians and Late Victorians*. English Institute Essays, 1959. New York: Columbia University Press, 1960.

Epperly, Elizabeth R. *Anthony Trollope's Notes on the Old Drama*. University of Victoria, 1988.

Epstein, Leonora. "Sale and Sacrament: The Wife Auction in *The Mayor of Casterbridge*." *English Language Notes* 24:4 (1987): 50–6.

Faber, Richard. *Proper Stations: Class in Victorian Fiction*. London: Faber and Faber, 1971.

Firor, Ruth A. *Folkways in Thomas Hardy*. New York: Russell & Russell, 1931.

Fisch, Harold. *The Dual Image: The Figure of the Jew in English and American Literature*. London: World Jewish Library, 1971.

Fisher, Philip. *Hard Facts: Setting and Form in the American Novel*. New York: Oxford University Press, 1987.

Flaxman, Rhoda. *Victorian Word Painting: Toward the Blending of Genres*. Ann Arbor: UMI Research Press, 1987.

[Fonblanque, A. W.]. "Jane Eyre." *Examiner* (27 November 1847): 756–7.

Forcade, Eugene. "De la Jeune Angleterre." *Revue des Deux Mondes* 5th series 7 (1 August 1844): 385–417. Rpt. in translation in R. W. Stewart, *Disraeli's Novels Reviewed, 1826–1968* 188–91.

Ford, George Harry, and Lauriat Lane, Jr., eds, *The Dickens Critics*. Ithaca: Cornell University Press, 1961.

Forster, E. M. *Aspects of the Novel*. New York: Harcourt, Brace, and World, 1927.
   Howards' End. 1910. London: Edward Arnold, 1973.
Forster, John. *The Life of Charles Dickens*. 2 vols. Ed. J. W. T. Ley. London: Cecil Palmer, 1928.
Fowler, Alastair. *Kinds of Literature: An Introduction to the Theory of Genres and Modes*. Cambridge, MA: Harvard University Press, 1982.
Frank, Joseph. *The Idea of Spatial Form*. New Brunswick: Rutgers University Press, 1991.
   "Spatial Form in Modern Literature." *Sewanee Review* 53 (1945): 221–46, 433–56.
Friedman, Susan Stanford. "Lyric Subversion of Narrative in Women's Writing: Virginia Woolf and the Tyranny of Plot," in Phelan, *Reading Narrative: Form, Ethics, Ideology* 162–85.
Frietzsche, A. H. "Action is Not For Me; Disraeli's Sidonia and the Dream of Power." *Utah Academy Proceedings* 37 (1960): 45–9.
Furedy, Viveca. "A Structural Model of Phenomena with Embedding in Literature and Other Arts," *Poetics Today* 10:4 (1989): 745–69.
Gallagher, Catherine. *The Industrial Reformation of English Fiction: Social Discourse and Narrative Form 1832–1867*. University of Chicago Press, 1985.
Garrett, Peter K. *The Victorian Multiplot Novel: Studies in Dialogical Form*. New Haven: Yale University Press, 1980.
Gaskell, Elizabeth. *Mary Barton: A Tale of Manchester Life* (1848). Ed. Stephen Gill. Harmondsworth: Penguin Books, 1970.
   North and South (1854–5). Ed. Dorothy Collin. Intro. Martin Dodsworth. Harmondsworth: Penguin Books, 1981.
   Wives and Daughters (1864–6). Ed. Frank Glover Smith. Intro. Laurence Lerner. Harmondsworth: Penguin Books, 1986.
Gelley, Alexander. *Narrative Crossings: Theory and Pragmatics of Prose Fiction*. Baltimore: The Johns Hopkins University Press, 1987.
Genette, Gerard. *Narrative Discourse, An Essay in Method*. Trans. Jane E. Lewin. Ithaca: Cornell University Press, 1980.
Gibson, James. "Hardy and his Readers," in Page, *Thomas Hardy: The Writer and his Background*. 192–218.
Gilbert, Sandra. "Plain Jane's Progress." *Signs* 2 (1977): 779–804.
Gilbert, Sandra, and Susan Gubar. *The Madwoman in the Attic: The Woman Writer and the Nineteenth-Century Literary Imagination*. New Haven: Yale University Press, 1979.
Gilead, Sarah. "Liminality and Antiliminality in Charlotte Brontë's Novels: *Shirley* reads *Jane Eyre*." *Texas Studies in Literature and Language* 29:3 (1987): 302–22.
   "Liminality, Anti-liminality, and the Victorian Novel," *ELH* 53:1 (1986): 183–97.
Gill, Richard. *Happy Rural Seat: The English Country House and the Literary Imagination*. New Haven: Yale University Press, 1972.
Glendinning, Victoria. *Anthony Trollope*. New York: Alfred A. Knopf, 1993.

Goodman, Nelson. *Ways of Worldmaking*. Indianapolis: Hackett, 1978.

Greene, Graham. *The Honorary Consul*. New York: Viking, 1973.

Gregor, Ian. *The Great Web: The Form of Hardy's Major Fiction*. London: Faber and Faber, 1974.

Gregor, Ian, ed. *The Brontës: A Collection of Critical Essays*. Englewood Cliffs, NJ: Prentice-Hall, 1970.

Gregory, Derek. *Ideology, Science, and Human Geography*. London: Hutchinson University Library, 1978.

Griest, Guinevere L. *Mudie's Circulating Library and the Victorian Novel*. Bloomington: Indiana University Press, 1970.

Guerard, Albert J. *Thomas Hardy: The Novels and Stories*. Oxford University Press, 1949.

Guerard, Albert J., ed. *Hardy: A Collection of Critical Essays*. Englewood Cliffs, NJ: Prentice-Hall, 1963.

Guillen, Claudio. *Literature as System*. Princeton University Press, 1971.

Hackett, Francis. *Horizons: A Book of Criticism*. New York: B. W. Huebsche, 1919.

Haggard, H. Rider. *King Solomon's Mines* (1885). Harmondsworth: Penguin Books, 1987.

She (1887). Ed. Daniel Karlin. The World's Classics. Oxford University Press, 1991.

Haight, Gordon. "Dickens and Lewes," *PMLA* 71 (1956): 166–79.

Halperin, John, ed. *Trollope Centenary Essays*. New York: St. Martin's Press, 1982.

Hammond, J. R. *H. G. Wells and the Modern Novel*. London: Macmillan, 1988.

An H. G. Wells Companion: A Guide to the Novels, Romances and Short Stories. London: Macmillan, 1979.

"The Narrative Voice in *Tono-Bungay*." *Wellsian* 12 (1989): 16–21.

"The Scenic Background of *Tono-Bungay*." *Wellsian* n.s. 1 (1976): 3–5.

"The Timescale of *Tono-Bungay*: A Problem in Literary Detection." *Wellsian* 14 (1991): 34–6.

Hamond, J. R., ed. *H. G. Wells: Interviews and Recollections*. London: Macmillan, 1980.

Hamon, Philippe. "The Rhetorical Status of the Descriptive." *Yale French Studies* 61 (1981): 1–26.

Hampton, Timothy. *Writing from History: The Rhetoric of Exemplarity in Renaissance Literature*. Ithaca: Cornell University Press, 1990.

Harbison, Robert. *Eccentric Spaces: A Voyage Through Real and Imagined Worlds*. New York: Alfred A. Knopf, 1977.

Hardy, Florence Emily. *The Life of Thomas Hardy 1840–1928*. London: Macmillan, 1962.

Hardy, Thomas. "The Dorsetshire Labourer." *Longman's Magazine* 2 (July 1883): 252–69.

The Mayor of Casterbridge (1886). Ed. Martin Seymour-Smith. Harmondsworth: Penguin Books, 1978.

Preface. *The Life and Death of the Mayor of Casterbridge: a Story of a Man of*

Character. Vol. v of *The Works of Thomas Hardy in Prose and Verse, with Prefaces and Notes.* The Wessex Edition. London: Macmillan, 1912.

"The Profitable Reading of Fiction." *Forum* (March 1888): 57–70.

Harpham, Geoffrey Galt. "Minority Report: *Tono-Bungay* and the Shape of Wells' Career." *Modern Language Quarterly* 39:1 (March 1978): 50–62.

Harson, Robert R. "H. G. Wells: The Mordet Island Episode." *Costerus* 8 (1973): 65–76.

Hartley, Allan John. *The Novels of Charles Kingsley: A Christian Social Interpretation.* Folkestone: Hour-Glass Press, 1977.

Harvey, Geoffrey. *The Art of Anthony Trollope.* London: Weidenfeld and Nicolson, 1980.

Hawthorne, Nathaniel. *The House of the Seven Gables* (1851). Ed. Milton R. Stern. Harmondsworth: Penguin Books, 1981.

Haynes, R. D. "The Multiple Functions of Alton Locke's 'Dreamland.'" *Cahiers Victoriens & Edouardiens* 25 (1987): 29–37.

Hayter, Alethea. *Opium and the Romantic Imagination.* Berkeley: University of California Press, 1968.

Hayward, A. "*Coningsby.*" *Edinburgh Review* 80 (October 1844): 517–25.

Heilman, Robert B. "Charlotte Brontë's 'New Gothic'" (1958), in Gregor, *The Brontës: A Collection of Critical Essays* 96–109.

Henighan, Tom. *Natural Space in Literature: Imagination and Environment in Nineteenth and Twentieth Century Fiction and Poetry.* Ottawa: Golden Dog Press, 1982.

Henkin, Leo J. *Darwinism in the English Novel: 1860–1910.* New York: Corporate Press, 1940.

Herbert, Christopher. *Culture and Anomie: Ethnographic Imagination in the Nineteenth Century.* University of Chicago Press, 1991.

Trollope and Comic Pleasure. University of Chicago Press, 1987.

Herbert, Lucille. "*Tono-Bungay*: Tradition and Experiment," in Bargonzi, *H. G. Wells: A Collection of Critical Essays* 140–56.

Hibbert, Christopher. *Disraeli and His World.* London: Thames and Hudson, 1978.

Hobsbaum, Philip. *A Reader's Guide to Charles Dickens.* London: Thames and Hudson, 1972.

Holloway, John. *The Victorian Sage: Studies in Argument.* London: Macmillan, 1953.

Homans, Margaret. *Bearing The Word: Language and Female Experience in Nineteenth-Century Women's Writing.* University of Chicago Press, 1986.

Hook, Andrew D. "Charlotte Brontë, the Imagination and *Villette*," in Gregor, *The Brontës: A Collection of Critical Essays* 137–56.

House, Humphrey. *The Dickens World.* Second edition. Oxford University Press, 1961.

House, Madeline, Graham Storey, and Kathleen Tillotson, eds. *The Letters of Charles Dickens.* 7 vols. The Pilgrim Edition. Oxford: Clarendon Press, 1965–93.

Howe, Florence, ed. *Tradition and the Talents of Women.* Urbana: University of Illinois Press, 1991.

Howells, William Dean. "Editor's Study." *Harper's New Monthly Magazine* (November 1886): 961–2.

Hughes, Thomas. "Prefatory Memoir." *Alton Locke, Tailor and Poet: An Autobiography*. Vol. VII of *The Life and Works of Charles Kingsley in Nineteen Volumes*. London: Macmillan and Co., 1902.

Hunt, Linda. "Sustenance and Balm: The Question of Female Friendship in *Shirley* and *Villette*." *Tulsa Studies in Women's Literature* 1 (1982): 55–66.

Hutchinson, Steven. *Cervantine Journeys*. Madison: University of Wisconsin Press, 1992.

[Hutton, Richard Holt]. "The Author of Heartsease and the Modern Schools of Fiction." *Prospective Review* 10:40 (1854): 460–82.

"George Sand." *National Review* 6 (January 1858): 37–68.

Ingersoll, Earl. "Writing and Memory in *The Mayor of Casterbridge*." *English Literature in Transition (1880–1920)* 33:3 (1990): 299–309.

Ingham, Patricia. *Thomas Hardy*. Feminist Readings. Ed. Sue Roe. Atlantic Highlands NJ: Humanities Press International, 1990.

Iser, Wolfgang. *The Act of Reading: A Theory of Aesthetic Response*. Baltimore: The Johns Hopkins University Press, 1978.

The Fictive and the Imaginary: Charting Literary Anthropology. Baltimore: The Johns Hopkins University Press, 1993.

Prospecting: From Reader Response to Literary Anthropology. Baltimore: The Johns Hopkins University Press, 1989.

Jackson, Rosemary. *Fantasy: The Literature of Subversion*. London: Methuen, 1981.

Jacobus, Mary. "The Buried Letter: Feminism and Romanticism in *Villette*." *Women Writing and Writing About Women*. Ed. Mary Jacobus. London: Croom Helm, 1979. 42–60.

Jakobson, Roman, and Morris Hale. *Fundamentals of Language*. The Hague: Mouton, 1956.

James, Henry. *The Art of the Novel*. Ed. R. P. Blackmur. New York: Scribners, 1934.

"The Death of the Lion" (1894). New York Edition, *The Lesson of the Master, The Death of the Lion, The Next Time, and Other Tales*. Vol. XV of *The Novels and Tales of Henry James*. New York: Charles Scribner's Sons, 1909. 99–154.

Partial Portraits (1888). New introduction by Leon Edel. Ann Arbor: University of Michigan Press, 1970.

Jameson, Frederic. *The Political Unconscious: Narrative as a Socially Symbolic Act*. Ithaca: Cornell University Press, 1981.

Jefferies, Richard. *After London, Or, Wild England* (1885). Intro. John Fowles. Oxford University Press, 1980.

[Jewsbury, Geraldine]. "New Novels." *Athenaeum* 1699 (19 May 1860): 681.

Johnson, E. D. H. "'Daring the Dread Glance': Charlotte Brontë's Treatment of the Supernatural in *Villette*." *Nineteenth-Century Fiction* 20 (1966): 325–36.

Johnson, Patricia E. "*Hard Times* and the Structure of Industrialism: The Novel as Factory." *Studies in the Novel* 21:2 (1989): 128–37.

Joyce, James. *Ulysses* (1922). Rpt. New York: Vintage Books, 1961.

Keen, Suzanne. "Narrative Annexes in Charlotte Brontë's *Shirley*." *Journal of Narrative Technique* 20:2 (1990): 107–19.

Keily, Robert. "Vision and Viewpoint in *The Mayor of Casterbridge*." *Nineteenth-Century Fiction* 23:2 (1968): 189–200.

Kendrick, Walter M. *The Novel Machine: The Theory and Fiction of Anthony Trollope*. Baltimore: The Johns Hopkins University Press, 1980.

Kestner, Joseph. *Protest and Reform: The British Social Narrative by Women, 1827–1867*. Madison: University of Wisconsin Press, 1985.

The Spatiality of the Novel. Detroit: Wayne State University Press, 1978.

Kettle, Arnold. *From Dickens to Hardy*. Vol. VI of *The Pelican Guide to English Literature*. Harmondsworth: Penguin Books, 1958.

"Introduction to *Tess of the d'Urbervilles*" (1966). *Twentieth-Century Interpretations of* 'Tess of the d'Urbervilles'. Ed. Albert J. LaValley. Englewood Cliffs, NJ: Prentice-Hall, 1969.

Kincaid, James R. "Hardy's Absences." in Kramer, *Critical Approaches* 202–14.

The Novels of Anthony Trollope. Oxford: Clarendon Press, 1977.

King, Helen Garlinghouse, ed. "Trollope's Letters to the *Examiner*." *Princeton University Library Chronicle* 26:2 (1965): 71–101.

Kingsley, Charles. *Alton Locke, Tailor and Poet. An Autobiography*. 1850. Ed. Elizabeth A. Cripps. The World's Classics. Oxford University Press, 1983.

Water Babies. London and Cambridge: Macmillan and Co., 1862–3.

Yeast, A Problem. New York: Harper and Brothers, 1851.

Kneiss, Earl. *The Art of Charlotte Brontë*. Athens: Ohio University Press, 1969.

Knoepflmacher, U. C. "The Counterworld of Victorian Fiction and *The Woman in White*," in Buckley, *The Worlds of Victorian Fiction* 351–70.

Kramer, Dale, ed. *Critical Approaches to the Fiction of Thomas Hardy*. London: Macmillan, 1979.

Kucich, John. "Moral Authority in the Late Novels: The Gendering of Art." *The Sense of Sex: Feminist Perspectives on Hardy*. Ed. Margaret R. Higonnet. Urbana: University of Illinois Press, 1993. 221–41.

Repression in Victorian Fiction: Charlotte Brontë, George Eliot, Charles Dickens. Berkeley: University of California Press, 1987.

"Transgression in Trollope: Dishonesty and the Antibourgeois Elite." *ELH* 56:3 (1989): 593–618.

Landow, George P. "And the World Became Strange: Realms of Literary Fantasy," in Schlobin, *The Aesthetics of Fantasy Literature and Art* 105–42.

Lanser, Susan S. *The Narrative Act*. Princeton University Press, 1981.

Lawrence, D. H. *Women in Love* (1921). New York: The Viking Press, 1966.

Lawrence, Karen. "The Cypher: Disclosure and Reticence in *Villette*." *Tradition and the Talents of Women*. Ed. Florence Howe. Urbana: University of Illinois Press 1991. 87–101.

Lemon, Lee T., and Marion J. Reis, trans. *Russian Formalist Criticism: Four Essays*. Lincoln: University of Nebraska Press, 1965.

Lerner, Laurence. *Thomas Hardy's "The Mayor of Casterbridge": Tragedy or*

Social History. London: Sussex University Press, 1975.

Levine, George. *Darwin and the Novelists: Patterns of Science in Victorian Fiction*. University of Chicago Press, 1988.

The Realistic Imagination: English Fiction from Frankenstein to Lady Chatterley. University of Chicago Press, 1981.

Levine, George, and Alan Rauch, eds. *One Culture: Essays in Science and Literature*. Madison: University of Wisconsin Press, 1987.

Levine, Richard A. *Benjamin Disraeli*. New York: Twayne, 1968.

Lévi-Strauss, Claude. *The Elementary Structures of Kinship*. Trans. James Bell *et al.* Boston: Beacon Press, 1969.

Lewalski, Barbara Keifer. Paradise Lost *and the Rhetoric of Form*. Princeton University Press, 1985.

[Lewes, George Henry]. "Currer Bell's 'Shirley.'" *Edinburgh Review* 91 (January 1850): 153–72.

"Disraeli." *British Quarterly Review* 10 (August 1849): 118–38.

"The Lady Novelists." *Westminster Review* 58 (July 1852): 129–41.

"Recent Novels: French and English." *Fraser's Magazine* 36 (December 1847): 686–95.

"Ruth and Villette." *Westminster Review* 69 (April 1853): 474–91.

"Villette." *Athenaeum* (12 February 1853): 186–8.

"A Word about *Tom Jones*." *Blackwood's Edinburgh Magazine* 87 (March 1860): 331–41.

Lodge, David. *Language of Fiction*. London: Routledge and Kegan Paul, 1966.

Nice Work. London: Secker and Warburg, 1988.

"*Tono-Bungay* and the Condition of England," in Bergonzi, *H. G. Wells: A Collection of Critical Essays* 110–39.

London, Bette. "The Pleasures of Submission: *Jane Eyre* and the Production of the Text." *ELH* 58:1 (1991): 195–213.

Lotman, Jurij. *The Stucture of the Artistic Text* (1971). Trans. Gail Lenhoff and Ronald Vroon. Michigan Slavic Contributions 7. Ann Arbor: University of Michigan Press, 1977. 209–31.

Lutwack, Leonard. *The Role of Place in Literature*. Syracuse: Syracuse University Press, 1984.

Lyons, John D. *Exemplum: The Rhetoric of Example in Early Modern France and Italy*. Princeton University Press, 1989.

McCarthy, Patrick A. "*Heart of Darkness* and the Early Novels of H. G. Wells: Evolution, Anarchy, Entropy." *Journal of Modern Literature* 13:1 (1986): 37–60.

MacDonald, George. *At the Back of the North Wind* (1871). Rpt. with illus. by Jessie Willcox Smith. Philadelphia: D. McKay, 1919.

"The Fantastic Imagination." *Fantasists on Fantasy: A Collection of Critical Reflections By Eighteen Masters of the Art*. ed. Robert H. Boyer and Kenneth J. Zahorski. New York: Avon Books, 1984. 14–21.

Phantastes (1858). In *Phantastes and Lilith: Two Novels by George MacDonald*. Intro. C. S. Lewis. Grand Rapids, MI: William B. Eerdmans, 1964.

The Princess and Curdie (1882). Philadelphia: J. B. Lippincott, 1883.

The Princess and the Goblin (1872). Rpt. with illus. by Jessie Willcox Smith. Philadelphia: D. McKay, 1920.

"The Wise Woman, or The Lost Princess: A Double Story" (1874). Rpt. *The Wise Woman and Other Fantasy Stories*. Grand Rapids, MI: Wm. B. Eerdmans Publishing Co., 1980. 1–108.

McGann, Jerome, ed. *Victorian Connections*. Virginia Victorian Studies. Charlottesville: University Press of Virginia, 1989.

MacPherson, Jay. *The Spirit of Solitude: Conventions and Continuities in Late Romance*. New Haven: Yale University Press, 1982.

Mallory, William E., and Paul Simpson-Housely, eds. *Geography and Literature: A Meeting of the Disciplines*. Syracuse University Press, 1987.

Manlove, C. N. *Modern Fantasy: Five Studies*. Cambridge University Press, 1975.

Martin, Wallace. *Recent Theories of Narrative*. Ithaca: Cornell University Press, 1986.

Martineau, Harriet. *Illustrations of Political Economy*. London: C. Fox, 1832–5.

Martinez-Bonati, Felix. *Fictive Discourse and the Structures of Literature*. Trans. Philip W. Silver. Ithaca: Cornell University Press, 1981.

"Toward a Formal Ontology of Fictional Worlds." *Philosophy and Literature* 7 (1983): 182–95.

[Masson, David]. "Literature and the Labour Question." *North British Review* 27 (February 1851): 207–27.

Mayhew, Henry. *London Labour and the London Poor* (1861–2). 4 vols. New York: Dover, 1968.

Maynard, John. *Charlotte Brontë and Sexuality*. Cambridge University Press, 1984.

Victorian Discourses on Sexuality and Religion. Cambridge University Press, 1993.

Mencken, H. L. "The Novels that Bloom in the Spring, Tra-la!" *The Smart Set* (April 1909): 154–5.

Meredith, George. *Diana of the Crossways* (1885). New York: Modern Library, n.d.

The Ordeal of Richard Feverel: A History of a Father and a Son (1859). Ed. John Halperin. The World's Classics. Oxford University Press, 1984.

Meyer, Susan L. "Colonialism and the Figurative Strategy of *Jane Eyre*." *Victorian Studies* 33:2 (1990): 247–68.

Miller, D. A. *Narrative and its Discontents: Problems of Closure in the Traditional Novel*. Princeton University Press, 1981.

The Novel and the Police. Berkeley: University of California Press, 1988.

Miller, Nancy K. "Emphasis Added: Plots and Plausibilities in Women's Fiction." *PMLA* 96:1 (1981): 36–48.

Millgate, Jane. "Jane Eyre's Progress." *English Studies Anglo-American Supplement* 50 (1969): xxi–xxix.

Millgate, Michael. *Thomas Hardy: A Biography*. New York: Random House, 1982.

Thomas Hardy: His Career as a Novelist. New York: Random House, 1971.

Mills, Nicolaus. *American and English Fiction in the Nineteenth Century: An Antigenre*

Critique and Comparison. Bloomington: Indiana University Press, 1973.

[Milnes, Richard Monckton]. "A Few Remarks on Coningsby." *Hood's Magazine* 1 (June 1844): 601–4. Signed "Real England."

Milton, John. *Complete Poems and Major Prose.* Ed. Merrit Y. Hughes. New York: Macmillan, 1957.

Minogue, Sally. "Gender and Class in *Villette* and *North and South.*" *Problems for Feminist Criticism.* Ed. Sally Minogue. London: Routledge, 1990. 70–108.

Mitchell, W. J. T. "Space, Ideology, and Literary Representation." *Poetics Today* 10 (1989): 91–102.

Modder, Montague Frank. *The Jew in the Literature of England to the End of the Century.* Philadelphia: The Jewish Publication Society of America, 1939.

Moglen, Helene. *Charlotte Brontë: The Self Conceived.* New York: Norton, 1976.

Molesworth, Mary Louisa. *The Cuckoo Clock* (1877). Philadelphia: J. B. Lippincott Co., 1914.

The Tapestry Room. Illus. by Walter Crane. London: Macmillan and Co., 1879.

Monahan, Melodie. "Heading Out is Not Going Home: Jane Eyre." *SEL* 28 (1988): 589–608.

Monod, Sylvere. "Dickens at Work on the Text of *Hard Times.*" *Dickensian* 64 (1968): 86–99.

Moore, George. *Literature at Nurse, or Circulating Morals.* London: Vizetelly and Co., 1885.

[Morley, Henry]. "Preventable Accidents." *Household Words* 9 (18 March 1854): 105–6.

Morson, Gary Saul. *The Boundaries of Genre.* Austin: University of Texas Press, 1981.

Muir, Edwin. *The Structure of the Novel* (1928). London: The Hogarth Press, 1957.

Murdoch, Iris. *A Message to the Planet.* London: Chatto and Windus, 1989.

Murfin, Ross. "The Gap in Trollope's Fiction: *The Warden* as Example." *Studies in the Novel* 14:1 (1982): 17–30.

"Novel Representations: Politics and Victorian Fiction." *Victorian Connections.* Virginia Victorian Studies. Ed. Jerome McGann. Charlottesville: University Press of Virginia, 1989. 31–59.

Swinburne, Hardy, Lawrence and the Burden of Belief. University of Chicago Press, 1978.

Naman, Anne Aresty. *The Jew in the Victorian Novel: Some Relationships Between Prejudice and Art.* New York: AMS Press, 1980.

Nardin, Jane. "The Social Critic in Anthony Trollope's Novels." *SEL* 30 (1990): 679–96.

Nation, W. H. C. *Under The Earth; Or, the Sons of Toil: A Romantic Drama, in Three Acts. Founded on a work by the late Charles Dickens* (1867). First produced at Astley's Theatre, 1867. Dick's British Drama 59. *English and American Drama of the Nineteenth Century.* New York: Readex Microprint, 1970.

Nelles, William. "Stories within Stories: Narrative Levels and Embedded Narrative." *Studies in the Literary Imagination* 25:1 (1992): 79–96.

Newsom, Robert. "*Villette* and *Bleak House*: Authorizing Women." *Nineteenth-*

Century Literature 46: 1 (1991) 54–81.

O'Kell, Robert, "Disraeli's 'Coningsby': Political Manifest or Psychological Romance?" *Victorian Studies* 23: 1 (1979) 57–78.

[Oliphant, Margaret]. "Charles Dickens." *Blackwood's Edinburgh Magazine* 77 (April 1855): 451–66.

"Modern Novelists – Great and Small." *Blackwood's Edinburgh Magazine* 77 (May 1855): 554–68.

Orel, Harold, ed. *Thomas Hardy's Personal Writings: Prefaces, Literary Opinions, Reminiscences* (1966). New York: St. Martin's Press, 1990.

Page, Norman, ed. *Thomas Hardy: The Writer and his Background*. London: Bell and Hyman, 1980.

Parama, Roy. "Unaccommodated Woman and the Poetics of Property in *Jane Eyre*." *SEL* 29:4 (1989): 713–27.

Paterson, John. "*The Mayor of Casterbridge* as Tragedy," in Geurard, *Hardy: A Collection of Critical Essays* 91–112.

Pavel, Thomas. *Fictional Worlds*. Cambridge, MA: Harvard University Press, 1986.

Payne, William Morton. "Recent Fiction." *Dial* (July 1886): 67.

Phelan, James, ed. *Reading Narrative: Form, Ethics, Ideology*. Columbus: Ohio State University Press, 1989.

Politi, Jina. "*Jane Eyre* Class-ified." *Literature and History* 8:1 (1982): 56–66.

[Pollack, F. W.]. "British Novelists – Richardson, Miss Austen and Scott." *Fraser's Magazine* 61 (January 1860) 20–38.

Pollard, Arthur. *Anthony Trollope*. London, Henley and Boston: Routledge and Kegan Paul, 1978.

"Hardy and Rural England." *Thomas Hardy Annual Number 1*. Ed. Norman Page. Atlantic Highlands, NJ: Humanities Press, 1982. 33–43.

The Landscape of the Brontës, with photographs by Simon McBride. New York: E. P. Dutton, 1988.

Poovey, Mary. *Making a Social Body: British Cultural Formation 1830–1864*. University of Chicago Press, 1995.

Uneven Developments: The Ideological Work of Gender in Mid-Victorian England. University of Chicago Press, 1988.

Porte, Joel. *The Romance in America: Studies in Cooper, Poe, Hawthorne, Melville, and James*. Middletown, CT: Wesleyan University Press, 1969.

Prickett, Stephen. *Victorian Fantasy*. Sussex: Harvester Press, 1979.

Prince, Gerald. *A Dictionary of Narratology*. Lincoln: University of Nebraska Press, 1987.

"The Disnarrated." *Style* 22:1 (1988): 1–8.

Purdy, Richard Little, and Michael Millgate, eds. *The Collected Letters of Thomas Hardy*. 5 vols. Oxford: Clarendon Press, 1978.

Rabinowitz, Nancy Sorkin. "'Faithful Narrator' or 'Partial Eulogist': First-Person Narration in Brontë's *Villette*." *Journal of Narrative Technique* 15:3 (1985): 244–55.

Rabkin, Eric S. *The Fantastic in Literature*. Princeton University Press, 1976.

Ragussis, Michael. *Figures of Conversion: "The Jewish Question" & English National Identity.* Durham, NC: Duke University Press, 1995.

Rauch, Alan. "The Tailor Transformed: Kingsley's *Alton Locke* and the Notion of Change." *Studies in the Novel* 25:2 (1993): 196–213.

Ray, Gordon N. "H. G. Wells Tries to be a Novelist." *Edwardians and Late Victorians.* Ed. Richard Ellmann. English Institute Essays, 1959. New York: Columbia University Press, 1960.

Reiter, Rayna R., ed. *Toward an Anthropology of Women.* New York: Monthly Review Press, 1975.

Richards, Thomas. *The Imperial Archive: Knowledge and the Fantasy of Empire.* London: Verso, 1993.

[Rigby, Elizabeth]. "*Vanity Fair* – and *Jane Eyre*." *Quarterly Review* 84 (December 1848): 153–85.

Rimmon-Kenan, Shlomith. *Narrative Fiction: Contemporary Poetics.* London: Methuen, 1983.

Robbins, Bruce. *The Servant's Hand: English Fiction From Below.* New York: Columbia University Press, 1986.

Robinson, Denys Kay. *The Landscape of Thomas Hardy*, with photographs by Simon McBride. Exeter: Webb and Bower, 1984.

Ron, Moshe. "The Restricted Abyss: Nine Problems in the Theory of *Mise en Abyme*," *Poetics Today* 8 (1987): 417–38.

Ronald, Ann. "Terror-Gothic: Nightmare and Dream in Ann Radcliffe and Charlotte Brontë." *The Female Gothic.* Ed. Juliann E. Fleenor. Montreal: Eden Press, 1983. 176–86.

Ronen, Ruth. "Space in Fiction." *Poetics Today* 7:3 (1986): 421–38.

Rossetti, Christina. *Goblin Market* (1862). London: Macmillan and Co., 1893.

Rowe, Karen E. "'Fairy-born and human-bred': Jane Eyre's Education in Romance," in Abel, Hirsh, and Langland, *The Voyage In: Fictions of Female Development.* 69–89.

Rubin, Gayle. "The Traffic in Women: Notes on the 'Political Economy' of Sex." *Toward an Anthropology of Women.* Ed. Rayna R. Reiter. New York: Monthly Review Press, 1975. 157–210.

Ruskin, John. *The King of the Golden River* (1851). New York: Charles T. Dillingham, 1889.

Ryan, Marie-Laure. *Possible Worlds, Artificial Intelligence, and Narrative Theory.* Bloomington and Indianapolis: Indiana University Press, 1991.

Sadleir, Michael. *Anthony Trollope: A Commentary.* Boston: Houghton Mifflin, 1927.

Said, Edward. *Beginnings: Intention & Method* (1975). New York: Columbia University Press, 1985.

Saintsbury, George. "The Mayor of Casterbridge." *Saturday Review* (29 May 1886): 757.

Schirmeister, Pamela. *The Consolations of Space: The Place of Romance in Hawthorne, Melville, and James.* Stanford University Press, 1990.

Schlobin, Roger C., ed. *The Aesthetics of Fantasy Literature and Art.* Notre Dame:

University of Notre Dame Press; Brighton: Harvester Press, 1982.

Schor, Hilary. *Scheherezade in the Marketplace: Elizabeth Gaskell and the Victorian Novel.* Oxford University Press, 1992.

Schwarz, Daniel R. "Beginnings and Endings in Hardy's Major Fiction," in Kramer, *Critical Approaches* 17–35.

Disraeli's Fiction. London and Guildford: Macmillan, 1979.

Schweik, Robert C. "Character and Fate in *The Mayor of Casterbridge*," in Draper, *Hardy: The Tragic Novels* 133–47.

Scott, Walter. *The Antiquary* (1816). Boston: Houghton Mifflin Co., 1923.

Miscellaneous Prose Works, vol. vi. Edinburgh: Adam and Charles Black, 1852.

Sedgwick, Eve Kosofsky. *The Coherence of Gothic Conventions.* New York: Arno Press, 1980.

Showalter, Elaine. "The Unmanning of *The Mayor of Casterbridge*," in Kramer, *Critical Approaches* 99–115.

Shuttleworth, Sally. "'The Surveillance of a Sleepless Eye': The Constitution of Neurosis in *Villette*," in Levine and Rauch, *One Culture: Essays in Science and Literature* 313–35.

Sidney, Philip. *An Apology for Poetry* (c. 1579). Ed. Forrest G. Robinson. New York: Macmillan/Library of Liberal Arts, 1970.

Silver, Brenda R. "The Reflecting Reader in *Villette*," in Abel, Hirsch, and Langland, *The Voyage In: Fictions of Female Development* 90–111.

[Sinnett, Jane]. "Belles Lettres." *Westminster Review* n.s. 6 (October 1854): 604–8.

Skilton, David. *Anthony Trollope and His Contemporaries: A Study in the Theories and Conventions of Mid-Victorian Fiction.* London: Longmans, 1972.

Smalley, Donald, ed. *Trollope: The Critical Heritage.* London: Routledge and Kegan Paul; New York: Barnes and Noble, 1969.

Smitten, Jeffrey R., and Ann Daghistany, eds. *Spatial Form in Narrative.* Ithaca: Cornell University Press, 1981.

Sommers, Jeffrey. "Wells' *Tono-Bungay*: The Novel within the Novel." *Studies in the Novel* 17:1 (1985): 69–79.

Spark, Muriel, ed., *The Letters of the Brontës: A Selection.* Norman: University of Oklahoma Press, 1954. Spark combines selections from Wise and Symington's four-volume edition with excerpts from Elizabeth Gaskell's *Life of Charlotte Brontë.*

Speirs, John. *Poetry Towards Novel.* London: Faber and Faber, 1971.

Stallybrass, Peter, and Allon White. *The Politics and Poetics of Transgression.* Ithaca: Cornell University Press, 1986.

Stang, Richard. *The Theory of the Novel in England, 1850–1870.* New York: Columbia University Press; London: Routledge and Kegan Paul, 1959.

Stevenson, Robert Louis, and Lloyd Osbourne. *The Wrecker* (1891). In *The Novels and Tales of Robert Louis Stevenson.* Vol. x (New York: Charles Scribner's Sons, 1919).

Stewart, J. I. M. *Thomas Hardy: A Critical Biography.* Edinburgh: Longman, 1971.

Stewart, R. W., ed. *Disraeli's Novels Reviewed, 1826–1968.* Metuchen, NJ: The Scarecrow Press, 1975.

Stoker, Bram. *Dracula*. New York: Grosset and Dunlap, 1897.

Storm, Melvin G. "Thematic Parallelism in *Tono-Bungay*: 'Night and the Open Sea' as a Structural Device." *Extrapolation* 18 (May 1977): 181–5.

Sutherland, John A. *Stanford Companion to Victorian Fiction*. Stanford University Press, 1989.

Victorian Novelists and Publishers. University of Chicago Press, 1976.

Swinfen, Ann. *In Defense of Fantasy: A Study of the Genre in English and American Literature since 1945*. London: Routledge and Kegan Paul, 1984.

Swingle, L. J. *Romanticism and Anthony Trollope: A Study in the Continuities of Nineteenth-Century Literary Thought*. Ann Arbor: University of Michigan Press, 1990.

Taft, Michael. "Hardy's Manipulation of Folklore and Literary Imagination: The Case of the Wife-Sale in *The Mayor of Casterbridge*." *Studies in the Novel* 13:4 (1981): 399–407.

Tatar, Maria M. "The Houses of Fiction: Toward a Definition of the Uncanny." *Comparative Literature* 33 (1981): 167–82.

[Taylor, Tom]. "The Novels and Poems of the Rev. Charles Kingsley." *National Review* 1 (July 1855) 124–61.

Terry, R. C. *Anthony Trollope: The Artist in Hiding*. London: Macmillan, 1977.

[Thackeray, William Makepeace]. "Coningsby." *Morning Chronicle* (13 May 1844): n.p.

"Sybil." *Morning Chronicle* (13 May 1845): n.p.

as B. de Shrewsbury, Esq. "Codlingsby." *Punch* (January–June 1847): 166, 198–9, 213–14, 223.

Thackeray, William Makepeace. *Vanity Fair: A Novel Without a Hero* (1847–8). Ed. Geoffrey and Kathleen Tillotson. Riverside Editions. Boston: Houghton Mifflin, 1963.

Thale, Jerome. "The Problem of Structure in Trollope." *Nineteenth-Century Fiction* 15 (1960): 147–57.

Thompson, Dorothy. *The Chartists: Popular Politics in the Industrial Revolution*. New York: Pantheon Books, 1984.

Thompson, E. P. *Customs in Common* (London: The Merlin Press, 1991).

Thorp, Margaret Farrand. *Charles Kingsley: 1819–1875*. Princeton University Press, 1937.

Tillotson, Kathleen. *Novels of the Eighteen-Forties*. Oxford: Clarendon Press, 1954.

Tindall, Gillian. *Countries of the Mind: The Meaning of Place to Writers*. London: Hogarth Press, 1991.

Todorov, Tzvetan. *The Fantastic: A Structural Approach to a Literary Genre* (1970). Trans. Richard Howard. Ithaca: Cornell University Press, 1975.

Tolkien, J. R. R. "On Fairy-Stories." Rpt. *The Tolkien Reader*. New York: Ballantine Books, 1966. 3–84.

Tracy, Robert. "'The Unnatural Ruin': Trollope and Nineteenth-Century Irish Fiction." *Nineteenth-Century Fiction* 37:3 (1982): 358–82.

Trilling, Lionel. *The Liberal Imagination: Essays on Literature and Society*. London: Secker and Warburg, 1964.

Tristram, Philippa. *Living Space in Fact and Fiction.* London: Routledge, 1989.

Trollope, Anthony. *An Autobiography* (1883). The Oxford Trollope, Crown Edition. General eds. Michael Sadleir and Frederick Page. Oxford University Press, 1950.

   Castle Richmond (1860). Photoreproduction. New York: Dover Publications, 1984.

   Cousin Henry (1879). Ed. Julian Thompson. The World's Classics. Oxford University Press, 1987.

   An Eye for an Eye (1879). Rpt. London: The Trollope Society, 1993.

   The Fixed Period. London: Blackwood, 1881–2.

   The Golden Lion of Granpere. New York: Harper and Brothers, 1872.

   Lady Anna. London: Chapman and Hall, 1873–4.

   The Last Chronicle of Barset (1866–7). Ed. Stephen Gill. The World's Classics. Oxford University Press, 1981.

   Linda Tressel (1867–8). New York: Arno Press, 1981.

   The Macdermots of Ballycloran (1847). Photoreproduction. Intro. Robert Lee Wolff. 3 vols. New York: Garland Publishing, 1979.

   Miss Mackenzie (1865). London: Oxford University Press, 1924.

   Nina Balatka. London: Blackwood, 1866–7.

   The Struggles of Brown, Jones, and Robinson, By One of the Firm (1861–2). New York: Arno Press, 1981.

   La Vendée. London: Colburn, 1850.

   The Warden (1855). The World's Classics. Oxford University Press, 1979.

   The Way We Live Now (1874–5). Ed. John Sutherland. The World's Classics. Oxford University Press, 1982.

Trollope, Frances. *The Life and Adventures of Michael Armstrong, Factory Boy.* London: Henry Colburn, 1839–40.

Tuan, Yi-Fu. *Space and Place: The Perspective of Experience.* Minneapolis: University of Minnesota Press, 1977.

Turner, Victor W. *The Anthropology of Performance.* New York: PAJ Publications, 1986.

   Dramas, Fields, and Metaphors: Symbolic Action in Human Society. Ithaca: Cornell University Press, 1974.

   The Forest of Symbols: Aspects of Ndembu Ritual. Ithaca: Cornell University Press, 1977.

   The Ritual Process: Structure and Anti-Structure. Ithaca: Cornell University Press, 1969.

Turner, Victor W., and Edward M. Bruner, eds. *The Anthropology of Experience.* Urbana: University of Illinois Press, 1986.

Underdown, David. *Fire From Heaven: Life in an English Town in the Seventeenth Century.* New Haven: Yale University Press, 1992.

Van Gennap, Arnold. *The Rites of Passage.* Trans. Monika B. Vizedom and Gabrielle L. Caffee. University of Chicago Press, 1960.

Vincent, John. *Disraeli.* Oxford University Press, 1990.

Vrettos, Athena. "From Neurosis to Narrative: The Private Life of the Nerves in *Villette* and *Daniel Deronda*." *Victorian Studies* 33:4 (1990): 551–79.

Warhol, Robyn R. *Gendered Interventions: Narrative Discourse in the Victorian Novel*. New Brunswick: Rutgers University Press, 1989.

Webb, Igor. *From Custom to Capital: The English Novel and the Industrial Revolution*. Ithaca: Cornell University Press, 1981.

Weintraub, Stanley. *Disraeli: A Biography*. New York: Dutton, 1993.

Wells, H. G. "A Complete Exposé of this Notorious Literary Humbug" (1945), in Hammond, *H. G. Wells: Interviews and Recollections* 108–17.

Experiment in Autobiography: Discoveries and Conclusions of a Very Ordinary Brain (since 1866). 2 vols. London: Victor Gollancz and the Cresset Press, 1934.

First & Last Things: A Confession of Faith and Rule of Life. London: Archibald Constable and Co., 1908.

The Island of Doctor Moreau (1896). *A Variorum Text*. Ed. Robert M. Philmus. Athens: University of Georgia Press, 1993.

Tono-Bungay (1909). New York: The Modern Library, 1935.

Westermarck, Edward. *The History of Human Marriage* (1881). New York: Macmillan and Co., n.d.

Wheeler, Michael. *English Fiction of the Victorian Period, 1830–1890*. London: Longman, 1985.

[Whipple, Edwin Percy]. "Novels of the Season." *North American Review* 67 (October 1848): 354–69.

White, Richard Grant. "The Styles of Disraeli and Dickens." *Galaxy* (NY) 10 (August 1870): 253–63.

Whitman, Walt. *Leaves of Grass: A Textual Variorum of the Printed Poems*, 3 vols. Ed. Sculley Bradley, Harold W. Blodgett, Arthur Golden, William White. New York University Press, 1980.

Williams, Merryn. *A Preface to Hardy*, 2nd ed. London: Longman, 1993.

Williams, Raymond. *The Country and the City*. New York: Oxford University Press, 1973.

Culture and Society 1780–1950 (1958). New York: Columbia University Press, 1983.

The English Novel From Dickens to Lawrence. London: Chatto and Windus, 1970.

Marxism and Literature. Oxford University Press, 1977.

Winfield, Christine. "Factual Sources of Two Episodes in *The Mayor of Casterbridge*." *Nineteenth-Century Fiction* 25:2 (1970): 224–31.

Wise, T., and A. Symington, eds. *The Brontës: Their Lives, Friendship and Correspondence*. 4 vols. Oxford: Shakespeare Head Press, 1932.

Woolf, Virginia. *Flush* (1933). New York: Harcourt Brace Jovanovich, 1961.

Orlando (1928). New York: Harcourt Brace Jovanovich, 1956.

Wotipka, Paul. "Ocularity and Irony: Pictorialism in *Villette*." *Word and Image* 8:2 (1992): 100–8.

Yates, E. H., and R. B. Brough, eds. *"Hard Times (refinished)* by Charles Diggins." *Our Miscellany*. London: Routledge and Co., 1856. 142–56.

Yeazell, Ruth Bernard. "The Boundaries of *Mansfield Park.*" *Representations* 7 (1984): 133–52.

Fictions of Modesty: Women and Courtship in the English Novel. University of Chicago Press, 1991.

"More True than Real: *Jane Eyre*'s 'Mysterious Summons,'" *Nineteenth-Century Fiction* 29 (1974): 127–43.

"Why Political Novels Have Heroines: *Sybil, Mary Barton,* and *Felix Holt,*" *Novel: A Forum on Fiction* 18:2 (1985): 126–44.

Zahorski, Kenneth J., and Robert H. Boyer. "The Secondary Worlds of High Fantasy," in Schlobin, *The Aesthetics of Fantasy Literature and Art* 56–81.

Index

CAMBRIDGE STUDIES IN NINETEENTH-CENTURY
LITERATURE AND CULTURE

General editors
Gillian Beer, *University of Cambridge*
Catherine Gallagher, *University of California, Berkeley*

Titles published